Who Killed Sir Walter Ralegh?

Who Killed Sir Walter Ralegh?

RICHARD DALE

The History Press

First published 2011

The History Press
The Mill, Brimscombe Port
Stroud, Gloucestershire, GL5 2QG
www.thehistorypress.co.uk

British Library Cataloguing in Publication Data.
A catalogue record for this book is available from the British Library.

ISBN 978 0 7524 5666 9

Typesetting and origination by The History Press
Printed in the EU for The History Press.

CONTENTS

LIST OF ILLUSTRATIONS

ACKNOWLEDGEMENTS

I would like to thank the staff of the National Archives at Kew, the British Library, Exeter Cathedral Library, the Cornish Studies Library at Redruth and, not least, Looe Library whose inter-library loan service is second to none. I would also like to express my gratitude to the Marquess of Salisbury and the Institute of Historical Research for making freely available the treasure trove of Cecil's State Papers at Hatfield House. I have had to do battle with the almost impenetrable 'secretarial' script of the late Elizabethan and early Jacobean period and in some cases I have been able to decipher this for myself. But elsewhere I have relied on the sterling efforts of others, notably the archival work of the historian Francis Edwards. Finally, I must thank Dr Mark Nicholls of Cambridge University who provided useful guidance on sources and whose carefully researched articles on the Winchester trials of 1603 first stirred my interest in Ralegh's conviction for treason.

The biography of Ralegh by Mark Nicholls and Penry Williams, *Sir Walter Raleigh in Life and Legend*, which was not yet published at the time of writing this book, takes a very different view of the role of Sir Robert Cecil in Ralegh's downfall from that presented here. It is therefore for readers to make their own judgement on the motivation and conduct of this brilliant but calculating politician.

Introduction

Brought to Bay

On 10 November 1603, the prisoner was taken from his lodging in the Tower of London to begin a 75-mile coach journey to Winchester. Ahead of him was a cavalcade of his co-accused, consisting of seven commoners travelling on horseback, two peers of the realm in their coaches and a cavalry escort of fifty men. There had been a severe outbreak of the plague in London: it was reported that 2,000 a week were dying and the streets were littered with infected bedding and straw, while 'carcass carriers' were out collecting bodies. Fear of infection had driven the royal court first to Hampton Court, then to Woodstock and finally to Wilton, while the Courts of Justice were now relocated to Winchester where preparations for a great trial were under way.

The coach journey from London to Winchester was slowed by muddy roads, the need for tight security and, above all, hostile crowds who gathered to jeer and throw tobacco pipes, sticks, stones, and mud. Sir William Waad, who travelled with the prisoner and was charged with his custody, later reported that it was 'hob or nob' whether he 'should have been brought out alive through such multitudes of unruly people as did exclaim at him'.[1]

The prisoner himself remained composed and contemptuous of the rabble, commenting only that 'dogs do always bark at those they know not'. At Wimbledon there was support from a small group of the prisoner's friends who had gathered to cheer him as he passed by. Thereafter, the country roads were quieter and it was possible for him to write some letters in relative peace.

It took three days to complete the coach journey to Winchester where the prisoner was given a cell behind the walls of Winchester Castle. This was the ancient stronghold originally built by William the Conqueror but then rebuilt and extended by Henry III in the thirteenth century. The city was crowded with visitors, so much so that, at the king's command, clerics and scholars of the cathedral and Winchester College had to vacate their lodgings in favour of the distinguished new arrivals. On 4 November Dr Harmer, warden of Winchester College, had acknowledged a letter from the king requiring him 'to remove myself, the fellows and scholars from the College … and forthwith to yield our house and lodgings to his Majesty's judges and serjeants …'[2] There being no alternative housing available he decided, reluctantly, to send the boys home.

The eminent visitors to the town included seven lord commissioners who were to try the case, together with their retinue of servants; four judges with their attendants; the Attorney General and his staff; and the twelve knights of the jury who had been brought down from Middlesex. There were also numerous courtiers and dignitaries who had come to witness the drama that was about to unfold, among them Lord Admiral Nottingham, who accompanied Lady Arabella Stuart, once a possible claimant to the crown of England.

The prisoner, whose health had already suffered from spending too many cold autumn nights in the damp confines of the Tower of London, had to endure a further four days of discomfort and anxiety before facing his accusers on the morning of 17 November. The trial was to be held in the Great Hall of Winchester Castle, an impressive early English Gothic structure, with Purbeck stone columns, pointed arches and plate-tracery windows, which survives to this day. The internal walls were at that time plastered and decorated with the most brilliant colours, there was a stairway at the east end leading to a gallery and at the west end there was a dais. King Arthur's round table hung on the wall then as it does now, reminding those present that the forensic combat that was about to begin was an echo of jousting of a different kind from a distant and more chivalrous past.

On the morning of 17 November the prisoner was taken from his cell by his guard to the Great Hall which was packed with spectators. Some had queued all night to get a place and now they thronged the aisles and filled the minstrels' gallery above.

The special commission which had been appointed for the trial included seven laymen and four judges. The laymen were Lord Mountjoy, Sir William Waad, the Earl of Suffolk, Lord Wotton, Sir John Stanhope, Lord Henry Howard and Sir Robert Cecil (recently made Baron of Essendon). The judges were Lord Chief Justice Sir John Popham, Chief Justice Anderson, and the justices Gawdy and Warburton.

Once silence had been called for and the crowded hall was hushed, the clerk read out the indictment. The general points of treason cited were 'that Sir Walter Ralegh, with other persons, had conspired to kill the King, to raise a rebellion with intent to change religion and subvert the government, and, for that purpose, to encourage and incite the King's enemies to invade the realm'.[3] The overt acts charged included conferring with Lord Cobham in order to support Lady Arabella Stuart's title to the throne and soliciting money from Spain in furtherance of this end.

Ralegh pleaded not guilty to the indictment and the Middlesex jury was duly sworn. The stage was now set for one of the most controversial state trials in English history which pitted a towering figure of the Elizabethan era against the closed ranks of the political and legal establishment appointed by the new Stuart monarchy.

Even before the trial Ralegh's sentence had been officially pronounced. In August he had been replaced as Governor of Jersey, the royal command citing as grounds for the forfeiture his 'grievous treason against us'. And a month later a council decree removed Ralegh from the lieutenancy of Cornwall, the original commission 'being void and determined'.

As he heard the indictment against him Ralegh must have realised that his chances of escaping the full horrors of a traitor's death were slim. Acquittal on charges of treason were rare and he would have known that of the seven alleged conspirators tried just two days before, all but one had been condemned to death. His turn had now come.

How did Sir Walter Ralegh come to this? How had a man renowned for his wit and political guile, a brilliant courtier who had espoused with patriotic fervour the English cause against Spain, who had seen heroic military action in the service of his country both on land and sea, now face charges of high treason against his sovereign and the realm? This is a 400-year-old mystery and it is the purpose of the chapters that follow to find an answer.

Sir Walter Ralegh

Ralegh doth time bestride
He sits twixt wind and tide
Yet uphill he cannot ride
For all his bloody pride.

London Ballad, 1601

As he contemplated his fate in his Winchester prison, Ralegh must have reflected that he had fallen from a very great height. For nearly twenty years up to the death of Queen Elizabeth in March 1603 he had enjoyed the life of a renaissance prince. As Captain of the Guard he was a familiar figure at court, always dressed exquisitely, renowned for his poetry and pithy sayings, and attracting around him a group of brilliant men who helped to plan his great voyages of discovery. When in London he lived a few minutes' horse ride from Whitehall Palace at one of the most desirable residences in London. This was Durham House, a great palace on the south side of the Strand where he had accommodation for forty servants and stabling for twenty horses. His country estate was at Sherborne where he had built a fine mansion which was conveniently located for his frequent trips into the West Country.

All this was far removed from the modest Devonshire farmhouse, Hayes Barton, where he been born in 1554. The Raleghs were a respectable family that had fallen on hard times after their involvement in the Cornish uprising of 1497. Squire Ralegh was a tenant farmer while his third wife, Katherine Champernowne – Walter's mother – had born three sons by her first husband, Otho Gilbert of Compton near Torquay. These three seafaring older half-brothers – John, Humphrey and Adrian – were to be an important influence on Walter in his early years.

So how had Ralegh emerged from his rural West Country origins to become one of the greatest figures of Elizabeth's court, enjoying a lifestyle and status surpassing that of the landed nobility? His early career had certainly been colourful.[1] At the age of 15 or thereabouts he fought in France with the Huguenots in a volunteer group led by his cousin, Henry Champernowne. By his own account, he was present at two great Huguenot defeats in 1569: the Battle of Jarnac and the retreat at Moncontour. As a boy soldier he was therefore exposed to the massacres, pillaging and merciless brutality of the continental religious wars.

Little is known about Ralegh's formal education. He appears to have attended Oriel College, Oxford, in 1572 after his continental adventures. He left without a degree and although in 1575 he was registered as a member of the Middle Temple, he later claimed that he never studied law.

A contemporary room-mate later referred to his 'riotous' and 'lascivious' companion, and there were other indications that Ralegh was enjoying a boisterous life in his early twenties. In 1577, when two of his servants were brought before magistrates on a charge of riotous behaviour, Ralegh described himself in the bail sheet as 'de Curia' or 'of the Court' suggesting that he was already on the fringes of the royal entourage. Two years later he would be committed to the Fleet Prison for a 'fray' with another courtier, Sir Thomas Perott, and in the same year he was sent to the Marshalsea Prison after coming to blows with a man named Wingfield beside the tennis court at Whitehall.

Ralegh's first big break came in 1578 when Queen Elizabeth granted to his half-brother and mentor, Sir Humphrey Gilbert, a six-year licence 'to discover, find, search out, … such remote, heathen and barbarous lands, countries and territories not actually possessed by any Christian prince or people.' Any land discovered could be disposed of according to the laws of England and settlers in the colonies would enjoy their full rights and privileges as subjects of the queen. This was an open-ended authorisation to colonise unclaimed territories in the New World and Ralegh, aged only 24, was chosen by Gilbert to be his partner in this great enterprise. The adventurers had plans for a little privateering on the side to help fund the expedition, but this was not publicised.

The would-be colonists set sail from Dartmouth in September 1578 with 365 men in ten ships. Ralegh was given command of the *Falcon*, a 100-ton vessel belonging to the queen, with seventy men on board. However, expectations of fame and fortune were to be disappointed: twice the fleet was driven back by autumn storms and after being forced to seek shelter, first in Plymouth and then in Dartmouth, those ships that had not already departed abandoned the cause. Only Ralegh in the *Falcon* continued on course for the West Indies. Yet after reaching the Cape Verde islands he was worsted in an encounter with the Spanish and was forced to return to Plymouth in May 1579, his ship severely damaged and many of his men killed. Ralegh had demonstrated his determination and courage but nothing had been gained and he would have to account for the near-loss of a royal vessel.

It was shortly after his return to London, following this naval setback, that Ralegh suffered his successive spells behind bars for breaching the peace. It may be thought that at such a juncture Ralegh would be the last person to deserve royal favours. Yet it was in 1580 that he now secured his first position at court, as an esquire of the Body Extraordinary – a group of young gentlemen required to wait upon the queen, particularly when she appeared in public. There is more than a suspicion that this was a reward for some political skulduggery at the behest of Queen Elizabeth's spymaster, Francis Walsingham, in which Ralegh had befriended the Earl of Oxford and his pro-Catholic set in order to report on their activities (two of the Oxford group, Charles Arundell and Lord Henry Howard, were later sent to the Tower for conspiring on behalf of Mary, Queen of Scots.) In any event Ralegh was sufficiently in favour to be appointed in July 1580 to serve under Lord Grey in Ireland, in command of 100 foot soldiers.

It was in Ireland that Ralegh established a reputation for military daring. He escaped an ambush and rescued a colleague when outnumbered twenty to one, he outmanoeuvred and defeated the rebel Lord Barry and, by a brilliant deception, infiltrated the castle of another Anglo-Irish rebel, Lord Roche, whom he humiliatingly brought to Cork in a perilous journey through enemy territory.

But the Irish episode also revealed the brutal side to Ralegh's soldiering. A party of Spanish and Italian mercenaries under the papal flag had landed on the west coast of Munster and Smerwick to support the Catholic cause against the English Crown. Holed up in their fort on this isolated peninsula, the invaders were overwhelmed by the forces of the puritan, Lord Grey. They capitulated following a bombardment of four days. As one of the two duty officers of the day, Ralegh received Grey's order to enter 'and full straight to execution'. Some pregnant women who attended the invading force were hanged and the soldiers, numbering around 600 and including some Irish, were systematically slaughtered using a technique known as 'hewing and punching' (slashing the neck, then stabbing the belly) after their armour had been removed and neatly stacked beside their pikes.[2] Judging from his later criticism of Lord Grey as being too soft in dealing with the Irish insurrection, it may be taken that Ralegh was in agreement with the massacre he helped to execute.

Another side of Ralegh's emerging personality to be revealed by the Irish episode was his deviousness and disloyalty to his superiors – at least when they stood in his way. First he wrote to Walsingham as well as to Grey criticising the Earl of Ormond, Governor General of Munster, for his organisational shortcomings: Ormond was recalled and, pending a replacement, Ralegh became part of a triumvirate appointed to discharge Ormond's duties. Ralegh also appears to have criticised his commanding officer, Grey, behind his back. In August 1581 he wrote to the queen's favourite, Leicester, to express his discontent: 'I have spent some time here under the deputy [Grey], in such poor place and charge, as, were it not for that I know him to be one of yours, I would disdain it as much as to keep sheep.'[3]

In 1582, after Ralegh and Grey had been recalled to London, further tensions between them were reported and it was related by Sir Robert Naunton, (later to become Secretary of State to James I) that, in briefing the Council on Irish affairs, Ralegh had 'much the better in telling of his tale'.[4] It was also on his return to the royal court that Ralegh began to attract the queen's attention, as Naunton describes:

> He had gotten the Queen's ear at a trice; and she began to be taken with his elocution, and loved to hear his reasons to her demands. And the truth is, she took him for a kind of oracle, which nettled them all; for those that she relied on began to take this sudden favour for an alarm, and to be sensible of their own supplantation.[5]

Ralegh's success as a courtier was achieved in the face of fierce rivalry for the queen's favour from men of higher birth and fortune. Yet he proved to be a master of the game of courtly love which Elizabeth played with her pretended suitors. The extremes to which these pseudo-romantic rituals could be taken is demonstrated by Sir Christopher Hatton, who, as a close confidante of the queen (he was later to become Lord Chancellor), wrote to her in language more appropriate to a lovesick sweetheart than a government official: 'Would God I were with you but for one hour. My wits are overwrought with thoughts. I find myself amazed. Bear with me, my most dear sweet Lady. Passion overcomes me. I can write no more. Love me, for I love you.'[6]

Ralegh's particular appeal to the queen lay in his physical allure and, above all, his 'wit'. Tall, with dark 'Spanish' looks, he was a flamboyant dresser who later set new standards for sartorial extravagance at court: he wore pearls in his hair, pearl studded clothes, jewels on his shoes and, by his own account, spent one hour each morning on his grooming. But it was above all his way with words that appealed to Elizabeth's sharp intellect: in his soft voice and rich Devonshire accent he wooed the queen with his quick repartee, forceful argument and colourful language. Whether or not Ralegh, when attending the court at Greenwich, really laid down his cloak so the queen could walk dry shod over a puddle, the legend still serves to portray the man: he knew how to employ chivalry to please his sovereign and did so at every opportunity. And when he was away from court he could, as an accomplished poet, continue to charm his middle-aged mistress with lines that expressed his love and idolatry.

> Those eyes which set my fancy on a fire,
> Those crispe'd hairs which hold my heart in chains
> Those dainty hands which conquered my desire,
> That wit which of my thought does hold the reins.[7]

Royal favours began to flow. In April 1582 he was given the command of a company of footmen in Ireland as a form of pension, since he was allowed to discharge his office by deputy and to remain at court. In February 1583 he was included in the prestigious escort sent to accompany the Duke of Anjou from England to the Netherlands. Two months later he was given the leases of two small estates belonging to All Souls' College, Oxford, and in March 1584 he began to make serious money when he was granted the licence to export woollen broadcloths in return for a fixed rent payable to the queen. Under this licence he received not only the duty payable on exports, but also a specified penalty due on all 'over-lengths' – that is, pieces which exceeded the maximum permissible length of 24 yards. When Lord Treasurer Burghley was later reviewing the tax system he calculated that Raleigh, in the first year of his grant, had received the staggering sum of £3,950 from a privilege for which he paid the state a rent of only £700.

But more was to come. In May 1584 Ralegh was given one of the great monopolies of state: the farm of wines. This enabled the holder to charge vintners £1 a year for the right to retail wine and Ralegh immediately sub-contracted the licence to his agent, Richard Browne, for seven years in exchange for a fixed payment of £700 per annum. Ralegh later discovered that Browne was making very substantial profits on the arrangement so he tried to renegotiate the deal. When Browne refused Ralegh persuaded the queen to call in his licence and reissue it to him so that he could sub-contract on much more favourable terms – thereby doubling his income from the monopoly.[8]

One may well ask at this point what was going on here? A young man from the West Country had arrived at court as something of a parvenu, he had performed some useful but relatively minor service in Ireland, and now he was being rewarded with great riches by his sovereign – putting him in income terms amongst the very wealthiest in the land, even though he had few assets to call his own.

The extent of royal patronage seemed limitless. In September 1583 Ralegh's half-brother, Sir Humphrey Gilbert, had drowned when his ship went down in a failed attempt to colonise North America. Ralegh had invested in this expedition by fitting out, at his own expense, a 200-ton ship of advanced design which he named *Ark Ralegh*. Now, in the spring of 1584, Elizabeth agreed to renew Gilbert's colonising charter in Ralegh's name but with expanded powers to 'inhabit or retain, build or fortify, at the discretion of the said W. Ralegh', any territory that he might find hitherto unoccupied by a Christian prince.[9] This was to become the basis of Ralegh's great colonising ventures, although for the time being, as favourite, he was not permitted to leave court.

The favours continued to be heaped on Ralegh. In January 1585 the queen bestowed on him a knighthood. In the same year he was appointed Lord Warden of the Stannaries (a position of profit), Lord Lieutenant of the county of Cornwall and Vice Admiral of the counties of Cornwall and Devon. At this time, too, he entered parliament as one of the two county members for Devonshire.

Meanwhile, Ralegh had moved into Durham House, a vast turreted palace overlooking the Thames. It was conveniently located off the Strand with its own waterfront, although he preferred to travel by coach rather than river boat or 'wherry'. Durham House was the fourteenth-century palace of the Bishops of Durham which had come into the possession of the Crown in the reign of Henry VIII and was now in the gift of Elizabeth. She granted it to her favourite to enjoy at the royal pleasure, although Ralegh did not have use of the ground floor which was occupied by Sir Edward Darcy. This stately pile became Ralegh's town house where he lived from 1584 to 1603. Here he was able to maintain a score of horses in the stables along the Strand, and up to forty servants in the outbuildings. He also had a study in the turret, as described by John Aubrey, the antiquarian: 'Durham House was a noble palace. I well remember [Ralegh's] study, which was a little turret that looked into and over the Thames, and had the prospect which is [as] pleasant, perhaps, as any in the world ...'[10]

Ralegh was now able to live a life of extraordinary privilege. However, he lacked one thing; nearly everything he possessed – Durham House, the farm of the wines and the licence for wool exports – was enjoyed at the royal pleasure and he had no extensive landed estates of his own.

This deficiency was, however, made good in 1586 when he became the beneficiary of confiscated property in both Ireland and England. Following the execution of the Earl of Desmond, whose rebellion Ralegh had helped to put down, the royal favourite was rewarded with 42,000 acres of the earl's forfeited lands in the southern Irish counties of Cork and Waterford. These Irish estates were the basis for Ralegh's first colonial settlement: West Country families were persuaded to become his tenant farmers and he cultivated his woodlands with a view to exporting hogsheads to wine merchants in France and Spain. Reflecting his enduring taste for grandeur and show Ralegh also acquired the lease of Lismore Castle, which was to be the jewel in the crown of his new little kingdom. The scale of the royal grant of Irish lands to Ralegh drew adverse comment from the Lord Deputy of Ireland, Sir John Perrot. Perrot was subsequently warned by Burghley that Ralegh 'is able to do you more harm in one hour than we are all able to do you good in a year'.[11] Such was the favourite's influence with the queen that a word in her ear could make or break a man.

In 1587 Ralegh enjoyed another windfall gain when he became the main beneficiary of the so-called Babington plot. This was a Catholic conspiracy, led by the wealthy young Anthony Babington, to put Mary Queen of Scots on the English throne with the help of troops brought over from the Netherlands. Ralegh appears to have played some minor role in the discovery of the plot but he was rewarded quite disproportionately with nearly all the estates forfeited by the Babington family. In this way he acquired extensive landholdings in Lincolnshire, Derbyshire and Nottinghamshire. He was now wealthy in his own right.

In the same year, when Sir Christopher Hatton was promoted to the office of Lord Chancellor, Ralegh was asked by Elizabeth to fill Hatton's vacated position as Captain of the Guard. This post carried no salary, but it involved close physical proximity to the queen at all times since the holder was entrusted with the safety and protection of her person. As Captain of the Guard, Ralegh also commanded the Yeomen of the Guard and the gentlemen pensioners – well-born young men who served the queen at meals and acted as royal messengers. As if this prestigious position was not enough, Elizabeth also appointed Ralegh to the court office of Master of the Horse.

Despite Ralegh's pre-eminence at court, and his special place in the queen's affections, he never achieved high political office nor was he appointed to the Privy Council. Part of the explanation is that Elizabeth drew a distinction between court favourites and government officials, the former seldom trespassing on the role of the latter – though Hatton was a notable exception. But a more persuasive reason for Ralegh's political exclusion lay in his personality: he was 'damnable proud' according to Aubrey and 'had that awfulness and ascendancy in his aspect over other mortals'.[12] Again 'He was such a person that ... a Prince would rather be afraid of than ashamed of'.[13] The Earl of Northumberland, in much the same vein, remarked that he 'desired to seem to be able to sway all men's fancies, all men's courses'.[14] It appears that Ralegh was not a team player, or someone who was prepared to defer to the majority view and no doubt there would have been considerable opposition from other privy councillors to this haughty and overbearing man becoming a member of Elizabeth's key governing body.

Yet Ralegh was keenly interested in policy making, as his parliamentary career testifies, and he advised the queen on political issues, ranging from Irish affairs to her own succession. It was a continuing source of frustration to him that he was excluded from government.

During the 1580s Ralegh established his interest in maritime expeditions. As a business sideline he built up a small fleet of privateering vessels, led by the 200-ton *Ark Ralegh*, which prayed on Spanish shipping and brought back valuable plunder in the form of spices, ivory, precious stones and hides. These activities were highly profitable but Ralegh's ambitions began to focus on much more grandiose projects involving the colonisation of North America.

Following the dispatch of two ships in 1584 to reconnoitre the inlet we now know as Chesapeake Bay, a much larger expedition, consisting of seven ships and nearly 600 men set sail from Plymouth in April 1585 with the aim of settling territory which Ralegh now named Virginia in honour of his sovereign. The queen herself had provided one of her prime ships, the Tyger, as a demonstration of her support and private backing was arranged through city financiers. Because Ralegh could not himself lead the expedition as, no doubt, he would have wished – his continued presence at court being required by Elizabeth – he placed his cousin, Sir Richard Grenville, in command. The expedition succeeded in settling the first group of colonists on Roanoke Island and, having plundered Spanish shipping on both the outward and return journeys, was able to distribute some £10,000 to investors.

In 1587 Ralegh sent out another expedition, this time under John White, with a view to establishing a new city of Ralegh in Chesapeake Bay. However, there was no follow-up because the Armada crisis intervened, the dispatch of further ships was forbidden and by the time a relief ship arrived in 1590 the colony was deserted and the settlers had mysteriously disappeared without trace.

Ralegh, as royal favourite, still not permitted to go to sea himself, continued to employ highly experienced seafarers to lead his expeditions. Durham House became a venue for learned discourses on maritime affairs and a training establishment for ship captains and navigators. Among those whose specialist services Ralegh acquired were Richard Hakluyt, clergyman turned geographer, and the brilliant young mathematician Thomas Hariot, who became his patron's close personal assistant and friend. Hariot gave a series of lectures at Durham House in 1583–84 on the application of mathematics to navigation, installed his optical instruments on the roof and prepared charts and maps for the use of Ralegh's sailing masters.

Ralegh arranged large-scale financial backing for his colonising expeditions through one of London's leading financiers, William Sanderson, who had married Ralegh's niece. Through Sanderson's city network Ralegh could raise what we today would call equity finance (effectively shares in profits from the expeditions) as well as straight loans. The scale of the financing needed for fitting out ships and paying crews is suggested by the claim that Sanderson, at one or more times, stood bound for Ralegh (was his guarantor) for over £100,000.[15] Certainly he was a key figure in Ralegh's maritime operations, guaranteeing his client's borrowings, borrowing money in his own name for Ralegh's use and investing his own funds directly in expeditions.

Despite his maritime interests and soldiering background Ralegh did not take part in the action against the Armada. However, as a member of the council of war he was heavily involved in defence strategy and took charge of coastal defences against a possible Spanish landing not only in the West Country but also in Kent and East Anglia. As a contribution to the naval effort he made available his own formidable warship, *Ark Ralegh*, which now became the naval flagship *Ark Royal*.

From the mid-1580s until 1591 Ralegh continued to enjoy the queen's favour, although he faced increasing competition from a younger rival in the form of Robert Devereux, Earl of Essex, the stepson of the Earl of Leicester. Then came an event which played into the hands of Ralegh's enemies at court; he had an affair with one of the queen's maids of honour, Elizabeth 'Bess' Throckmorton, daughter of Sir Nicholas Throckmorton. Ralegh secretly married the pregnant Bess towards the end of 1591 and a son was born in March the following year. The union was a double affront to the queen because Ralegh had failed to seek her permission to marry, and her maids of honour were supposed to be untouchable.

Bess was to become Ralegh's life-long partner, sharing his love of stately living as well as his political and financial ambitions and, ultimately, his tribulations.[16] But the couple were first brought together by physical passion which Ralegh captured in verse:

> Her eyes he would should be of light,
> A violet breath and lips of jelly
> Her hair not black, nor over-bright,
> And of the softest down her belly;
> As for her inside, he'd have it
> Only of wantonness and wit.[17]

Ralegh hoped to get away with his indiscretion by keeping his marriage secret. In the spring of 1592 he prepared to embark on an ambitious privateering expedition to the Azores in which he had invested everything he had, while Bess returned to court at the end of April to resume her duties as a maid of honour. Rumours began to circulate and Ralegh felt obliged to write to Sir Robert Cecil, soon to become the queen's Principal Secretary, denying the reports of his marriage and assuring him that 'if any such thing were I would have imparted it unto yourself before any man living'.[18]

Ralegh had hoped to lead this great privateering expedition himself but he was peremptorily recalled to court by Elizabeth. In his own words he had set out 'to seek new worlds, for gold, for praise, for glory', but his hopes had been dashed:

> When I was gone she sent her memory [reminder]
> More strong than were ten thousand ships of war
> To call me back, to leave honours thought,
> To leave my friends, my fortune, my attempt
> To leave the purpose I so long had sought
> And hold both cares and comforts in contempt.[19]

When the truth about Ralegh's marriage came out the queen's fury erupted. The favourite was put under house arrest while Bess was placed in the custody of the Vice Chamberlain, Sir Thomas Heneage. After some prevarication both husband and wife were sent to the Tower of London on 7 August. There is no further mention of Ralegh's baby son who presumably did not survive.

Ralegh remained in the Tower for only five weeks and on 15 September he was given a temporary release. This was to enable him to sort out the near-anarchy that had broken out in the West Country when the largest ever privateering prize, the Portuguese carrack *Madre de Dios*, was brought into Dartmouth. The vessel had been captured by the Azores fleet which had been fitted out, financed and manned under Ralegh's direction. The carrack, carrying a cargo valued at some

£150,000, was being systematically pillaged by the returning sailors and since these were Ralegh's men, they responded to his command. Under his supervision order was restored and the distribution of the spoils could proceed.

The queen in effect struck a deal: Ralegh was allowed to get back what he and his partners had invested in the project, while she took the lion's share of the profits, some £80,000. Ralegh had committed £6,000 of his own money and borrowed a further £11,000 to finance an expedition which had cost around £40,000 to prepare and whose joint stock or equity capital amounted to £18,000. If he had remained in command of the fleet he might have expected to receive up to one third of the spoils. The queen, on the other hand, was rewarded with an extraordinary gain on her outlay of only £1,800.[20] On his return to London Ralegh was liberated, but he had paid dearly for his freedom while Elizabeth had exacted heavy tribute from his disgrace.

Just before Christmas Bess was also released from the Tower and husband and wife were reunited – though banished indefinitely from court. It was fortunate for Ralegh that shortly before his disgrace he had been given a country estate in Dorset through yet another act of royal generosity. This was the old castle of Sherborne and its associated manors which belonged to the Bishops of Salisbury. Ralegh had long coveted this property which he passed on his journeys into the West Country and, in January 1592, the queen had acquired a ninety-nine-year lease on Sherborne which she immediately sublet to her favourite for the remainder of her term. Ralegh and Bess now restored the castle, cultivated the gardens, stocked the pastures and began to build an ambitious new 'lodge' – in fact a splendid country house of innovative design with plastered exterior walls and hexagonal towers at each corner. Towards the end of 1593 Ralegh's second child, Walter, was born at Sherborne and baptised nearby at Lillington.

Ralegh's sudden expulsion from court and the royal presence prompted an outpouring of verse – possibly written while in the Tower and in the weeks during which he was separated from Bess. Ralegh was not a compulsive poet nor did he seek to publish his work, though copies of his manuscripts were circulated at court. He did, however, write for a purpose which was to promote himself as a courtier and, above all, to ingratiate himself with the queen. When he fell out of favour he embarked on an epic poem, the *Book of the Ocean to Cynthia*. Cynthia (Elizabeth) was a name for the cold, chaste moon which held sway over the movements of the ocean (Ralegh). Ralegh implied that he intended to write twelve books of verse to cover each of the twelve years he had been at court and had attended the queen:

> Twelve years entire I wasted in this war
> twelve years of my most happy younger days,
> but I in them, and they now wasted are
> of all which past the sorrow only stays.[21]

Ralegh wrote the last book first – a poem of over 500 lines – but then discontinued the project. What remains is a powerful expression of the joy he experienced when in favour with Elizabeth and the torment in which he found himself when she cast him aside. The purpose, no doubt, was to stir the queen to have compassion on him and to recall him to court. But he made the mistake of entrusting his work to Sir Robert Cecil, who declined to present the manuscript to Elizabeth as was presumably intended. Instead, Cecil filed the poem among his papers where it remained, unread, until its discovery nearly 400 years later.[22]

The self-pity displayed in the *Book of the Ocean to Cynthia* was, perhaps, a little contrived, for Ralegh had not been stripped of his offices, his perquisites or his property. He had fallen from the summit of royal favour onto a very comfortable lower slope where he could continue to enjoy the income from his wine licence, his various appointments in the West Country, his London palace and, of course, his newly acquired estate at Sherborne. The royal bounty had not been cut off as it well might have been if Elizabeth had been truly outraged by his behaviour.

At this juncture Ralegh could have settled down to a life of domestic pleasures amid the beautiful surroundings of Sherborne. However, for a man of such restless spirit and soaring ambition, this was not enough. He had obtained letters patent to explore and commercially exploit unclaimed territories in the New World, and he now became preoccupied with a vision of untapped riches in South America that was to become an obsession.

From travellers' reports he had become convinced that the fabled empire of El Dorado was to be found in Guiana (Venezuela today), and that un-mined gold and the treasures of lost cities were waiting to be discovered along the upper reaches of the Orinoco. Outside investors were persuaded to participate and with the help of financier Sanderson, who appears to have raised over £30,000 for this voyage alone, four ships were fitted out which set sail under Ralegh's command in February 1595.[23]

Ralegh was embarking on an expedition into the wild interior of South America in his early 40s – late middle-age for those times. His motivation was to rebuild his fortune which had been depleted by previous loss-making voyages as well as his lavish lifestyle and his building projects at Sherborne. Always the gambler, he was doubling his stakes in order to recoup his losses. As he himself put it:

> The fruit ... was long before fallen from the tree and the dead stock only remained. I did therefore even in the winter of my life, undertake these travels, fitter for bodies less blasted with misfortunes, for men of greater ability, and for minds of better encouragement, that thereby, if it were possible, I might recover but ... the least taste of the greatest plenty formerly possessed.[24]

Ralegh's South American expedition, described graphically in his best-selling tract *The Discovery of the Large, Rich and Beautiful Empire of Guiana*, failed to yield the promised gold and his little flotilla returned to Plymouth eight months later empty-handed except for some dubious ore samples. Ralegh and his co-adventurers faced heavy financial losses but his faith in Guiana's untold riches remained undiminished.

It was around this time that Ralegh was forced to liquidate much of his landed wealth in order to meet the cost of his grandiose maritime projects. A will dated July 1597 shows that his only major remaining assets consisted of his Irish lands (shortly to be much reduced in value due to the Irish uprising of 1598), his Sherborne estate and a single privateering vessel, *Roebuck*. His extensive Babington estates, the lands he had acquired from All Souls' College and the bulk of his privateering fleet had all been disposed of to pay his debts.

Shortly after his return from Guiana, Ralegh's maritime skills were however given recognition when he was recalled to the queen's service to take command of a naval squadron in the planned assault on Cadiz harbour. The attack was a military success, but the opportunity for plunder was missed because the Spanish merchantmen in port carrying a cargo valued at some 12 million ducats, were scuttled before they could be seized. Ralegh's quick thinking and leadership qualities had played a major role in the success of the naval operation but he suffered a serious leg wound and was once again denied the chance to enrich himself. He complained that although he had received much acclaim he had 'possession of nought but poverty and pain'.[25]

The queen's fallen idol had, however, done enough to be restored to royal favour and reinstated at court. In 1597, as a follow up to Cadiz, Ralegh was again called upon to command a naval squadron in an attack on Spanish shipping in the Azores. Once more there were opportunities for plunder but a combination of bad weather and poor co-ordination between the commanders meant that the expedition was a costly failure.

Ralegh enjoyed some consolation when he managed to obtain the freehold on his Sherborne estate in 1599. But as Elizabeth's reign drew to a close he was under considerable financial pressure. He later commented that 'I found my fortune at court towards the end of her Majesty's reign to be at a stand ...'[26] He owed the Crown money and there were unresolved financial issues arising out of his Guiana voyage which were later to resurface in a fiercely contested court case between Ralegh and his financial agent, Sanderson.[27] It was a bitter disappointment to Ralegh that as an absentee landlord he had failed to turn his huge Irish estates to advantage, despite heavy expenditure on his part, and in 1602 he was obliged to sell out to Richard Boyle, the future Earl of Cork, at a knock-down price of £1,500.

Through the profligate generosity of his queen Ralegh had acquired in the 1580s a great fortune in the form of landed wealth and an income from perquisites to match. But he had then dissipated most of this wealth in fruitless but epic endeavours to acquire vast riches from the New World. He himself calculated the cumulative losses on his maritime ventures at £40,000, a sum equivalent to over twelve times his estimated annual income. The net result was that on the death of his great benefactress, Ralegh was financially vulnerable.

He was also politically exposed, and outside the West Country he was a much-hated figure. This was attributable to his reputation for arrogance, his opulent lifestyle and his farm of the wines which, along with other great monopolies of state, was viewed as an imposition on the public. It did not help that he was widely regarded as an atheist at a time when atheism was a more odious sin than heresy and when a man's character was judged by his piety. Robert Parsons, a Jesuit, further promoted this popular perception of Ralegh and his Durham House set when, in 1592, he wrote a tract denouncing 'Sir Walter Ralegh's School of Atheism ... and ... the conjuror that is Master thereof' (a reference to Thomas Hariot).[28] Finally, Ralegh was widely believed to have played a role in the down-fall and execution of his court rival, the Earl of Essex, who had a loyal following among Londoners.

To all outward appearances Ralegh's good fortune was undimmed as the Elizabethan era came to its natural end. He continued to live in great style with a retinue of servants at Durham House and Sherborne, to adorn the court with his almost regal presence and to fulfil his various offices in the West Country with customary panache and vigour. But behind the façade Ralegh was troubled: his great wealth had gone and he was more than ever dependent on royal favour; he was frustrated at his exclusion from government; and he was ill prepared for the transition to a new and unknown monarch.

In reality his position was under much greater threat than he knew. He had placed his trust in a man he considered to be his close friend – a man who held the reins of power under Elizabeth and who was undoubtedly the cleverest politician of his generation. But Sir Robert Cecil, far from being the friend of Ralegh he used to be, had every intention of taking him down; and even as the queen lay dying Cecil was planning to unseat the unsuspecting favourite.

2

Sir Robert Cecil

Little Cecil trips up and down
He rules both Court and Crown
With his brother Burghley clown,
In his great fox-furred gown,
With the long proclamation
He swore he saved the town.
Is it not likely!

London ballad, 1601

Pre-eminent among the commissioners sitting in judgement on Ralegh at Winchester was Sir Robert Cecil, Principal Secretary to King James. Born on 1 June 1563 he was eleven years younger than Ralegh but he had enjoyed a meteoric rise to prominence under Elizabeth and at the time of the Winchester trial held sway in both domestic and foreign affairs under his new sovereign.

Cecil had begun life with one great advantage. He was the second son of Lord Burghley, Lord Treasurer of England, and Elizabeth's most trusted adviser who, by the queen's own acknowledgement, had held 'the first place in her realm' since 1565.[1] Thomas Cecil, Burghley's elder son by his first wife, was a disappointment to his father, having little inclination or capacity for intellectual endeavours and a preference for seemingly less worthy pursuits. On his first wife's early death Burghley had remarried Mildred, daughter of Sir Anthony Cooke, a considerable scholar whose love of learning he passed on to his children. It was Mildred's son, Robert, who showed early promise and it was Robert, therefore, who Burghley identified as his political heir and in whom he placed all his hopes for future worldly success.

Robert Cecil was educated at home under the tutelage of distinguished scholars and the watchful eye of his solicitous parents. He studied the Classics, French,

Italian and Spanish as well as mathematics, music and religion. In his mid-teens he was entered at Grays Inn where he kept a few terms but without any intention of taking up law as a profession. He also attended St John's College, Cambridge, intermittently – though Burghley continued to retain private tutors for his son's home studies. At the age of 21 Cecil's education was rounded off with a stay in France where he was entertained by diplomats and courtiers. He used this opportunity to send to Walsingham, Elizabeth's then Principal Secretary, a forty-page analysis of the marriage alliances and political sympathies of the princes of the blood and other leading families.[2]

Sometime before Cecil's visit to France, Burghley wrote a memorandum to his younger son giving 'such advice and rules for the squaring of thy life as are gained rather by long experience than by much reading'. This distilled wisdom was set out in the form of ten commandments, but the content consisted not of moral imperatives but rather Machiavellian advice to a man wishing to make his way in the world. On choosing a wife Burghley pointed out that 'a man can err but once' and warned that nothing could be bought 'in the market with gentility'. He condemned drunkenness and commented that to carry liquor well was 'a better commendation for a brewer's horse than a gentleman'. He counselled 'be sure to keep some great man thy friend', but in Cecil's case the advice was needless because he could always look to his father for patronage. In the dog-eat-dog world of Elizabethan court life it was also prudent to 'trust not any with thy life, credit or estate'. Finally, worldly guidance was offered on dealing with men of varying status: 'Towards thy superior be humble yet generous, with thy equal familiar yet respectful, towards thy inferior show humility and some familiarity … the first prepares the way to thy advancement, the second makes thee known for a man well bred, the third gains a good report.' But then Burghley added the following caveat: 'I advise thee not to affect popularity too much: seek not to be E [Essex] and shun to be R [Ralegh].'[3]

In view of what was later to transpire this last caution is of particular interest. Ralegh most emphatically did not court popularity, so what Burghley appears to be warning against here is the favourite's flamboyance and desire to impress with his sartorial splendour, overbearing manner and acid wit. The comment is significant because it betrays the tension that must have existed between the worker bees in Elizabeth's court, of whom Burghley was the foremost, and the favourites or drones like Ralegh who owed their position to personal magnetism rather than to back-breaking work in the service of the state. The warning about Ralegh also foreshadowed the final showdown between Cecil, the self-humbling master of statecraft, and his dazzling rival.

It was Cecil's good fortune that his father was determined to give him the best start in life through a rigorous education and sound worldly advice. Burghley was also able to pass on to his younger son some of the considerable wealth that he had acquired through the perquisites of office. Burghley House in Northamptonshire went to Thomas Cecil, but Robert inherited his father's beloved mansion, Theobalds, in Hertfordshire, as well as property that generated an annual income of around £1,600. At the time of his marriage in 1589 Cecil was also given a number of properties in Edmonton, including a small manor house at Pymmes, while his well-connected wife, Elizabeth, daughter of Lord Cobham, Warden of the Cinque Ports, brought a dowry of £2,000.[4] Cecil, unlike Ralegh, was therefore independently wealthy, although his later acquisitiveness showed that he was just as determined as his court rival to improve his lot.

While Cecil was born into privilege, he started life with one severe natural disadvantage which might have broken a lesser man. He was short and slight, around 5ft high, and he was a hunchback. Furthermore the curvature of his spine affected his walk and this in turn meant that his feet were splayed. The family story was that he had fallen as an infant from the arms of a careless wet nurse but the truth lay elsewhere. There was genetic weakness on the Cooke side for his mother was herself slightly hunchbacked and Cecil's own daughter, Frances, had a physical deformity that required medical treatment.

In a superstitious world which associated deformity with malign spirits, and at an Elizabethan court which lauded physical beauty and marshal prowess above intellect, Cecil was heavily handicapped. He was excluded from the traditionally manly sports such as archery and he could not join in the dancing that was so popular among those who waited on the queen. He was therefore an outsider, knowing that he was the subject of cruel jests behind his back and no doubt aware that in French diplomatic circles he was called 'Monsieur Le Bossu' and in Spanish circles 'Robertus Diabolus'. Elizabeth herself gave Cecil the nickname of 'Pygmy' but he resented this so strongly that he wrote to a cousin, John Stanhope, a letter that he knew would be shown to the queen, saying 'I mislike not the name only because she gives it'.[5] This tactful hint of the hurt that had been felt prompted the queen to change his pet name to 'Elf'. Limited in his leisure pursuits, Cecil's great sporting passion was hawking. Watching a raptor seek out, circle and swoop on its prey was, perhaps, not too far removed from the struggle for supremacy at court where ambitious men learned how to hunt down their rivals. Certainly the heraldic meaning of the hawk as 'one who does not rest until his objective is achieved', fitted well the single-minded determination of Cecil.

Through his drive, industry and intellectual brilliance Cecil overcame his physical handicap in a manner that was neatly described by his cousin and political adversary, Francis Bacon. In his *Essay on 'Deformity'* (published after Cecil's death) Bacon explained how physical disfigurement could help a man in his rise to power:

> Whosoever have anything fixed in his person that doth induce contempt, have also a perpetual spur in himself to rescue and deliver himself from scorn: therefore all deformed persons are extreme bold … also it stirreth in them industry,

and especially in this kind, to watch and observe the weakness of others, that they may have somewhat to repay. Again in their superiors, it quencheth jealousy towards them, as persons that they think they may at their pleasure despise: and it layeth their competitors and emulators asleep; as never believing, they should be in the possibility of advancement till they see them in possession. So that, upon the matter, in a great wit, deformity is an advantage to rising.[6]

In penning these words it is clear that Bacon had Cecil very much in mind. According to his contemporary, John Chamberlain, scholar and man of letters: 'Sir Francis Bacon hath set out new essays where, in a chapter of "Deformity" the world takes notice that he paints out his little cousin to the life'.[7]

Cecil's rise began modestly enough. While his boyhood companion, Robert Devereux, Earl of Essex, shot to prominence in 1587 when he displaced Ralegh as the queen's favourite, Cecil assisted his father at court and performed some minor services for Walsingham, the queen's Principal Secretary, who was a Cecil family protégé. Then, in April 1590 Walsingham died leaving a key vacancy in the administration to be filled. A power struggle followed in which Essex pressed openly for his own nominee while Burghley fought behind the scenes to ensure that such a crucial appointment remained within the Cecil sphere of influence. In the ensuing stand off Burghley became de facto acting Principal Secretary – a vast extension of his already heavy responsibilities – while Cecil played an increasingly important role as his informal administrative assistant.

The office of Principal Secretary, to which Cecil aspired, had during Elizabeth's reign become considerably more important than that of Lord Chancellor. In modern terms it combined the roles of Foreign and Home Secretary, and when liaising between the queen and the Privy Council (whose meetings Elizabeth did not attend), the Principal Secretary acted in effect as prime minister. The office carried a derisory salary of £100 per annum for life but there were, of course, almost limitless opportunities for self-enrichment for the holder of such a powerful position. As for the qualifications required to discharge the heavy responsibilities, these were set out by a clerk of the Privy Council, Robert Beale, who concluded that 'it is convenient for a Secretary to understand the state of the whole realm'.[8] In other words, an effective secretary would need to have the compendious knowledge of domestic and foreign affairs that Cecil quickly began to acquire as his father's industrious deputy.

At the time of Walsingham's death, Cecil, not yet 30, was too young and had insufficient status or experience in public affairs to be a serious candidate for the vacant office, but by buying time Burghley was able to manoeuvre his son into the position. After ten festive days spent at Theobalds in May 1591 the queen, on the last day of her visit, bestowed a knighthood on Cecil and less than three months later, while Essex was away in France, Cecil was admitted to the Privy Council. According to one observer, with Burghley in poor health and overburdened with work 'the whole management of the Secretary's place' was put into Cecil's hands.[9] As Francis Bacon no doubt discerned, the diminutive privy councillor was creeping up on the unsuspecting Essex in a fateful game of grandmother's footsteps. From now on Cecil was to be seen passing through Whitehall Palace to the queen's apartments 'his hands full of papers and head full of matter', so intent on Her Majesty's business that he was oblivious to all those around him.[10]

It was around this time that Francis Bacon cautioned Essex that Cecil was a man who played both sides and whose face could turn two ways – like a boatman rowing up the Thames who 'looketh toward London Bridge when he pulleth toward Westminster'.[11]

On his return from France, Essex had cause to heed this warning. He made a bid for the chancellorship of Oxford University and found that he needed to enlist the support of Cecil – whose influence in such matters was now acknowledged. When the appointment was given to another in July 1592, Essex wrote to Cecil accusing him of double dealing:

Sir R. I have been with the Queen and have had my answer. How it agrees with your letter you can judge, after you have spoken with the Queen.

Whether you have mistaken the Queen or used cunning with me I know not. I will not condemn you, but leave you to think if it were your own case whether you would not be jealous.

Your friend, if I have cause, R. Essex.[12]

Essex nevertheless continued to press his cause. The queen evidently found it difficult to resist the demands of her favourite when he was around her, for in February 1593 he was sworn of the Privy Council. Essex also campaigned to pack as many of his supporters as he could muster into the parliament of 1593 but it was Cecil, now Senior Knight of the Shire for Hertfordshire, who played the dominant role.

It was a sign of his new importance that Cecil was chosen to give the opening parliamentary address and he proceeded to demonstrate great skill and tact in steering the queen's subsidy bill through the Upper and Lower Houses. By the end of the session he had established himself as a trusted manager of parliamentary business. Cecil was on the threshold of great power – but he was not yet quite there. He therefore set about strengthening his position, first by placing his nominees in positions of influence, second by building up a formidable intelligence network and finally by neutralising his main rivals at court – which in the first instance meant Essex.

In 1594 Cecil, backed by his father, won a fierce tussle with Essex over who should be Attorney General, with Anthony Bacon, the earl's nominee, losing out to the Cecil's protégé Sir Edward Coke. Then in July 1596, while Essex was at sea on his Cadiz expedition, Cecil was formally sworn in as Principal Secretary to the queen. The pattern was familiar: the queen was always influenced by those immediately around her and it was easier to slip through things which might cause upset when her favourite was out of sight and earshot.

In the early months of 1597, when Burghley was incapacitated through illness and Essex was away from court having one of his periodic sulks, Cecil's growing intimacy with the queen as her chief adviser was noted. He was, according to one observer, 'in greatest credit, the Queen passing the most part of the day in private and secret conference with him'.[13] Cecil used the opportunity to secure a clutch of appointments that would extend his territorial reach: Lord Burgh was made Lord Deputy of Ireland; Richard Bancroft became Bishop of London, and in that capacity sole licensor of printing and publishing in the capital; while later in the year Henry Brooke, the new Lord Cobham and sworn enemy of Essex, was appointed to his late father's position of Warden of the Cinque Ports – despite opposition from the earl.

In August 1598 Cecil's great patron and protector, Burghley, died leaving his son to do battle on his own against Essex. As one noted historian put it: 'with his tiny stature, crooked back and white, quiet face, what chance had he, for all his cleverness, against the generous young warrior earl either in court or country?'[14] But Cecil's sway was now such that his appointees appeared to be going through on the nod and more were to follow. In 1599 his half-brother, the new Lord Burghley, became President of the North, an important administrative post which was later matched by the appointment of Lord Zouch, Cecil's good friend, as Warden of the Welsh Marches. The little hunchback's influence was now felt throughout the land and it was said that the queen 'is wholly directed by Mr Secretary who now rules as his father did'.[15]

Realising that private information conferred political power, Cecil strengthened his hold on the state by developing his own proprietary intelligence network. Walsingham had adopted the practice of using agents to gather information from abroad and Cecil built on his predecessor's intelligence gathering by establishing agents in all the major continental European centres as well as Scotland and Ireland. He was perhaps aided by Walsingham's files; his papers and books, both public and private, mysteriously disappeared immediately after his death, an incident widely attributed to the Cecils.

The agents were generally part-time and received payments of £50 to £100 per annum; it seems that Cecil used his own funds to supplement the £800 per annum that was specifically allocated to this service. Of course, the reports received from abroad were in the service of the queen but they also gave Cecil inside information which he could use at Council meetings to support his policies. This was at a time when the word 'news' was just coming into use, but Cecil's understanding of news was information deliberately withheld, for once it was imparted to others it ceased to confer political advantage.

As Principal Secretary Cecil had responsibility for identifying threats to the queen and the state not only from abroad but also at home. Here the usual techniques of surveillance and interception of correspondence were used. When he was first appointed secretary his aunt, Lady Bacon, wrote a warning letter to her son, Anthony, who was no friend of the Cecils:

> Now that Sir Robert is fully installed in his long-longed-for Secretary's place
> … you had more need now to be more circumspect and advised in your dis-
> coursings, doings and dealings … Walk more warily … the father and son are
> affectionate joined in power and policy.[16]

She added that Cecil would now have 'strength to intercept' and to 'prevent'.[17] Evidently, it was not just enemies of the state who had to fear the investigative reach of Cecil's intelligence service, but also his political rivals.

Cecil was, however, much more than a spymaster. He was also actively involved in interrogation and the extraction of confessions when those suspected of treason had been placed in custody. In 1594 he was involved in the investigation of an alleged plot centring around Elizabeth's Portuguese physician, Dr Lopez, who was believed to be planning to poison the queen on behalf of his Spanish paymasters. The Doctor and two of his collaborators were hung at Tyburn but a fourth convicted conspirator appears to have been reprieved in return for testifying against his confederates.[18]

Suspected traitors were induced to confess through fear of death, torture and hope of lenience. As for torture, Cecil could not only order the rack, or whatever else was to be used against un-co-operative suspects, he was also able to view the agonies of his victims with apparent equanimity. When the Jesuit, Robert Southwell, was being questioned under torture in 1595 Cecil visited him in the company of other members of the Council. Riding away he observed: 'We have a new torture which it is not possible for a man to bear. And yet I have seen Robert Southwell hanging by it, still as a tree trunk and no-one able to drag one word from his mouth.'[19] Of course Cecil was a man of his time, but anyone who mistook his somewhat dainty appearance for delicacy of feeling or lack of steel was under a dangerous misapprehension.

Cecil sought to gather all power to himself by ensuring that his followers were placed in key positions and by building up his own intelligence and investigative capability. But he also needed to contain and, if possible, eliminate his main rival at court, namely Essex. The earl represented everything that Cecil despised and his father had warned against: self-glorification, an unstable temperament that was reflected in periodic tantrums, administrative incompetence and a passion for soldiering and war.

Outright confrontation with the queen's favourite would be far too dangerous so Cecil played a patient waiting game, knowing that Essex's vaulting ambition and personal failings were liable to get him into serious trouble sooner or later. The secretary cleverly sought to divert the favourite away from domestic policy

making and influence by encouraging him to accept strictly military posts, notably the Master of the Ordinance, the Master of the Horse and the Office of Earl
Marshall – positions which typically involved grandiose ceremonial duties rather
than executive authority. Cecil also took advantage of the earl's military expeditions by extending his power base through appointments while the favourite was
away and by ensuring that Essex was made fully accountable on his return.

The Cadiz expedition of 1596 was generally acclaimed as a great military feat
for which Essex was anxious to get all the credit. He therefore had printed an
account of the voyage in which he featured as the true hero of the day. However,
Cecil pre-empted him by ensuring that a more objective version of events was
circulated to the Privy Council. When Essex returned to the court he was asked
to explain how it was that an expedition that had cost the queen over £50,000
to equip had yielded so little by way of plunder. It transpired that £11,000 sitting
in the coffers of Cadiz Castle had been overlooked by the raiding party, and that
some £12,000 of loot had been distributed to the earl's followers, of whom no
less than sixty-four were also knighted. Cecil eventually managed to recover a
total of £28,000 but the queen would have been made aware that the voyage had
failed financially and Essex reported to Anthony Bacon that 'I was more braved
by your little cousin than ever I was by any man in my life'.[20]

Essex's next naval expedition against Spain, the so-called Islands Voyage in
1597, was such a manifest fiasco that Cecil had no need to draw attention to its
failure. The intention was to capture the Canary Islands, to intercept and seize
Spanish treasure ships and to attack the Spanish fleet. The English ships, crippled
by a combination of bad weather and feuding among the commanders, limped
back without any of its objectives achieved and Essex on his return went into a
prolonged sulk.

The end for the unruly Earl of Essex came when, with some reluctance and
considerable foreboding, he accepted command of an army of 16,000 men to
be sent over to Ireland to put down a rebellion led by the Earl of Tyrone. That
shrewd observer, Francis Bacon, warned his friend that his mission, though
worthy, was full of peril, and privately he forecast the favourite's downfall. In
March 1599 Essex set off from London and Cecil, as usual, seized the opportunity of his absence to implement policies and appointments which would have
been anathema to his court rival. He pursued peace initiatives with Spain, he was
instrumental in securing the vacant office of Lord Treasurer for Lord Buckhurst,
a man already beholden to the Cecils, and he obtained for himself the highly
desirable office of Master of the Wards. Essex had himself coveted and openly
contested this last appointment since it offered opportunities for considerable
self-enrichment. The fact that it was given not to a nominee of Cecil but to the
Principal Secretary himself was a double strike against the earl.

Essex failed to engage Tyrone and with his army dwindling through illness and
desertions he breached the instructions of his command, first by entering into

a truce with the rebel leader and second by deserting his post and returning to England. When in September 1599 he arrived at court, still filthy from his journey, he burst into the queen's chamber while she was dressing, later complaining bitterly that he was the victim of a smear campaign by his enemies.

Then came the decisive blow: Essex's fortune was based on his licence to import sweet wines which was due for renewal in October but the queen, no doubt advised by Cecil, decided to administer this monopoly for the benefit of the Crown instead. Essex, who had pressing debts of £16,000, now faced financial ruin. Already in disgrace and subsequently beset by creditors, Essex gathered his followers to Essex House in the Strand. From there, in February 1601, he led a cavalcade of some 200 men through the city in an attempt to rally the London mob in his support. Cecil showed great presence of mind by instructing his brother, Burghley, to follow Essex with a herald proclaiming the earl to be a traitor to Her Majesty the Queen. The rebellion failed, Essex returned by boat to Essex House and then gave himself up.

Charged with high treason Essex was arraigned on 19 February at Westminster Hall before a jury of twenty-five peers selected by Cecil. The secretary himself was not among them and, indeed, not visibly present at the trial. He was, however, standing behind a tapestry in readiness to intervene if any false allegation should be made against him. When Essex accused Cecil of telling one of his counsellors that 'none in the world but the Infanta of Spain had right to the Crown of England',[21] Cecil suddenly emerged from behind the screen. In a shrill voice he repeatedly demanded to know the source of the allegation. Essex reluctantly divulged the name of Sir Francis Knollys, the queen's comptroller, but when Knollys was brought from the city he denied that Cecil had made any such claim.

Cecil then used the opportunity to make a blistering attack on Essex and all that he stood for, accusing him of trying to provoke war against Spain for no other reason than it gave importance to himself and his followers. Cecil also accused him of seeking to depose the queen and have himself declared king. 'The Secretary,' wrote one onlooker 'cried out at the top of his voice, the [jury of] peers showing in their faces more fear of this little man than of their conscience and their Queen.'[22] Well might the Venetian emissary describe Cecil as a man 'readier for revenge than for affection'.[23]

After Elizabeth had signed the warrant for his execution, Essex was brought to the scaffold on 23 February. He had asked for a private execution within the Tower and only a few of his peers attended, among whom was Ralegh in his capacity of Captain of the Guard. The Council had authorised two headsmen so that 'if one faint, the other may perform it to him',[24] but this proved to be an unnecessary precaution, the executioner's third stroke of the axe severing the earl's head from his body.

Cecil was now indisputably in charge. With the elimination of the queen's favourite he was the unchallenged political supremo and he was able to devote himself more freely to affairs of state. But just as he had systematically gathered political power into his hands so too did Cecil set about accumulating huge personal wealth. His official emoluments from the various offices he held were modest but he was able to exploit his position to generate by far the largest private income in the country, bar the Crown.

He engaged in privateering in partnership with, among others, Ralegh and the Lord Admiral and was able to get the state to pay for some of the outlays. Cecil's share of captures by just two privateering boats, *Lioness* and *Refusal*, amounted to some £7,000 in the two years 1601–2.[25] Privateering was later to be suspended, however, when peace negotiations with Spain began in 1603 and the letters of marque that authorised the capture of enemy ships were withdrawn.

The late Lord Burghley had made a little over £1,000 per annum as Master of the Wards. Under this anachronistic regime landed heirs who were under age (21 for male heirs and 14 for heiresses) were subject to the wardship of the Crown – which had custody of their property and the right to arrange their marriage. These rights could be sold in the open market for the benefit of the monarch, but more often for the enrichment of the office holder. When Cecil succeeded his father as Master of the Wards, he milked the system for all it was worth, raising his take to around £3,000 per annum.[26]

In 1601 Elizabeth granted Cecil the farm of the customs on imported silks and satins for ten years, which was later renewed by King James I. An annual rent was paid to the Crown for this privilege and the farm then sublet to others. Initially the net yield to Cecil averaged around £1,300 per annum. But he used state powers to clamp down on smuggling in order to boost his revenue, and when silk and satin imports boomed despite a rise in tariffs, Cecil's net take soared to the staggering sum of £7,000 per annum.[27] In 1605, when tenders were invited for the lease of the 'Great Farm' (general customs duties), Cecil was on the selection committee as well as a participant in one of the bidding syndicates. Unsurprisingly his syndicate won the tender whereupon he sold his interest for £6,000 cash to the other participants.[28]

Cecil also traded heavily in real estate. He was able to buy property from the Crown, often at knock-down prices – in one instance purchasing an estate valued at 1514 prices, since when land values had risen fourfold. Where his speculation did not work out he could sell the properties back to the Crown at cost – a 'put option' that effectively eliminated his risk. He built up a property portfolio along the Strand up to St Martins Lane and then, in 1601–3, he engaged in a frenzy of purchases, borrowing heavily in order to buy manors and estates in Cornwall, Dorset, Wiltshire, East Anglia, Northamptonshire and the immediate environs of London. In all, his land purchases in just three years amounted to over £35,000: some of these investments were quickly resold at a profit but others were retained and 'fines' or premiums exacted on rent renewals – a practice that raised £4,400 in just four years.[29]

Of course, Cecil himself did not have much time to devote to his property interests and relied to a large degree on his faithful steward, Roger Houghton, to look after his affairs. On his most spectacular commercial development, however, Cecil was closely involved. This was the so-called 'New Exchange', a shopping mall sited on the Strand, west of Salisbury House, which was officially opened by James I in April 1609. The project was intended to provide a Westminster alternative to Sir Thomas Gresham's Royal Exchange in the city. The 100 shops within the mall were open from 6.00 a.m. to 8.00 p.m. and were permitted to sell only high-class merchandise such as perfumes, oriental silks and porcelain with no perishables allowed. The rental income from the shops had to pay for the project's financing costs of some £11,000 per annum and the scheme seems to have done little more than break even before going into decline after 1620 when the top floor of the two-tiered bazaar was converted into flats.[30]

It is estimated that by the end of his life Cecil's total income from his official offices as well as all perquisites, but excluding dealings in land, amounted to some £25,000 per annum – this at a time when the greatest landed income in the country was less than £8,000 per annum.[31] Clearly it was not just political power that was concentrated in Cecil's grasp: he also took into his possession any source of revenue or profit that lay within his very long reach.

In his personal appearance and conduct Cecil always displayed modesty. As befitted someone of his stature and misshapen physique he chose not to compete with the peacocks at court. On the other hand, he was able to indulge his passion for grandiose buildings and it was here that he showed a very different face to the world. The great mansion he inherited at Theobalds was the largest residence in England apart from Westminster Palace and Hampton Court, and it was within its walls, celebrated gardens and parklands that Cecil, like his father before him, entertained the queen and the court.

For his London house Cecil wanted a grand residence on the fashionable south side of the Strand with a waterfront that would give easy river access to Whitehall Palace. He managed to buy a property for £1,000 in a prime position between Russell House and Ivy Bridge Lane. Moving the lane slightly to the west to accommodate his development, Cecil demolished the existing building and replaced it with a three-storey courtyard house with four storey corner towers that he named Cecil (later Salisbury) House. He moved in during October 1602 though the plasterwork was still damp, and he gave a sumptuous house-warming party in December at which the queen was present. Among his West Country property purchases Cecil selected Cranborne Manor as a country estate which made him a neighbour of Ralegh at Sherborne. In 1608 he decided to demolish and replace the original building and later on King James I, attracted by the hunting offered at Cranborne Chase, paid several visits to his secretary's rural retreat.

On his accession James also took a fancy to Theobalds, with its opportunities for hunting and easy access to London; and in 1607 Cecil was persuaded to exchange his family seat for the former palace of the Bishops of Ely at Hatfield. This transaction presented Cecil with an opportunity to build a great house in his own image – an edifice whose grandeur would celebrate his achievement and his status far more powerfully and enduringly than the passing flamboyance of a Ralegh or an Essex. He built in the latest Jacobean style at the colossal cost of some £40,000 the magnificent palace that still stands today, thereby fulfilling his ambition to 'show himself a good architectour'.[32] Cecil could by the end of his life justly claim to be 'the greatest builder of an age which itself was the greatest period of country house building in English history'.[33]

Cecil's great building projects were a pleasurable distraction from the day to day burdens of high office and the ever pressing need for political vigilance. Cecil's father had advised him 'seek not to be Essex and shun to be Ralegh' and this warning was to prove prophetic. The execution of Essex marked the final dissolution of what had at one time been a powerful faction both at court and within the Privy Council. Yet as Francis Bacon so astutely remarked in his essay *Of Faction:* 'When one of the factions is extinguished, the remaining subdivideth … and therefore those that are seconds in factions do many times, when the faction subdivideth, prove principals …'[34]

So it was with the destruction of the Essex party. Some of those who had joined with Cecil to defeat the earl peeled off as soon as the mission was accomplished and formed their own faction in opposition to Cecil. Therefore as Elizabeth's reign drew towards a close, Cecil became preoccupied with two related concerns: his own prospects for continuance in office under the queen's successor; and the need to snuff out those recalcitrant spirits, notably Ralegh and his friend Lord Cobham, who were threatening to get in his way. He would eventually use the same techniques that destroyed Essex in his efforts to eliminate his new rivals – the difference being that Ralegh was a much more formidable opponent than the earl.

3

SHIFTING ALLIANCES

When factions are carried too high, and too violently, it is a sign of weakness in Princes, and much to the prejudice both of their authority, and business.

Francis Bacon, *Of Faction*

As Cecil and Ralegh faced each other across the Great Hall of Winchester Castle on that fateful day in November 1603, everyone present would have been aware of their earlier intimacy. They had been close friends, political allies, colleagues in the queen's service and neighbours in both town and county. Yet beneath the veneer of social familiarity there had always been a deep-seated rivalry between the two men. Now it was out in the open as they engaged in what amounted to a deadly personal duel in which the strengths and weaknesses of the one were known only too well to the other.

Cecil's animosity towards Ralegh had deep roots. There was an understandable tension at the Elizabethan court between those high government officials who had worked their way to the top, and the royal favourites who could sway the queen's opinions and influence policy outside the Council chamber. Add to this Elizabeth's own unpredictable nature and we have what Francis Bacon aptly described as 'that deep and inscrutable centre of the court which is her Majesty's mind'.[1]

When Ralegh was riding high in the queen's esteem, even the most powerful councillor might need to beg his favour in order to gain the royal ear. So it was that Cecil's father, Lord Burghley, humbled himself in May 1583 by asking Ralegh to intervene on behalf of his son-in-law, the Earl of Oxford, who had disgraced himself by fathering an illegitimate child by Anne Vavasour, a lady of the court. Ralegh was able to oblige the Lord Treasurer and his reply is indicative of the extraordinary influence the young favourite exercised over the queen at this time:

The evening after receipt of your Lordship's letter, I spake with Her Majesty and ministering some occasion touching the Earl of Oxford, I told Her Majesty how grievously your Lordship received her late discomfortable answer ... What I said further, how honourable and profitable it were for Her Majesty to have regard to your Lordship's health and quiet, I leave to the witness of God, and good report of Her Highness. And the more to witness how desirous I am of your Lordship's favour and good opinion I am content, for your sake, to lay the serpent before the fire, as much as in me lieth, that having recovered strength myself may be most in danger of his poison and sting [Oxford and Ralegh being court enemies]. For answer Her Majesty would give me non other but that she would satisfy Your Lordship, of whom she ever had, and would ever have, special regard. Thus being unfeignably willing to deserve Your Lordship's good favour, I humbly take my leave.[2]

As the greatest councillor in the land, Burghley must have bitten his tongue when he received this patronising response – which also makes very clear Ralegh's expectation of favours in return.

While Burghley may have courted Ralegh in the early 1580s, the shoe was on the other foot when his son began his extraordinary rise to power nearly a decade later. By then Essex was in the ascendant, Ralegh's star was on the wane and it was he who sought Cecil's favour. In early 1592 Ralegh, after secretly marrying Bess, was preparing his privateering expedition to the Azores when rumours of the marriage threatened to derail his plans. In a letter to Cecil dated March 1592, he said that he had promised the queen (who still wanted him around her) that he would return to court once he had persuaded his men to accept the command of Sir Martin Frobisher. He added:

I mean not to come away, as they say I will, for fear of a marriage and I know not what. If any such thing were, I would have imparted it unto yourself before any man living; and, therefore, I pray believe it not, and I beseech you to sup-press what you can any such malicious report. For I protest before God, there is none, on the face of the earth, that I would be fastened unto.[3]

This assurance to Cecil was clearly a barefaced lie, but it may not be quite as brazen and insulting to his new wife as it seems. The letter was evidently written in haste and it has been suggested that the last sentence, which in the manuscript is incomplete, may have omitted the single word 'sooner', so that it should read: 'for I protest before God, there is none on the face of the earth, that I would sooner be fastened unto.'[4] This makes sense, because Ralegh was undoubtedly courting Cecil's favour at this time and was shortly to address him as 'my very loving friend'. Whatever the true intent, Ralegh soon had need of all the help he could get. When the queen's fury erupted over his marriage and he was committed to the Tower, it was again to Cecil that Ralegh wrote. But here he was trying to use his friend as an intermediary with the queen, and it was for her eyes that his extravagant prose was clearly intended:

> My heart was never broken till this day, that I hear the Queen goes away so far off [on Progress, a journey around her kingdom] – whom I have followed so many years with so great love and desire, in so many journeys, and am now left behind her, in a dark prison, all alone … I that was won't to behold her riding like Alexander, hunting like Diana, walking like Venus, the gentle wind blowing her fair hair about her pure cheeks like a nymph; sometime sitting in the shade like a goddess; sometime singing like an angel; sometime playing like Orpheus.[5]

When the Cecils did intervene it was for reasons of state, not the cloying sentimentality of the kind Ralegh occasionally indulged in. The privateering expedition organised and part-financed by Ralegh, but now commanded by Frobisher and Sir John Borough, successfully attacked the Spanish treasure fleet and brought back into Dartmouth harbour the great carrack, *Madre de Dios*, laden with spices, pepper, silk, ivory and precious stones. The uncontrolled pillaging of this booty by West Country men had to be stopped and it was Sir John Hawkins, who wrote to Burghley in September that 'to bring this into some good effect Sir Walter Ralegh is the especial man'.[6]

Cecil had, on 15 September, already been appointed Her Majesty's commissioner with a remit to protect the queen's interest in the carrack's spoils of war. Burghley, while securing Ralegh's release from the Tower to help in this urgent task, also ensured that his son was despatched immediately so that he could gain credit for taking firm action ahead of Ralegh's arrival. The competitive element in the situation is revealed by Cecil's correspondence with his father, where he assures him that 'Her Majesty's captive comes after me, but I have outrid him, and will be at Dartmouth before him'.[7] Moreover in a letter written just after Ralegh's arrival, he reveals his spite to Sir Thomas Heneage, the Vice Chamberlain: 'I do grace him [Ralegh] as much as I may, for I find him marvellous greedy to recover the conceit of his brutish offence.'[8] Clearly Cecil is already playing his familiar two-faced game.

Cecil's misgivings about Ralegh may have been prompted by old-fashioned jealousy. While Cecil was effective in tracking down the carrack's pilfered cargo through the interrogation of suspects and the searching of all bags and mail coming from the west, he could only look on with amazement at the response of the rough West Country sailors to their commander's arrival. As Cecil himself reported to Heneage: '… All the mariners are come to him [Ralegh] with such shouts and joy, as I never saw a man more troubled to quiet them in my life.'[9] Ralegh was a born leader of men while Cecil, though a good ferret, knew he could never be that.

Ralegh's handling of the *Madre de Dios'* spoils earned him his release from captivity, but he was still to be banished from court for the next five years. During this period he continued to correspond with Cecil on a variety of matters, ranging from Irish politics, the defences of the West Country, plans for a voyage of discovery to Guiana and his own personal affairs. Ralegh was no longer a court rival and his role was that of petitioner and subordinate, a status which he openly acknowledged. In May 1593 he wrote to Cecil: 'wherever I be, and while I am, you shall command me,'[10] and his letters were typically signed off 'and so, being always your servant to be commanded.' When he wrote to Cecil in September 1594 Ralegh referred to 'your most honourable friendship towards me,' and went on to say 'how much for such respect I may be bound you know and which I will acknowledge and perform to the end of my life.'[11] Ralegh was safely penned in to his West Country domain and when he came up to London it was to pursue his passion for maritime adventures and not to engage in court politics. Cecil could therefore afford to offer friendship and a degree of patronage to the disgraced royal favourite. He was also persuaded to become an investor in Ralegh's expedition to Guiana in 1595, and Ralegh dedicated his work *The Discovery of the Large, Rich and Beautiful Empire of Guiana* to Cecil and the Lord Admiral, Charles Howard.

When the Cadiz expedition was being prepared under Essex's command in the spring of 1596, Ralegh was recalled into active service. He was given the thankless task of rounding up men and supplies around London, but he went about the business with furious energy and made regular reports of his progress to Cecil. Essex showed generosity to Ralegh, and he welcomed his participation in the navel venture as a squadron commander. He assured him that 'this is the action and the time in which you and I shall be both taught to know and love one another'.[12] Meanwhile, Burghley and Cecil, persuaded of the need for a strike against Spain, gave their full support to the mission.

Here were the beginnings of a triumvirate of power involving three very different men: the boyish, enthusiastic but erratic royal favourite, Essex; the older, shrewder and much cleverer former favourite, Ralegh; and the wily, calculating and ever watchful hunchback, Cecil. In this military expedition their interests were bound together, but they were also rivals for power and favour.

Some six months after the successful attack, Cecil's wife Elizabeth died, and the letter of condolence that Ralegh wrote to the grief stricken secretary says something about the two men's intimacy at this time:

> I had rather be with you now than at any other time, if I could thereby either take off from you the burden of your sorrows, or lay the greater part thereof on mine own heart … it is true you have lost a good and virtuous wife, and myself an honourable friend and kinswoman. But there was a time when she was unknown to you, for whom you then lamented not. She is now no more yours nor of your acquaintance, but immortal, and not needing or knowing your love

or sorrow. Therefore you shall but grieve for that which now is as then it was, when not yours; only bettered by the difference in this, that she hath passed the wearisome journey of this dark world, and hath possession of her inheritance.

Ralegh went on to say that 'the mind of man is that part of God which is in us,' and that the more we allow ourselves to be ruled by our emotions, the further removed we are from our maker: 'Sorrow draws not the dead to life, but the living to death.'[13] This is a remarkable and paradoxical letter because it was written by a man capable of great passion and emotional turmoil to another whose defining characteristic was his iron self-control and clinical calculation. The bleak under-lying philosophy – that death is an obliteration which severs all claims on the sentiments of the living – was to be reflected again in Ralegh's own farewell letter to his wife, Bess.

Following Cecil's bereavement, Bess offered to help in raising Will – the sec-retary's oldest son – and this gesture was gratefully received. Will was to spend long periods with the Raleghs at Sherborne, which became a second home to him. Significantly, when Will wrote to his father he did so in Latin and spoke only of his studies; when he wrote to Ralegh he wrote in English and said that in his absence he felt he had lost his 'captain'. Whether Cecil felt in any way slighted by his son's manifest affection and admiration for his new guardian can only be guessed at. Bess clearly saw Cecil as the key to Ralegh's rehabilitation and she not only took great trouble with Will but also offered solace to the widowed secretary. She made dinner for him, she sent him porcelain and she accompanied him to plays and banquets.[14] She was also a faithful correspondent and, on one occasion, sent Cecil a pair of gloves with a teasing instruction that 'it is indented [stipulated] that if they serve not your own hands you must of your grace return them again'.[15] Ralegh, in his own letter to Cecil a week later, added a message from Bess to the effect that 'she must envy any fingers whosoever shall wear her gloves but your own'.[16]

In the spring of 1597 the rapprochement between Ralegh, Essex and Cecil was made explicit. On 18 April Ralegh and Cecil attended a dinner at Essex House in the Strand and, according to one correspondent, 'after dinner they were very private all three for two hours, where the treaty of peace was confirmed'.[17] The agreement that emerged was that Essex should be made Master of the Ordinance, Ralegh should resume his office as Captain of the Guard and Cecil should gain the Chancellorship of the Duchy of Lancaster. The three also committed themselves to the so-called Islands Voyage, which involved an attack on Spanish possessions and ships in the mid-Atlantic.

The three men each had their own reasons to embrace one another. Essex wanted Cecil's support for his grandiose military ambitions, and valued Ralegh's active involvement so long as he was subordinate. Cecil was happy to see Ralegh back at court as a potential counterbalance to Essex who had such a powerful hold on the queen. And Ralegh was content to ally himself with those who could help to restore his former position at court. As they sought their own advantage, the three manoeuvred around each other, balancing common interests against innate mistrust and mutual rivalry.

The coming together of Ralegh, Essex and Cecil made possible Ralegh's rehabilitation with the queen. When his five years of banishment were over, in May 1597, he made his reappearance at court and on 2 June it was Cecil who brought the fallen favourite to the queen's presence so that she could authorise him to resume his duties as Captain of the Guard. According to one observer, 'In the evening he rid abroad with the queen, and had private conference with her; and now he comes boldly to the Privy chamber, as he was wont'.[18] Essex had evidently made no objection to this reunion, but still found reason to busy himself in Chatham rather than witness the reinstatement of his old rival.

Behind the overt displays of unity other considerations weighed. Ralegh was a clear beneficiary of the new entente and in July 1597 he wrote gratefully to Cecil:

> I hope it shall never alter, and whereof I shall be most glad of it, as the true way to all our good, quiet and advancement and most of all for her sake, whose affairs will thereby find better progression. Sir, I will ever be yours, it is all I can say, and I will perform it with my life and with my fortune.[19]

Once again Ralegh was prepared to subordinate himself to the younger man whom he saw as his benefactor and patron. Cecil, for his part, no doubt viewed Ralegh as a means of neutralising Essex. It is clear that the secretary did not want either man to hold too much sway and he was also nervous that they might combine against him. He was therefore prepared to play one off against the other, as he did when he wrote to Essex deriding 'good Mr Ralegh who wonders at his own diligence, because diligence and he are not familiars'.[20]

The biggest potential loser in the peace agreement was Essex. He had allowed Ralegh back to court and was now allied to the wily Cecil. He was excited by the prospect of heroic military action against Spain, but friends of the earl were more cautious. His uncle, the experienced courtier Sir William Knollys, wrote to his impetuous nephew in June: 'If we lived not in a cunning world I should assure myself that Mr Secretary were wholly yours – I will hope the best, yet will I observe him as narrowly as I can.'[21] In the same month, Knollys reported 'Mr Secretary remaineth in all show firm to your Lordship and no doubt will, so long as the Queen is well pleased with you'.[22]

The Islands Voyage undertaken in the autumn of 1597 was not only a financial and military failure, but also led to an explosive confrontation between Essex as commander and Ralegh his subordinate. After the English fleet's return, however, relations between the two were smoothed over when Ralegh proposed that Essex should be given the vacant position of Earl Marshall.

Ralegh was now hoping to be admitted to the Privy Council, but he appears to have been blocked by Essex. In early 1598 it was reported that Cecil was ready to agree that Sir Robert Sydney, an Essex supporter, should be appointed to the Council provided Ralegh was admitted at the same time.[23] This was presumably unacceptable to Essex because nothing happened. Clearly there were tensions between the Essex and Cecil factions within the Council, and in October there was talk of what would have amounted to a coup against the earl: the appointment of four new councillors, Cobham, Ralegh, Stanhope and Thomas Howard, all of whom were potential Essex opponents.[24] The standoff continued and the vacancy on the Council created by Burghley's death in the summer of 1598 was left unfilled. Ralegh, though restored to royal favour, remained conspicuously outside the magic circle of political advisors.

Ralegh's standing with Essex was not helped by the close friendship and political alliance he had formed with Henry Brooke, the new Lord Cobham. Cobham was a court rival of the earl who had succeeded his father as Warden of the Cinque Ports against the Essex nominee, Sir Robert Sydney. Although he was no intellectual match for Ralegh, Cobham had the queen's ear, powerful connections (Cecil had been married to his sister) and he was ambitious for his own political advancement.

During his disastrous military commission in Ireland Essex became convinced that a new alliance, consisting of Ralegh, Cobham and Cecil, was plotting against him. In a letter from Ireland in June 1599 he injudiciously harangued the queen:

> Is it not lamented by your Majesty's faithfullest subjects, both here and there, that a Cobham and a Ralegh – I will forebear others for their places' sakes – should have such credit and favour with your Majesty, when they wish the ill success of your Majesty's most important action [the Irish Campaign], the decay of your greatest strength and the destruction of your faithfullest servants?[25]

Such paranoia was not calculated to endear the royal favourite to his mistress.

The old triumvirate had fallen apart, but for the time being Ralegh and Cecil remained close. Ralegh was on several occasions admitted to the Council Chamber to advise on Irish affairs and on the military threat from Spain. Both he and Cobham were now looking for a political opening, and Essex's return from Ireland and subsequent treason provided the opportunity. In a now infamous letter to Cecil, written at the time of the earl's disgrace, but before his insurrection, Ralegh in effect urged the secretary to finish off the royal favourite while he was down:

> If you take it for a good counsel to relent towards this tyrant, you will repent it when it shall be too late. His malice is fixed and will not evaporate by any of your mild courses. For he will ascribe the alteration to her Majesty's pusillanim-

ity and not to your good nature; knowing that you work but upon her humour, and not out of any love towards him. The less you make him the less he shall be able to harm you and yours. And if her Majesty fail him he will again decline to a common person.

Ralegh was saying that if Essex forfeited the protection of the queen he would decline to a 'common person' and it would then be in Cecil's power to do what he wished with him. Ralegh goes on to make it quite clear what the earl's fate should be: 'for after – revenges fear them not' he says. He then cites three cases, among many more he says he could mention, where noblemen were put to death without their heirs taking revenge upon those responsible. If Essex were eliminated, 'his son shall be the youngest Earl of England but one and, if his father be now kept down, Will Cecil [Cecil's heir] shall be able to keep as many men at his heels as he, and more too'. In other words, Will would be in a position to take care of himself. On the other hand, 'if the father continue, he will be able to break the branches and pull up the tree, root and all. Lose not your advantage'.[26]

The overall chilling message from Ralegh was that Cecil should take it upon himself to secure the execution of Essex while he had the chance. Otherwise the fallen idol, on regaining the queen's favour, would have it in for Cecil – and, of course, for Ralegh too. At this highest level of court rivalry it was 'kill or be killed', but little did Ralegh know that the advice he was giving to the diminutive hunchback would be fully taken on board when dealing with Ralegh himself less than three years later.

What Cecil made of this advice we do not know, but he would have been only too aware that he was being asked to take a huge personal risk. To initiate treason proceedings against Essex, before his open rebellion had put him beyond the pale, would be to endanger the secretary's standing with the queen. Cecil knew only too well how much the royal favourite meant to his mistress. When Essex was arraigned after his insurrection, Cecil was no doubt happy to be excluded from the panel of twenty-five peers who sat in judgement, knowing full well that the queen would mourn the loss of her beloved earl even after she had signed his death warrant.

Ordinary Londoners, to whom Essex remained something of a hero, blamed Ralegh for rejoicing in the earl's fate. As Captain of the Guard Ralegh was present at the execution and it was said that he had joked and puffed his pipe as his rival was decapitated. But Ralegh was insistent that to avoid the impression of triumphalism he had withdrawn discreetly to the armoury before the axe fell; from here he could witness the execution unseen. Ralegh later commented on the downfall of his adversary in his tract *Prerogative of Parliaments*, where he referred to Essex's reported response to the queen's refusal to renew his farm of sweet wines. The offending remark was that Elizabeth's 'conditions were as crooked as her carcass', and Ralegh asserted that these words 'cost the Earl his head, which his insurrection had not cost him, but for that speech'. The lesson was that 'the undu-tiful words of a subject do often take deeper root than the memory of ill deeds'.[27]

During the year or so of the earl's disgrace leading up to his execution, Ralegh and Cobham had been confidently anticipating political favours from Cecil. Indeed so much so that in February 1600, Cobham was hoping to be made a privy councillor before celebrating his marriage to Frances Howard, widow of the Earl of Kildare. But the call did not come, and when in May of that year John Herbert – a loyal assistant to Cecil but a man lacking both status and experience – was made a councillor, both Ralegh and Cobham must have been affronted. Meanwhile, Ralegh, excluded from peace negotiations with an embassy from the Spanish Netherlands, and relegated to the role of entertaining the emissaries, decided to retire to the countryside. That summer Ralegh wrote a letter to Cecil from Sherborne which betrayed his frustrations: 'Bess returns you her best wishes, not withstanding all quarrels'.[28]

The execution of Essex in February 1601 led to the disbandment of his fac-tion at court; some of his key followers betrayed each other while others, such as Francis Bacon, changed sides. The disappearance of the Essex party created a power vacuum which Ralegh and Cobham were ambitious to fill. However, they badly misunderstood Cecil's own political perspective. He had been happy to restore Ralegh to favour and ally himself with the queen's old favourite, but only because he had wanted a powerful counterweight to Essex with his danger-ous ambitions and strong court following. Now that Essex and his faction were destroyed, he had no need of Ralegh. Furthermore, Ralegh once again had access to the queen, as did his friend Cobham, and Cecil was no doubt concerned that these two could become a disruptive force if they became councillors. Ralegh was also, like Essex, a warmonger, while Cecil was now committed to peace with Spain. Finally, behind all the politeness, consideration and camaraderie, it is clear that Cecil did not trust Ralegh; he disliked his conceit and harboured long-stand-ing feelings of jealousy towards him.

In July 1600, excluded from national politics, Cobham and Ralegh had already taken matters into their own hands when they visited Ostend while a peace con-ference was in session. Evidently Cecil was put out: he was unaware of their true purpose in going and no doubt viewed their visit as an unauthorised intervention in foreign affairs.[29] If, as has been suggested, the two travellers made contact with the Count of Aremberg – the Spanish Minister in the Netherlands – Cecil's anxi-ety was fully justified.

Ralegh was eager to grasp the one bone that was thrown to him. Three months after his return from Ostend he was offered the governorship of Jersey, a respon-sibility which he assumed with his usual frenetic energy. The appointment also kept him away from court and this no doubt suited Cecil: the secretary was happy to see such an ambitious man loaded with regional responsibilities in Devon, Cornwall and now the Channel Islands, so long as he did not interfere in national affairs. Now that mutual suspicion between Ralegh and Cecil had taken root the secretary, determined as always to safeguard his monopoly of political power, had decided to do whatever was necessary to keep Ralegh out. This is revealed in a letter Cecil wrote to his confidante, Sir George Carew, President of Munster, in June 1601. He referred to 'the mutinies of those I do love' and went on to say that Ralegh 'shall never have my consent to be a Councillor, without he surrender to you the Captainship of the Guard …'[30] That same month, Shrewsbury, Worcester and Stanhope were sworn of the Council – a clear signal to Ralegh and Cobham that the doors of the Council Chamber were to be closed to them so long as Cecil was in charge. If Ralegh were a councillor and also had direct access to the queen in his official capacity, he would have too much influence.

Ralegh now declared his hand. When parliament met on 27 October 1601 he openly opposed Cecil on the subsidy bill. In an eloquent speech he proposed that the poorest, or 'three pound men', should be exempt and that all those above them should pay proportionately more. This radical idea was unacceptable to Cecil, but in the unruly debate that followed the secretary lost his command of the house. When Ralegh later argued powerfully against a government bill for the compulsory sewing of hemp, Cecil was forcefully reminded what a disruptive influence Ralegh could be when he chose. Cecil's close ally, Henry Howard, observed that Ralegh was frustrated by finding his political aspirations blocked, and was pursuing wrecking tactics in the hope, perhaps, that Cecil might relent. Howard noted that Ralegh 'cares not at what rate he purchase opportunity to vex others, having no great hope of ascending to his own altitude'.[31]

In the privacy of his own London residence Ralegh appeared to be forming a rival faction, much as Essex had done at Essex House. He and Cobham had developed an increasingly close relationship with Henry Percy, 9th Earl of Northumberland, and these three were constantly in conference at Durham House. That the triumvirate intended the secretary no good was confirmed when, towards the end of 1601, Cobham attempted a direct assault on Cecil by maligning him to the queen – a clumsy initiative for which he received a royal snub.[32]

The difficulties Cecil experienced in the 1601 parliament, and the emergence of what appeared to be an opposition group at Durham House, persuaded Cecil that something had to be done about his new adversaries. Yet during the following year he was careful not to disclose his intentions. On the contrary, he continued to collaborate with Ralegh in privateering ventures and the social niceties between the two men were preserved. But in a letter written to Carew in June 1602, Cecil swore to take revenge on Ralegh and Cobham: 'Know it we will be merry, and yet believe me two old friends use me unkindly, but I have covenanted with my heart not to know it, for in show we are great, and all my revenge shall be to heap coals on their heads.'[33]

Cecil's preferred approach was to avoid outright confrontation; instead he was prepared to bide his time and then to undermine and, ultimately, destroy his opponents through clandestine use of his powerful intelligence and political network. For Cecil's objective had moved well beyond that of keeping Ralegh out of the Privy Council and confined to the political wilderness. From his point of view, Ralegh had shown gross ingratitude and broken his vow of loyalty to the benefactor who had helped to bring him back to court and the queen's favour. He now decided that Ralegh, and his junior partner Cobham, were deliberately obstructing him and the 'coals' that were to be heaped on their heads meant nothing less than their elimination from court politics. The secretary had found a sinister new ally to excavate the ground under their feet, and following the advice that Ralegh himself had given to Cecil on dealing with Essex, he would seek to reduce them to 'common men', leaving them unprotected by their sovereign and exposed to whatever fate Cecil might choose for them.

4

PREPARING FOR THE GREAT DAY OF MART

Treason doth never prosper, what's the reason?
For if it prosper, who dare call it treason

Sir John Harrington, 1561–1612

Elizabeth was never willing to discuss the succession to her throne, but towards the end of her reign there was a widespread assumption in court and country alike that an existing monarch – James VI of Scotland – would be crowned King of England when she died. Other possible claimants included Lady Arabella Stuart, James' first cousin; the Infanta Isabella Clara Eugenia of Spain, who inherited the claim of her father Philip II; and Edward Seymour, Lord Beauchamp, who was descended from the younger daughter of Henry VII. James may have been the front-runner in the succession stakes, but there was always the danger that a rival would emerge, particularly if the queen refused to name her heir.

For holders of high office and ambitious men around the court, the accession of a new sovereign presented opportunities but also great risks: old favourites would have to make way for new; royal patronage would be exercised in unpredictable ways; the entire Privy Council would have to resign and be reappointed; and office holders would be confirmed in their positions or replaced. In short, on the 'Great Day of Mart' or 'Exchange' – as Cecil neatly described the day of the queen's death – the distribution of honours, sinecures, offices of state, royal licences and favours were all up for renegotiation. There would be big winners and big losers, and Elizabeth's Principal Secretary was determined to ensure that the political pre-eminence he had worked so hard to achieve would not be put in jeopardy.

Well before his downfall, Essex had been in secret correspondence with Scotland. His purpose was both to ingratiate himself with the future King of

England and to undermine his enemies at court by questioning their loyalty to the Scottish claimant. According to the earl's secretary, Henry Cuffe, Essex had tried to blacken Cecil's name by giving a detailed account of his alleged intention to support the Infanta's claim to the crown and of his malice towards James.[1] James was therefore prejudiced against Cecil but he was also a realist, and after Essex's execution he instructed his two emissaries to England, the Earl of Mar and Edward Bruce, to sound out 'Mr Secretary, who is king there in effect'.[2] James wanted to smooth his path to the English throne and his informants had told him that Cecil was the man.

Towards the end of April 1601, Mar and Bruce met Cecil privately, away from the court at the offices of the Duchy of Lancaster in the Strand. This was the beginning of a negotiation of utmost delicacy which eventually led to an historic understanding between the Principal Secretary and Elizabeth's would-be successor. Cecil undertook to bring James to the English throne after Elizabeth's death, and for this purpose he would communicate with James on the basis of guaranteed secrecy. A simple numerical code was agreed for future correspondence, each major player being designated by a number: Northumberland was 0, Ralegh 3, Cobham 8, Cecil himself 10, Mar 20, Elizabeth 24 and James 30.

James's first letter to Cecil made clear that the quid pro quo for the secretary's co-operation was an assurance that he would enjoy as much royal favour under James as he had under Elizabeth. Since the two men had never met and had no bond of personal friendship or shared political ideology, the deal between them was pure power-broking:

> When it shall please God that 30 [James] shall succeed to his right, he shall no surelier succeed to the place than he shall succeed in bestowing as great and greater favour upon 10 [Cecil] as his predecessor doth bestow upon him, and in the meantime you may rest assured of the constant love and secrecy of your most loving and assured friend, 30.[3]

In his reply, Cecil was anxious to stress his continued loyalty to Elizabeth and excused his deceitful behaviour on the grounds that 'faithful ministers' must sometimes 'conceal thoughts and actions from Princes, when they are persuaded it is for their own greater service'.[4] Cecil was engaged in what could be viewed as treasonable conduct, but as he said, it was all for the good of the realm. As a further token of his loyalty, Cecil arranged for the Scottish king's pension from Elizabeth's hard-pressed treasury to be raised from £3,000 to £5,000 a year.[5]

Cecil had three objectives in mind when dealing with James: first to ensure a smooth transition to the new regime after the queen's death; second to protect his own position as the most powerful political figure in England; and third to vilify his enemies at court, of whom Ralegh and Cobham were the chief targets. In this last task he was to be greatly assisted by an unlikely ally and correspondent. For although Cecil himself was to write to James from time to time, his main instrument of communication was Henry Howard, a man already known to and trusted by James. This arrangement brought into play, as a close confidante of Cecil, one of the most sinister and venomous figures at the Elizabethan court.

Lord Henry Howard's family had experienced mixed fortunes. His father, the Earl of Surrey, had been executed by Henry VIII; his grandfather, the Duke of Norfolk, had been sent to the Tower; and his brother, the fourth Duke of Norfolk, had been executed by Elizabeth for plotting on behalf of Mary Queen of Scots. His fellow kinsmen Charles Howard, Earl of Nottingham, and Thomas Howard, later Earl of Suffolk, had fared much better, but Howard himself had languished on the outer fringes of Elizabeth's court – denied the financial rewards, status and royal favour to which he believed his talents and birth entitled him.

Howard was certainly outside the mainstream. He was suspected of Catholic leanings, he was a homosexual, he had an intense interest in astrology and at one time lectured on rhetoric at Cambridge University – an unusual occupation for a nobleman. He was prepared to toady in the most extravagant language to those who might offer him preferment, and he used intrigue as well as his vitriolic pen against those whom he considered his enemies. He had initially attached himself to the Essex faction as a follower of the Earl of Southampton, to whom he wrote, when he was serving in Ireland, that he bowed his knees 'thrice a day to God for the prospering of your safe return'.[6] After the fall of Essex, Howard cultivated Cecil's favour in order to safeguard his own future, and James' proposal to use him as an intermediary with the secretary gave him the break he was looking for.

Howard and James had much in common. They were both considerable scholars who enjoyed philosophical musings, flowery language and bawdy humour dressed up in Latin phrases. They also shared the same sexual preferences, had a deep-seated antipathy to militarism and indulged in self-righteous religiosity. Cecil, for his part, may have had a hold over his new ally because Howard had previously compromised himself by sending secret dispatches to Southampton which, through interception or other means, had found their way into Cecil's files.[7] The secretary, having such sensitive material in his possession, could therefore rely on Howard's compliance and loyalty which was essential in the mission he was now engaged in.

Howard's venom was directed in particular at Ralegh, for whom he appears to have nurtured an unabashed loathing. His hatred was due in part to the fact that, as a nobleman denied office and royal favour, he found it difficult to stomach Ralegh's meteoric rise from relatively humble origins. Ralegh's reputation as an atheist would not have gone down well with Howard, who had deep religious convictions, nor would the former favourite's military prowess and advocacy of war with Spain. Whatever the root cause of his enmity, this shadowy figure, whom Lady Bacon described as a 'subtle serpent', was a dangerous enemy – and especially so now that he was allied with Cecil and had the Scottish king's ear.

Howard's ideas for dealing with Ralegh and Cobham were set out in an undated memorandum, written in the spring or early summer of 1602, which appears to have been the basis of the advice he gave to Cecil.[8] According to Howard, Ralegh was manipulating Cobham and using the latter's favour with the queen to criticise others – presumably meaning Cecil. He felt the queen needed to be reminded of Ralegh's deep unpopularity in the country, and of the fact that any representations made by Ralegh and his two allies, Cobham and Northumberland, were motivated by their own personal grievances. The way to bring down Cobham, Howard wrote, was to give him some commission connected with Spain which, 'either may reveal his weakness or ensnare his ambition'.[9] Howard goes on to say:

> Be not unwilling … to engage him in traffick with suspected ministers … I account it impossible for him to escape the snares which we may set and weakness is apt to fall into. The Queen did never yet love man that failed in a project of importance put into his hand.[10]

The cynicism of this advice, which amounted to suggesting that Cobham be given an important task in the service of the state so that he could fail spectacularly, provides an interesting insight into court intrigue.

To destroy Ralegh, Howard suggested that the source of his income (which must mean his wine licence) be cut off. Howard cites here the example of Leicester, though he might equally well have chosen Essex: 'By stopping the springs of bounty … it stirred him so forcibly … as in a passion he grew – twice or thrice in my time – to speak those words to the Queen which lost him absolutely that advantage …'[11] Howard said Ralegh's over-weaning pride made him 'the greatest Lucifer that hath ever lived in our age,' and 'by so much shall he sooner run himself aground in rage, and make the Queen more sensitive in scorning so great sauciness in so great infirmity.' There was a clear hint here too, that if Ralegh's income was cut off he might resort to dangerous measures 'which will bring him into that snare which he would shun otherwise'.[12]

Finally, Howard raised the possibility that both Ralegh and Cobham might be severely damaged if James were to encourage them to open direct communications with him. This correspondence could then be intercepted, and the underhand dealings of the pair exposed to the queen.[13] However, Howard believed that James would not entertain such an idea, not least because the disclosure of secret correspondence would discourage others from dealing with him. Nevertheless, it says something about Howard that he would consider tempting Ralegh and Cobham into a course of conduct that he and Cecil were already engaged in, and then denounce them when the trap was sprung and their dealings made public.

Howard's thoughts on dealing with Cecil's enemies, which were no doubt shared with the secretary himself, turned out to be prophetic: Cobham was later to be ensnared in a Spanish plot and Ralegh was to be destabilised by the with-drawal of his main source of income. Also prophetic was a letter which Howard wrote to Mar at this time:

> The glass of time being very far run, the day of the Queen's death may be the day
> of their [Ralegh's and Cobham's] doom, if they do not agree with their adversary
> [Cecil] upon the way, lest he deliver them to the judge, and the judge to prison ...[14]

The implication contained in this letter, as well as the memorandum, is that Ralegh and Cobham were to be 'set up' by inducing them to engage in danger-ous practices; upon discovery of which they would be arraigned, convicted and imprisoned. This is precisely what was to transpire a little more than a year later.

Whereas Howard's memorandum focused on discrediting Cobham and Ralegh in the eyes of the queen, the correspondence he and Cecil conducted with Scotland was aimed at blackening the two men's characters in the eyes of James. The letters sent back and forth by couriers over hundreds of miles could have also brought Cecil down, had they been intercepted or fallen into the wrong hands. He was taking a huge, calculated risk, the only safeguards being an easily decoded cipher, the fact that most of the correspondence was conducted by intermediar-ies, (Howard, Mar and Bruce) and the mistaken belief on the part of Howard and Cecil that their letters were immediately burned after they had been read.

Howard's letters were verbose, discursive and often impenetrable, so much so that James himself was prompted to comment on 'all your ample Asiatic and end-less volumes'.[15] Cecil's letters by contrast were clear, concise and to the point. How far the secretary scrutinised and approved Howard's correspondence is an open question, since in one letter Howard says he is writing as Cecil's amanuensis, and in another he states explicitly that his comments are 'without commission' from Cecil.[16] However, when it came to Ralegh and Cobham, the sentiments expressed by the two men were very similar, the main difference being in the calculated malice shown by Cecil and the unrestrained ferocity of Howard's lan-guage. Both men sought to undermine their two opponents by ridiculing their thwarted ambition and by questioning their support for James' succession – in the same way that Essex had tried to undermine Cecil at the Scottish court by alleg-ing his commitment to the Infanta.

When Howard wrote directly to James, rather than to his agents, he indulged in extravagant flattery as in the following letter of August 1602:

> It is impossible for any other pen than that which the Prophet calleth *calamum*
> *scribe velociter scribentis*, Most Excellent Most Gracious, and most Redoubted
> King James, to present any figure of humble thankfulness proportionable to the
> merit of your matchless mind ... with a sweetness suitable to those true and
> humble affections that are born to you.

He then ended his letter with a sycophantic flourish: 'I humbly take my leave and most affectionately kiss your gracious and sacred hand, resting evermore yours than it is possible for you to conceive or imagine.'[17]

More often, Howard wrote to Mar or Bruce, reporting in tedious detail on the political wrangling at the Elizabethan court. He was particularly scathing about the conferences being held at Durham House, as is reflected in a letter dated November 1601:

> You remember also, that I gave you notice of the diabolical triplicity, that is
> Cobham, Ralegh and Northumberland, that met every day at Durham House,
> where Ralegh lies in consultation, which awaked all the best wits of the town
> out of suspicions of sundry kinds, to watch what chickens they could hatch out
> of these cockatrice-eggs that were daily and nightly sitten on.[18]

Howard accused Bess, Ralegh's wife, of presiding over the machinations at Durham House, adding for good measure that 'she is a most dangerous woman and full of her father's inventions'[19] – a reference to the alleged treasonable activities of Sir Nicholas Throckmorton. She was said to be in league with Lady Shrewsbury and using her connections to 'bring her into the Privy Chamber to her old place'.[20] Meanwhile, Cobham and Ralegh, together with their accomplices, were said to 'hover in the air for an advantage, as kites do for carrion'.[21] But according to Howard the queen was very wary of both Northumberland and Ralegh; she was reported as saying that 'Ralegh had made [Northumberland] as odious as himself, because he would be singular [independent], and such were not to be employed by princes of sound policy'.[22] Here there may be more than a grain of truth: Ralegh was, perhaps, too much his own man to be a loyal servant of the state.

No opportunity was missed to poison James' mind against the Durham House faction. The Scottish king had made an offer to Elizabeth to provide soldiers to serve in Ireland, but according to Howard this goodwill gesture had been disparaged by Ralegh and Cobham: 'for both Ralegh and Cobham ... have argued against the peril of the Queen's accepting the King's offer of the Highlandmen; Ralegh proving by his own experience, that they are mutinous, rebellious, and dangerous.'[23] For the King of Scotland to be told that his fellow countrymen made poor soldiers was an insult he was unlikely to forget.

Cecil was evidently fully aware of Howard's vilification of Ralegh, for in a letter to James he wrote that he left 'the best and the worst of Ralegh to Howard's relations' and on another occasion he said he had read over letters from Howard.[24] However, Cecil was also happy to make his own contribution to the smear campaign against his old friend, as is evident from a letter he wrote to James:

> I do profess ... that if I did not sometimes cast a stone unto the mouth of
> those gaping crabs [Ralegh and Cobham] ... they would not stick to confess

daily how contrary it is to their nature to resolve to be under your sovereignty;
though they confess – Ralegh especially – that (rebus sic stantibus) natural
policy forceth them to keep on foot such a trade against the great day of mart.
In all which light and sudden humours of his, though I do no way check him,
because he shall not think I reject his freedom or his affection, but always use
contestation with him ... Yet, under pretext of extraordinary care of his well
being, I have seemed to dissuade him from engaging himself too far, even for
himself ... Would God I were as free from offence towards God in seeking, for
private affection, to support a person [Ralegh] whom most religious men do
hold anathema.[25]

Cecil here contrived to inflict maximum damage on Ralegh, while claiming to
befriend and protect the target of his malevolence. According to the secretary,
Ralegh was disinclined to accept James as king and professed loyalty only because
it was good politics to do so – at least as things then stood ('rebus sic stantibus').
Cecil claims in the letter to support his friend and try his best to keep him from
disloyalty – though it is difficult to accept the obligations of friendship towards
someone of notoriously atheistic views. This is Cecil in his most devious mode,
but the subtlety of his betrayal of Ralegh had the desired effect on James.

While the secret correspondence with Scotland was in the very early stages, the
Duke of Lennox, a favourite of James, arrived in England via France in November
1601 to make soundings at the English court on behalf of his sovereign. Lennox was
not party to the secret correspondence, and was indeed a rival of Mar for James'
favour. He was unaware that Ralegh and Cobham were already damaged goods as
far as James was concerned, and he was therefore keen to enlist their support.

Cobham, as Warden of the Cinque Ports, was able to have a private interview
with Lennox when he disembarked at Dover. According to Howard, Cobham
sought to remove any suspicions that he opposed James' succession and to assure
the duke of his loyalty to the English king-in-waiting. Emboldened by his interview, Cobham then went to Cecil and suggested that advantage should be taken
of the duke's presence to establish friendly relations with James on the grounds
that 'there is no wisdom in being taken sleeper when the game determines'.[26] But
Cecil, in a masterly display of deceit, reminded Cobham of his previous assertion
that it was impossible for a man to be a loyal subject and at the same time to pay
respects to the Scottish king. He also warned Cobham that it would be awkward
for him if James chose to disclose his conversation with Lennox to the queen.
Cecil said that for his part he sincerely hoped that Elizabeth would outlive him
and that he remained uncommitted on the question of succession.

The next day, following a conference at Durham House, Ralegh went to Cecil
and revealed that Lennox had requested a private meeting with him. He said he
had declined such an interview because he was 'too deeply engaged ... to his
own mistress to seek favour elsewhere'.[27] Again Cecil dissimulated, saying that

Ralegh had done well 'and as I myself would have made answer if the like offer had been made to me.'[28] When Ralegh then asked Cecil to inform the queen of his refusal to go behind her back by engaging with James' emissary, the secretary replied sharply that such a message 'would be thought a motive to pick a thank'.[29] Besides which, it might be thought that Lennox would not have sought such a meeting unless he suspected a weakness in Ralegh that would be better concealed from the queen.

These exchanges, reported by Howard to James' agents, are revealing. Firstly, they show that despite the mistrust between them and the secretary, Ralegh and Cobham were prepared to deal with Cecil on what they mistakenly assumed to be a matter of common interest – that is, fostering good relations with the future King of England for their collective advantage. Secondly, following Cobham's reprimand from Cecil, Ralegh was dissuaded from opening up a line of communication with Lennox – presumably for fear that Cecil, if he got to hear of it through his intelligence network, would straight away inform the queen. Finally, it is clear that Cecil was most anxious to prevent a separate and rival channel of communication developing between the English and Scottish courts, especially one involving the Ralegh faction at one end and Lennox at the other. This would threaten to undo much of the hard work that Cecil and Howard had put in to prejudice James against the Durham House clique.

Yet Cecil could not be sure that he had succeeded in discouraging Ralegh and Cobham from dealing with Scotland. Could these rivals be ingratiating themselves with James by confiding to Lennox, and might Lennox persuade his king of the two men's merit and loyalty? Howard's letters reflect these concerns: he entreated Bruce to ensure that any advice given by Lennox in favour of a correspondence between Cobham or Ralegh and the king should not be acted upon:

> If the Duke crave traffic with these gallants of intelligence by correspondency of King James, Cecil desires him not to yield to it in any sort; for the first beginning King James may find that their intentions are traitorous, and only seek, like sirens, by sweet songs, to draw those passengers within the compass of their danger.[30]

Howard went on to ridicule Cobham's protestations of loyalty to James, likening him to a bird that alights 'on this tree [James' favour] until he might make a further flight.'[31] And in case there was any doubt about Cecil co-operating with his rivals in any future government, Howard reported to Bruce Cecil's insistence that 'Duo erinacii [two hedgehogs, Ralegh and Cobham], that is, he and they would never live under one appletree'.[32]

In Howard's view, Ralegh and Cobham, in dealing with Lennox, had acted independently of their ally Northumberland. Whatever the truth of that, Northumberland appears to have abandoned his friends at Durham House when he tried, unilaterally, to establish communications with James. He apparently decided in the spring of 1602 that Cecil was, after all, the man to follow. He wrote directly to James offering his support and then showed Cecil the favourable response he received from the Scottish king (which he need not have troubled to do because Bruce sent a transcript to the secretary). Northumberland then wrote again to James suggesting that it was essential to win Cecil over to his side, offering himself as intermediary with the secretary with whom he claimed to maintain 'ancient familiarity and inward trust'.[33] Cecil and James were content to play the poor duke along for a time but, unsurprisingly, Northumberland's initiative came to nothing.

During this brief correspondence Northumberland provided a short profile of Ralegh which, though not altogether complimentary, gave a balanced view of the man:

> I must needs affirm Ralegh's ever allowance of your right [to the English throne] and although I know him insolent, extremely heated, a man that desires to seem to be able to sway all men's fancies, all men's courses, and a man that out of himself, when your time shall come, will never be able to do you much good nor harm, yet must I needs confess what I know, that there is excellent good parts of nature in him … and whom I wish your Majesty not to lose, because I would not that one hair of a man's head should be against you that might be for you.[34]

All this correspondence reflects the extreme edginess that characterised both the English and Scottish courts as Elizabeth's life was coming to its natural end. Cecil and Howard were determined to exclude all their rivals from Scottish favour, but could not be sure if any of these had opened up a channel of communication with James. From their standpoint there was the continuing danger, too, that the ageing and increasingly unpredictable queen might suddenly return to her old court favourite, Ralegh, or find some other, such as Cobham. There was also the ever present risk that their own treacherous cross-border correspondence with James might be discovered.

Ralegh and Cobham, for their part, were in a dilemma. Should they present themselves as a rival faction to Cecil or, like Northumberland, try to cooperate with the most powerful politician in England in the hope that together they might all find Scottish favour when the fast approaching 'day of mart' arrived? A postscript to a letter from Ralegh to Cecil, dated August 1602, suggests that Ralegh was anxious to patch up the quarrel between them:

> It is your destiny to be troubled with your friends and so must all men be. But what you think unfit to be done for me shall never be a quarrel, either internal or external. I thank you ever more for the good, and what cannot be effected [so be it].[35]

The message is clear; if Cecil cannot admit his friend to the Privy Council, or secure some worthwhile preferment, Ralegh will no longer hold it against him. But Cecil still did not trust Ralegh, and so there was no let up in the undercover campaign to unseat the former royal favourite.

What seems certain is that Ralegh and Cobham had no idea the secretary was systematically wrecking their reputations with the future King of England. Still less did they imagine that he was planning to eliminate them from the political life of the country after Elizabeth's death. In all his outward dealings with the two men, Cecil was determined to remain courteous and friendly. He had also asked Carew not to make any reference to his complaints about the conduct of Ralegh and Cobham in any letter he might write to either of them.[36] The smooth surface of their relations was to be undisturbed until a later, more propitious time, when the true destructive intent of their undeclared adversary would be revealed.

A few months before her final illness, Cecil and Ralegh conferred privately with the queen on the policy to be adopted towards Munster rebels. Even as late as January 1603, Cecil was writing to Ralegh in confidential terms about helping to finance a new privateering expedition:

> I pray you as much as maybe, conceal our adventure, at the least my name above any other. For though I thank God I have no other meaning than becometh an honest man in any of my actions, yet that which were another man's pater noster would be accounted in me a charm [black magic].[37]

To all appearances, therefore, it was business as usual. Although Ralegh had had his differences with Cecil since Essex's downfall, he was to be taken completely unawares by the succession of blows that were about to fall. For it never occurred to him that his old friend and former political ally would set out to destroy him, and that the queen's life and his own fate hung by the same fraying thread.

5

THE DEATH OF A QUEEN

Upon Thursday it was treason to cry God Save King James of England, and upon Friday, high treason not to cry so.

Thomas Dekker, *The Wonderful Year*, 1603

As she approached 70 years of age Elizabeth lost much of her old zest. The death of Essex had hit her hard and she suffered periodic bouts of depression. She was also becoming increasingly frail, and at the opening of her last parliament in November 1601 she nearly fell under the weight of her robes and had to be supported. In what was to be her last speech to the House of Commons she betrayed her exhaustion: 'to be a King, and to wear a Crown, is a thing more glorious to them that see it, than it is pleasant to them that wear it.'[1] In June 1602 she told the French ambassador that she was weary of life. She also lamented the fact that she had failed to curb the late Earl of Essex's impetuosity and that he had ignored her warning to take care not to touch her sceptre.[2] A court correspondent wrote to James that the queen would, on occasion, sit in the dark and shed tears over the loss of her former favourite.[3] Then in the bitterly cold January of 1603 Elizabeth retired to Richmond Palace where, bizarrely insisting on wearing summer clothes, she caught a chill and became seriously ill.

By early March the queen was fading fast. She had lost the will to live but feared to die. She scarcely ate, became feeble and emaciated, and rejected all medication. She refused to go to bed because she thought she would never get up again. Instead, she sat on cushions for several successive days – sleepless, barely capable of speech, deeply disturbed and staring at the floor, often with her finger in her mouth like a child in need of comfort.[4] Only when she was too weak to resist was she taken to her bed, where she lay semi-comatose for three days attended by John Whitgift, the Archbishop of Canterbury, and other church dignitaries. At around 3.00 a.m. on

24 March, Elizabeth turned on her side and stopped breathing, departing this life 'easily like a ripe apple from the tree', according to her chaplain.[5]

When news spread that the queen was dying the state was exposed to danger because there was still no declared successor. Precautions were therefore taken: eight armed ships lay in the Thames, each carrying 500 troops; leading Catholic recusants were taken into safe-custody; the ports were closed; and Cecil's intelligence network was put on full alert. The Council and leading nobility were meanwhile summoned to Richmond to bear witness to the last days of England's greatest monarch.

Cecil well understood that to pre-empt any threats from rival claimants, armed usurpers, foreign interference or civil unrest, he must ensure the legitimacy of the succession and also act with utmost speed. The queen had refused to name her successor until the very last. But on 22 March (so it was reported) she was asked directly by Cecil, in the presence of the Lord Keeper and the Lord Admiral, about her wishes. She responded 'who should succeed me but a King?' and when further pressed added, 'Who but our cousin in Scotland?'[6] On the following day, when the queen was no longer able to speak, leading councillors assembled around her bed and she was asked to confirm by some sign her approval of the King of Scots. It was reported that she raised her arms above her head – which was enough for those present to believe that James was her chosen successor.[7] Whether or not this was the true royal intent, a smooth transition required that it be so interpreted.

As soon as the queen's death had been confirmed, Cecil orchestrated events to ensure the rapid and uncontested succession of James. The councillors and nobility who had attended the queen at Richmond departed at dawn for Whitehall Palace. Once assembled at Whitehall, Cecil presented them with a draft proclamation declaring James to be the new King of England. This had been prepared, sent up to Edinburgh and approved by the Scottish king some days before.[8] By anticipating the queen's death, Cecil was guilty of a final act of treachery, but one which might be excused on grounds of expediency. The lords and councillors approved the proclamation which was then read out by Cecil himself, sitting on his horse in front of the Palace gates. The new ruler was proclaimed as:

James the First, King of England, Scotland, France and Ireland, Defender of the Faith, linearly and lawfully descended from Margaret, daughter of the high and renowned Prince Henry VII, his great-grandfather; the said Lady Margaret being lawfully begotten of the body of Elizabeth, daughter of King Edward IV.[9]

A procession of heralds followed by the Council, lords and courtiers then moved down the Strand from Westminster and entered the city at Ludgate. After the proclamation had been read out at St Paul's and at Cheapside, the procession reached the Tower of London. Here, the ancient palace-stronghold was claimed in the new sovereign's name, thereby completing the ceremony that secured the throne for James. The crowds along the way were subdued, no doubt because they had lost their queen of forty-five years while gaining an unknown king.

In the last hours of Elizabeth's life post-horses had been stationed along the Great North Road so that the news, when it came, could be carried immediately to Scotland. James could then make arrangements for the journey south to claim his inheritance. The queen died on Thursday morning and by the following Saturday night, 26 March, the courtier Sir Robert Carey had ridden the 395 miles to Edinburgh to deliver his momentous message – for which service he was duly rewarded. On the following day James wrote to Cecil, authorising the Council to retain their offices and adding a postscript in his own hand: 'How happy I think myself by the conquest of so faithful and so wise a Councillor I reserve to be expressed out of my own mouth to you.'[10]

On 5 April James left Holyrood on a triumphal progress south, staying at the country houses of nobility, enjoying his hunting where he could, acknowledging the excited crowds along the route and showing profligate generosity in the creation of over 300 knights. The Council had to stay in London to attend to government business, but others from the court sped northwards hoping for favours. Ladies of the court also joined the rush north to meet the new queen, Anne of Denmark; Lady Anne Clifford reporting that she and her mother had killed three horses in one day in their haste to meet the royal party travelling south.[11]

Having ensured the orderly change of regime, Cecil himself set out on a two day journey to York, where on 18 April he met for the first time the man whom he had been corresponding with over the previous eighteen months, and to whom he had now safely delivered the Crown of England. Cecil conducted what business he could with James – who was more intent on enjoying the hospitality and entertainments offered to him by the northern nobility. The secretary left the new king at Burghley, the Northamptonshire seat of his half-brother, on 25 April and hastened back to London, having arranged to accommodate James at his own palace, Theobalds, in early May. The first formal mark of the king's gratitude came shortly after when, on 13 May, Sir Robert became Lord Cecil of Essendon. Cecil had not only master-minded a peaceful succession; he had also ensured an unrivalled position for himself in the new order.

James himself was in no hurry to reach London because he did not wish to attend the queen's funeral, due to take place on 28 April. 'They say,' reported the Venetian ambassador, 'he wishes to see her neither alive nor dead, for he can never expel from his memory the fact that his mother was put to death at the hands of the public executioner.'[12]

The funeral itself was a solemn but magnificent occasion. After her death, Elizabeth's body had been embalmed, placed in a lead coffin and taken down the Thames by barge from Richmond Palace to Whitehall where she lay in state for a month. On the day of the funeral the coffin was covered in purple velvet and drawn by four horses draped in black. A life-size wax effigy of the queen, dressed in her full regalia and complete with crown and sceptre, was placed on her funeral hearse. The mourning crowds thronged the funeral route from Whitehall to Westminster Abbey, as witnessed by the antiquarian, John Stow:

> Westminster was surcharged with multitudes of all sorts of people in their streets, houses, windows, leads and gutters, that came to see the obsequy and when they beheld her statue lying upon the coffin, there was such a general sighing, groaning and weeping as the like hath not been seen or known in the memory of man, neither doth any history mention any people, time or state to make like lamentation for the death of their sovereign.[13]

Elizabeth was initially buried in the vault of her grandfather, Henry VII, in the Abbey. James was later to erect a large white marble monument to her memory in the north aisle of the Lady Chapel, and her body was reburied there in 1606. The inscription reads:

> To the eternal memory of Elizabeth, Queen of England, France and Ireland, daughter of King Henry VIII, granddaughter of King Henry VII, great grand-daughter to King Edward IV. Mother of her country, a nursing-mother to religion and all liberal sciences, skilled in many languages, adorned with excellent endow-ments both of body and mind, and excellent for princely virtues beyond her sex. James, King of Great Britain, France and Ireland, hath devoutly and justly erected this monument to her whose virtues and kingdoms he inherits.

In 1612 James ordered that the body of his mother, Mary Queen of Scots, be removed from Peterborough Cathedral to Westminster Abbey, where she was laid to rest alongside the woman who had put her to death.

Ralegh had been preoccupied in the West Country on official as well as priva-teering business when the queen died. As soon as he heard the news he headed north to meet his new sovereign. A proclamation was issued at this time to deter office holders from pestering the king and crowding his court as he progressed slowly towards London. Cecil had, for this purpose, received blank forms signed by James which he could fill in to authorise whatever was necessary for the des-patch of government business. The move was widely believed to have been aimed specifically at Ralegh and Cobham to prevent them journeying north, but what-ever the intent may have been, Ralegh made his way to Northamptonshire where he met the king at Burghley House.

This was a meeting between two men of irreconcilable opposites. James was slovenly and seldom washed, whereas Ralegh was always meticulous about his appearance. James was physically unimpressive and awkward in manner, while Ralegh was suave and ever the polished courtier. Ralegh was a battle-hardened soldier and never afraid to get into a fight; James, on the other hand, was fearful and could not abide violence in any form. Ralegh had a reputation as a ladies man, whereas James' sexual preferences were in the other direction. James spoke and wrote in convoluted phrases, often indulging in elaborate puns, while Ralegh was always direct and pithy in his conversation and prose. James was self-righteously religious; Ralegh was a sceptic where religion was concerned. Add to these stark contrasts the deep distrust which had been successfully embedded in James' mind by Cecil and Howard, and it is easy to see that the new king and the late queen's former favourite would be uncomfortable in each other's company.

The interview reportedly began with one of James' dreadful puns ('Rawly! Rawly! True enough for I think of thee very rawly'[14]), and was then very quickly over after Ralegh had explained that he needed royal authority for continuance of legal process in the Duchy of Cornwall. When James subsequently gave instructions to Sir Thomas Lake, acting as his secretary on the journey south, to prepare the necessary letters, he added: 'Let them be delivered speedily that Ralegh may be gone again.'[15] The following day, Lake reported to Cecil that 'to my seeming he [Ralegh] hath taken no great root here'.[16] After his wearisome journey of several days from the West Country to court royal favour, Ralegh had been snubbed.

The two men were to meet again at Beddington Park, Surrey, when the king visited Sir Francis Carew, Lady Ralegh's uncle, on his Progress around the kingdom. Ralegh had already submitted a pamphlet to James entitled *A discourse touching a war with Spain, and of the protecting of the Netherlands*, which argued the case for continuing the military offensive against Spain in alliance with Holland. At Beddington, Ralegh offered to raise 2,000 men at his own expense and to take command of them in an offensive against the enemy – a misjudged initiative in which he assumed the role of warlord, no doubt further alienating the king.

Cobham was meanwhile having no better luck in his dealings with the new regime. He was a signatory to the proclamation and within a week of the queen's death he, like Ralegh, was heading north. On 30 March John Chamberlain wrote:

> The Lord Cobham is even now taking post to go towards the King, and do his wonted good offices. But the Lords [the council, which was detained in London] do so little like his going, that I think his errand will be there before him or soon overtake him.[17]

Some ten days later the same observer reported that 'the Lord Henry Howard was sent thither to possess the King's ear and countermine the Lord Cobham'.[18] Cobham had high hopes because Count Aremberg, Philip III's minister in the Spanish Netherlands, had just written to him expressing the hope that he would assist in negotiations for a peace settlement. Having been sounded out as though he were someone who had authority to forward the peace, he sought to ingratiate himself with James by sending the letter to him and raising the matter at his first audience. But a letter Cobham wrote to Cecil after his interview with the king shows that his plan had misfired:

> The Duke [of Lennox] telling the King of my coming, and that I was desirous to know his pleasure touching that letter [of Aremberg], he made him an angry answer, and told him I was more busy in it than I need to be, though to me he said no such matter, but only that at the coming of the Council I should know his pleasure.[19]

Cobham was meddling in foreign affairs, which was the secretary's preserve, and it was a little naïve of him to think that he could stake a claim to be a major player in any peace negotiations. Neither the king nor Cecil would allow him to be a go-between in dealings with Aremberg.

Following this rebuff, Cobham was in a state of febrile uncertainty regarding his future prospects and in a further letter to Cecil he wanted to know how he and his wife stood with the king:

> If that you will favour me so much as to let me know how the King used my Lady of Kildare [his own wife] I will greatly thank you, and whether the King have spoken of me unto yourself, and what the reports be of the speeches between the King and me. In London they be very strange and falsely reported.[20]

The 'strange' reports which Cobham referred to were noted by the French ambassador, de Beaumont, who told his master that at his audience with the king, Cobham had tried, futilely, to undermine Cecil – the irony being, of course, that Cecil had already inflicted irreparable damage on Cobham. Cobham had now played his peace card and been rejected, just as Ralegh had tried his war policy on James without success. The two allies were clearly involved in complex political manoeuvring, as Howard had already observed: 'We see that these two gallants … divide their provinces with so great artifices, as, if the peace go forward, Cobham prospers by his industry; if it do not, Ralegh by his opposition.'[21]

While neither Ralegh nor Cobham were aware of the calculating way in which Cecil had prepared the ground against them, they must have sensed after their first audiences that they were out of favour with the king. Cobham was apparently incensed with Cecil and, according to the reports of the French ambassador de Beaumont, insulted the secretary behind his back.[22] Ralegh, for his part, may have heard rumours that he was to be replaced as Captain of the Guard scarcely two weeks into James' succession. The beginning of the new reign was proving inauspicious for both men who may have begun to feel that they were under threat.

It seems that Ralegh had already anticipated possible dangers ahead after the queen's death. In the last months of Elizabeth's reign he had drawn up a deed transferring his estates at Sherborne to his son, Wat, while reserving to himself a life interest. This meant that if Ralegh's properties were for any reason confiscated, Sherborne would no longer be legally his and could therefore remain in his possession via his son. There were three possible motivations for such a precautionary move. First, he might have been safe-guarding his estate against possible personal bankruptcy, realising that if he lost royal favour he might lose his income too. Second, he could have been concerned that if he ceased to enjoy the protection of the Crown his enemies might try to get him on some trumped up charge of treason – in which case his attainder would result in confiscation of all property held in his name. Finally, there is a more sinister interpretation of Ralegh's move to put his estate beyond reach. Was he perhaps already contemplating, at the end of Elizabeth's reign, the possibility of treasonable actions against her successor that would carry high risks for himself and his family? Subsequent dramatic events suggest that any or all of these motives may have played a part in Ralegh's decision to try to ring-fence his beloved Sherborne estate.

6

THE LION PROVOKED

Poverty is a shame, an imprisonment of the mind. Poverty provokes a man to do infamous and detested deeds

Ralegh's advice to his son

As King James moved south to claim the throne of England, Ralegh's world began to fall apart. As early as 12 April John Chamberlain gave a detailed account of the reports of new appointments that were circulating around the court: it was being said that Ralegh was to be replaced by Mar's brother, Sir Thomas Erskine, as Captain of the Guard.[1] This was confirmed some days later when Ralegh was summoned to attend in the Council Chamber where he was told that it was his Majesty's pleasure to use Erskine's service in that office whereupon, according to the Council book, Sir Walter 'in very humble manner did submit himself'.[2] As compensation for his loss of office Ralegh was allowed £300 per annum which was payable to him as Governor of Jersey, but which had been withheld by Elizabeth.

It might seem natural that James should wish to have a Scotsman from his own entourage occupying such a personal office as that of Captain of the Guard. After all, he appointed other Scotsmen as Master of the Wardrobe and as Gentlemen of the Bedchamber. But according to the French ambassador, de Beaumont, Ralegh was privately furious at his dismissal and blamed the behind the scenes machinations of Cecil for prejudicing the king against him.[3] De Beaumont believed this to be the case: he informed his court that Cecil had prompted the king to make the change because of Ralegh's alleged unpopularity, and the fact that his dismissal would go down well in the country.[4] The financial compensation was hardly the point: Ralegh had lost his position at court, his access to his sovereign and a privileged status which he had continued to enjoy (albeit in absentia) even when in disgrace with Elizabeth.

Then came an even bigger blow. The great bulk of Ralegh's income – nearly £3,000 per annum – derived from his wine licence. While staying at Cecil's own palace at Theobalds on 7 May, James issued a proclamation calling in all monopolies until such time as the beneficiaries could satisfy the Council that they were not prejudicial to the king's subjects. Until the Council made a final determination the levy of all dues, including those relating to Ralegh's wine licence, were suspended. Ralegh's income was immediately cut off, just as Henry Howard had suggested it should be in his memorandum to Cecil written the previous year. Adding to Ralegh's financial difficulties was James' early inclination to make peace with Spain. As a preliminary move, a royal proclamation was issued prohibiting the capture of Spanish prizes.[5] This removed another source of profit for Ralegh at a time when he was investing heavily in his privateering interests. Ralegh's political isolation was further underlined when, shortly after his arrival in London, James made new appointments to the Privy Council. The two Howards, Thomas and Henry, along with five Scottish nobles were admitted to an enlarged Council which Cecil continued to dominate through his close allies – notably the Howards and Worcester.[6] Ralegh and Cobham were again left out in the cold.

Ralegh faced financial and political oblivion but the greatest humiliation was yet to come. Elizabeth had granted a lease of Durham House to her favourite in 1584, and Ralegh had occupied this great London palace for nearly twenty years, spending considerable sums on its repair despite the insecurity of his tenure. On James' accession, Tobias Matthew, Bishop of Durham, claimed the house of his ancient predecessors – apparently prompted by Cecil. In a brief letter to Cecil written from Berwick in early April, Matthew makes clear that the secretary had already been in touch with him about the future of the property: 'I have had conference with the bearer, John Taylor, sent by you to deal with me as to my house called Durham Place in The Strand'.[7] He goes on to say that he cannot give an immediate reply but intends to look into the matter.

James was about to cross the border on his journey south and Matthew was among the first to welcome him, preaching a congratulatory sermon before the new king at Berwick. It seems that the bishop, encouraged by the communication with Cecil, made an application for the return of Durham House to his bishopric. This request was favourably received by James and at the end of May, after some legal argument about rights of occupancy and ownership, a royal warrant was issued in the following terms:

James R – Right trusty and well beloved Counsellors, we greet you well. Forasmuch as upon examination before you of the matter between the Bishop of Durham and those that now dwell in his house, touching the right of the House called Durham Place, it appeareth that neither the said dwellers have any right therein, nor we, whom they sought to entitle to it; and that thereof we are certified by you, we think it reasonable the said Bishop should have quiet possession of his house. Wherefore we require you to give order to our Attorney General, or some other of our learned Council, to give warning and commandment in our name to Sir Walter Ralegh, Knight, and Sir Edward Darcy, to deliver quiet possession of the said house to the said Bishop of Durham, ... And that they and all others there abiding do, within such time as you shall think good to limit, avoid the house, removing thence themselves and all their goods within that time which you shall appoint ... Given under our Signet at our Manor of Greenwich, the last day of May 1603, in the first year of our reign.[8]

Matthew, no doubt aware by now that Ralegh was a broken force, pushed to have immediate possession of the property. On 7 June he complained to Sir Thomas Egerton, Keeper of the Great Seal, that Ralegh was planning to occupy the house until Michaelmas (the end of September), and asked that he be given possession 'with what celerity may conveniently be granted'. He explained the need for haste:

... the supposed tenants seek nothing else but to gain time to deface the house more than is justifiable by law, or to shuffle in some noble or otherwise gracious person thereinto ... whom to remove it may be harder for me than I am willing to assay. I hear that Sir Walter Ralegh doth earnestly labour to continue his habitation there until Michaelmas, a design nothing reasonable, considering that the commodity of the summer will be lost, a time most fit for me to repair the delapidations and decays which he by some many years' space hath made or suffered ...[9]

Matthew's request met with an immediate response, the Lord Keeper delivering a warrant to Ralegh requiring him to vacate the house by midsummer's day, which fell on 24 June. This summary eviction elicited an almost pathetic response from Ralegh who understandably felt shocked and humiliated:

I received a warrant from your Lordships, my Lord Keeper and my Lord Chief Justice, and signed also by Mr Attorney General, requiring me to deliver the possession of Durham House to the Bishop of Durham, or to his attorney, before the 24th day of June next ensuing, and that the stables and garden should be presently put into his hands; and that I should not remove any ceiling, glass, iron etc. without warrant from your Lordships or any two of you. This letter seemeth to me very strange, seeing I have had possession of the house almost 20 years, and have bestowed well nigh £2,000 upon the same out of mine own purse. I am of the opinion that if the King's Majesty had recovered this house, or the like, from the meanest gentleman and servant he had in England, that his Majesty would have given six months time for the avoidance, and I do not know but that the poorest artificer in London hath a quarter's warning given him by his landlord. I have made my provisions for 40 persons in the spring

... and the like for almost 20 horse. Now to cast out my hay and oats into the streets, at an hours warning, and to remove my family and stuff in 14 days after, is such a severe expulsion as hath not been offered to any man before this day. But this I would have written to any that had not been of your Lordships' place and respect, that the course taken with me is both contrary to honour, to custom, and to civility, and therefore I pray your Lordships to pardon me till I have acquainted the King's Majesty with this letter; and then, if his Majesty shall think it reasonable, I will obey it.[10]

Ralegh's letter – which was to no avail – was undated, but it was recorded as having been received by Keeper Egerton on 9 June.[11] The implication is that Ralegh received the peremptory notice to quit his house on 8 June – or a day either side. The timing is very significant, as will later appear, because it was on 9 June that Ralegh was alleged to have had a crucial meeting with Cobham at which regime change was discussed.

Ralegh's abrupt removal from Durham House was the culmination of a sequence of blows which left him financially ruined, politically isolated, relegated to the outer fringes of the court and homeless in London. He and Bess were given just two weeks to pack their bags, dismiss their servants, sell their horses and provisions and transport whatever was left of their London belongings to Sherborne. The greatest courtier of Elizabeth's reign had been kicked out of his house without notice.

A later declaration by Ralegh regarding his remaining property and income shows just how dire his finances were. His total revenue from the wine licence, his governorship of Jersey and Wardenship of the Stanneries was put at around £3,000 per annum, of which the wine licence contributed much the greater part. The Sherborne estate, even when fully stocked with sheep, yielded less than £700 per annum, but out of this he had to pay the Bishop of Salisbury £260 per annum in perpetuity. Sherborne apart, Ralegh calculated that his assets amounted to less than £1,000 marks (£666) to be set against his debts of £3,000.[12]

Most of Ralegh's fortune had disappeared in overseas ventures and, stripped of the wine licence, he was now left with a few hundred pounds a year. This might be sufficient to provide a comfortable living for a country gentleman, but it could go nowhere near to supporting the kind of lifestyle to which Ralegh was accustomed – whether attending court, adventuring abroad or living in London like a renaissance prince. Ralegh therefore faced a critical choice. He could have retired from court, contented himself with his responsibilities in the West Country and Jersey, and abandoned London in favour of Sherborne. But he was not a man to confine himself to genteel life in the country, nor would his pride allow him to accept the humiliation that had been heaped upon him. For he remained what he had always been: a man driven by ambition, vanity and a need for great projects in which to sink his boundless creative energy. He might also have reflected that since his house, his income and his official position at court could be so easily taken from him, perhaps it would not stop there. If his enemies were really out to get him he could no longer regard his position in the West Country as secure.

Cobham was in a very different situation. He was independently wealthy and nothing had been taken from him. But he nevertheless resented the way in which he had been treated: excluded yet again from the Privy Council, denied a role in the Spanish peace negotiations and generally side-lined by the new regime. But above all, Cobham took his cue from Ralegh, and Ralegh had been systematically taken apart.

How far was Cecil responsible for Ralegh's spectacular downfall? The answer is that his hand can be seen at every stage: it was Cecil who enlisted Howard to destroy Ralegh in the eyes of James; it was Cecil who seems to have played a part at Theobalds in having Ralegh's wine licence called in; it was Cecil who kept Ralegh out of the expanded Privy Council; it was Cecil who advised James on changing the Captaincy of the Guard; and it was Cecil who prompted Bishop Matthew to apply to have Durham House restored to his use. In short, having removed Ralegh's royal protection and, to use Ralegh's own phrase, reduced him to a 'common man', Cecil was free to determine his fate. Cecil had used this power to heap coals on Ralegh's head, just as he said he would.

Ralegh and Cobham now became 'discontented persons'. Cobham incautiously gathered around him an assortment of similarly disenchanted individuals – disillusioned Catholics, place-seekers who had been denied preferment and some who resented the influx of Scottish courtiers and office holders. Ralegh remained more circumspect, but his alliance with Cobham became closer and more conspiratorial. Cecil would have known that Ralegh, in particular, was unlikely to take his humiliation meekly. A man of his temperament would certainly react. And Cecil, who knew him as well as anybody, was fully prepared for his victim's next move.

7

Treason: The Raptor Strikes

When a falcon hunts first it targets a prey, it circles high above it and, suddenly, the falcon aims and dives straight down at 200 miles per hour. After striking its prey, the falcon circles back, grabs the falling victim with hook like talons and carries it off.

The Sport of Falconry, 2008

During the last desperate days of Elizabeth's reign – when the queen refused to take to her bed for fear of dying – and the first uncertain weeks of James' accession, the country was swept by rumours and suspicions. At one point it was reported that Lord Beauchamp was gathering followers to enforce his claim to the crown; there were fears that the Jesuits were planning some violent action against the state; and the tensions between the Spanish and anti-Spanish factions at court reflected broader political and religious divisions in the country at large. Shortly after the queen's death, one close observer of the political scene, John Chamberlain, lamented the uncertainties of the times: 'I know not how nor what to write, the postages being stopped, and all conveyance so dangerous and suspicious'.[1] No doubt Cecil's spy network was operating at full stretch as he sought to flush out potential dissidents and to establish himself and his sovereign as the unchallenged twin pillars of the new political order.

It was in this atmosphere of mistrust that the Bishop of London, Dr Bancroft, was at the end of June given information by a priest named Barnaby about a plot to overthrow the government and seize the king. The Bishop immediately sent a dispatch to Cecil and by 9 July the conspirator originally responsible for the leak, Anthony Copley, was in the Tower and under interrogation. Copley, a member of a Catholic family of some standing, had fought for Spain against the Dutch and their English allies, and was now involved with a group of malcontents, misfits and oddballs in a plot to seize power. In a series of confessions, culminating in a full statement made on 14 July, Copley revealed the details of an ill-conceived plot against the king while also implicating his co-conspirators. The chief of these were William Watson and William Clarke, both Catholic priests; Sir Griffin Markham, a soldier who had fought in the Dutch and Irish wars; and George Brooke, younger brother of Lord Cobham.[2]

The two priests, Watson and Clarke, were actuated by the desire for religious toleration and hatred of the Elizabethan recusancy laws that penalised Catholics. Markham, although from a land-owning family, was in desperate financial straits having failed to secure any recent preferment or favours from the Crown; and Brooke, as the high-spending younger son of the wealthy Cobham dynasty, was also in urgent need of a remunerative sinecure. He had previously hoped, in vain, for the patronage of his brother-in-law, Robert Cecil, and was particularly disappointed by the refusal of King James to implement Queen Elizabeth's promise to appoint him to the mastership of the Hospital of St Cross at Winchester. This group also enlisted the help of Lord Grey of Wilton, an impulsive Puritan, who resented the favour being shown to the Scottish upstarts in James' train, as well as the pardon given by James to Grey's bitter personal enemy, the Earl of Southampton.

The plot itself was little more than fantasy, given the insufficiency of armed men to carry it through. The plan was to seize the person of the king and leading members of the government, to take the Tower of London and to hold the king there in protective custody until he met the plotters' demands. These were: a pardon for their actions; toleration of their religion; and the removal of those ministers, notably Robert Cecil, associated with the policy of religious repression. The high offices of state would then be distributed among the conspirators, with Markham appointed Earl Marshall, Brooke Lord Treasurer and Watson Lord Keeper. The king was to have been taken on midsummer's day while staying at the Palace of Greenwich, but an element of farce was introduced into the proceedings when, due to a late change of plan, the court moved on to Windsor via Hanworth, leaving the plotters stranded.

Copley's revelations about the planned surprise of the king at Greenwich did not suggest a credible threat to the state. However, the interrogation of Brooke disclosed links to another, murkier, but potentially much more dangerous conspiracy allegedly involving Brooke's older brother, Lord Cobham, and as it later transpired, Ralegh. Named in Copley's initial confessions, Brooke was arrested and taken into the custody of Bishop Bancroft at Fulham on 14 July, before being moved to the Tower five days later. He was then subject to a series of interrogations in which he confessed, very freely, not only to his own involvement in the Priests' Plot, but also to his brother's central role in a separate conspiracy. Brooke was eventually to confirm the testimony of Watson, the priest, who reported a conversation in which 'Lord Cobham said that Mr Brooke and the rest were upon the Bye, but he and Sir Walter were upon the Main, which was to destroy the King and all his cubs'.[3] This characterisation of the Priests' Plot as 'the Bye', and Cobham's separate treason as 'the Main', has passed into the vernacular of history. The infamous allusion to 'the King and all his cubs' was also to resurface many times in the months ahead.

The method of interrogation in such cases traditionally involved the full range of inducements: from torture or the threat of torture at one extreme, to the hope of royal mercy at the other. Certainly, Cecil was familiar with the use of the rack and his reputation for 'severity' is suggested by the remark attributed to Cobham on learning of Copley's arrest: 'By God my Lord Cecil will play his prize to fetch the truth out of Copley's fingers' ends.'[4] However, it seems that Copley was willing to talk without either 'torture or threatening' according to his examiners[5] and there is no evidence that other suspects were tortured – though Kemys, Ralegh's trusted aide, said he was threatened with the rack.[6]

Brooke had connections with both the Bye and the Main plots and was therefore targeted by Cecil as an especially valuable witness. Terror-stricken by the prospect of the scaffold, and believing that by condemning his brother he might save himself, he was prepared to divulge all. He was further encouraged by Cecil who allowed him special privileges in the Tower including visits by his wife. But above all, it is clear that Brooke was convinced that he had been offered not only forgiveness by Cecil but also positive financial rewards in return for exposing the scheming of his brother. In a letter to Cecil dated 18 November 1603 (four days before Cobham's trial) he pleads for life which he believes has been promised to him:

> She that loved me, and whose memory you yet love, [Cecil's late wife, who was Brooke's sister] beholds from heaven the extreme calamity of her father's house … 'Tis all but weak if I pray you to cancel injuries past; you have promised to do so, and I believe if I promise you anything of myself, you may truly say you need it not nor care for it. Therefore I must stand only upon your free disposition, and shall be so much the more assured, because nothing binds you. Leave now, I beseech your Lordship, to be nice and stick not to dissever yourself in my relief but above all give me leave to conjure your Lordship to deal directly with me what I am to expect after so many promises received and so much conformity and accepted service performed on my part to you. Your Lordship's brother in law to command, – G. Brooke.[7]

In a more peremptory letter written to the Privy Council at about the same time, Brooke again refers to the promise of life and rewards: 'In the behalf of justice and honour, that your Lordships will believe that whilst I breathe, if not after, I shall claim those promises I have received both from the King and your Lordships in several manner assuring more than life …'.[8] There is also evidence that Brooke told those in his inner circle that he had been given an undertaking from the king (presumably meaning Cecil, his first minister) that 'he shall lose neither life, lands, nor goods but be recompensed for his troubles'.[9] Driven by fear for his life and hope of lenience, Brooke sealed the fate of his brother. On 17 July he said that Cobham was aware of the Priests' Plot, and on the following day – in a confession subsequently confirmed on 19 July by eight privy councillors – there came the breakthrough Cecil had been looking for. Brooke revealed that Cobham was involved in a plot to overthrow James and put a rival Stuart claimant, Lady Arabella Stuart, on the throne. According to Brooke:

> divers letters passed of late between the Count Aremberg and the Lord Cobham, carried by one La Renzi, touching the value of certain crowns to the value of 500,000 or 600,000. The intent, so far as I know, or was acquainted, was to assist and furnish a several action for the surprise of his Majesty. I saw an answer of the Count of Aremberg to one of them promising he should be furnished of that he wrote for, but requiring to know how to send them over, and how they should be distributed, he [his master] being beyond the seas.[10]

Charles de Ligne, Count of Aremberg, an elderly nobleman afflicted with gout, was an ambassador to London. He represented the Archduke Albert – joint sovereign of the Spanish Netherlands with his wife, the Infanta Isabel. He was also Cobham's long-standing friend, and any suggestion that these two men had been conspiring against the Crown would be not only fatal to Cobham but also highly embarrassing for Cecil who, as the central plank of his foreign policy, was at great pains to stitch together a peace settlement with Spain. Any public disclosure that Aremberg had been plotting against James on behalf of Philip III would give the anti-Spanish faction powerful ammunition in their opposition to the peace.

In his confession on 18/19 July Brooke added that Cobham, having already approached Lady Arabella Stuart to prepare the way, had asked his brother to persuade her to write three separate letters: to the King of Spain, the Infanta and the Duke of Savoy, requesting their assistance to enforce her claim to the English crown. In return she was to promise religious toleration, peace with Spain and a husband chosen by her Spanish sponsors. Following these disclosures, Cobham was quickly reeled in. Already under suspicion because of his brother's complicity, he was placed under house arrest. On his first examination on 16 July he denied everything.[11] Upon his second examination the following day Cobham did admit to what he described as a polite and innocent correspondence with Lady Arabella, though he must have raised deep suspicions when he said that his letters had been returned to him and burned.[12] Cobham also refused to sign his responses to questions on the grounds that 'being a baron of the realm … he is not bound to do it', a conceit of which the Lord Chief Justice was later to disabuse him by insisting that to decline to subscribe was a high contempt.

On 19 July, Cobham was further interrogated on his communications with Count Aremberg since the latter's arrival in England on 4 June. In testimony that was now signed but not written in his own hand, he admitted that he had visited Aremberg's house on the south bank of the Thames, and had engaged in an exchange of letters which were taken across the river by La Renzi, an Antwerp merchant, who was one of the count's entourage.[13] However, he insisted that his dealings with the count were confined to routine domestic concerns such as 'dogs and ambling mares and suchlike things', and had nothing to do with matters of state. He had burned Aremberg's letters immediately after receiving them since 'he made no account of them'.[14] He continued to deny any knowledge of the Priests' Plot.

Meanwhile, Ralegh had come under suspicion in circumstances which continue to mystify historians. On 14 July (or a day either side – the precise date is not known) Ralegh had accompanied the court to Windsor Castle and was walking on the terrace in anticipation of joining the king's hunting party. At this point the hand of fate intervened in the diminutive form of the Secretary of State, who suddenly appeared on the terrace and told Ralegh 'as from the King' that he was to stay behind and to answer some questions to be put to him by the lords in the Council Chamber. This was the decisive moment of Ralegh's fall. Nearby were the new Elizabethan buildings with the inscribed date of 1583, a year which marked the high-water mark of Ralegh's favour with the queen as well as his first visit to Windsor Castle. In the twenty years since then he had travelled the world, founded Virginia, taken Cadiz, played his part in the defeat of the Spanish Armada, enjoyed the spoils of war and the bounty of royal patronage, and adorned the Elizabethan court with his wit, poetry and style. Now, as he waited on the terrace for the king, he unknowingly performed his last act of courtiership and enjoyed his final moments as a free man.[15]

After the summons from Cecil, Ralegh was examined by four or five councillors on any knowledge he might have of the Priests' Plot – which he firmly denied. Nevertheless he was immediately detained at the house of Sir Thomas Bodley in Fulham, pending further investigations. Nothing more is known of the fateful examination that day except that Ralegh and Cecil appear to have discoursed privately outside the Council Chamber.

At this point it is necessary to pause the chronology of events and consider in some detail the background to Cecil's decision to have Ralegh examined, and the various letters that Ralegh wrote in response to his detention. At the time of Ralegh's arrest (on or around 14 July) Cecil would, on the face of it, have had no evidence of either Cobham's or Ralegh's involvement in any conspiracy since Brooke's confession implicating his brother was made several days later on 18 July. Why, then, did Cecil have Ralegh examined? The 400-year-old mystery deepens when we learn that Cecil questioned Ralegh at Windsor about Cobham's dealings with Aremberg – which he surely could not have known about before Brooke's revelations. The main trial reports, on which historians and others have relied, give little indication that Ralegh was questioned about Cobham or Aremberg

at his initial examination at Windsor. However, these reports were not true tran-
scripts — shorthand was not fully developed until the following century — and
were therefore compressions of the trial proceedings. But Sir Thomas Overbury's
report of Ralegh's trial provides the key additional material that the others omit.
According to the Overbury version, Ralegh claimed that he was asked by the
Lords about Cobham's possible involvement in treasonable activity and also about
his dealings with Aremberg. But he then corrected himself and said it was Cecil,
talking to him privately at Windsor, who asked about Cobham. He conceded that
when called before the Lords:

> though he were not examined of my Lord Cobham, yet he talking with My
> Lord Cecil, and his Lordship telling him he was glad there were no more in
> the action [the Priests' Plot] than there appeared, and he hoped that such a one
> [Cobham] was not in, Sir Walter said that my Lord Cobham was absolutely
> clear, and my Lord Cecil replied he did hope so and thought no less: all of
> which was said in regard my Lord Cobham was thought to be discontented.[16]

Ralegh also stated at his trial that he was asked about 'Lord Cobham's practices
with the Count Aremberg' and 'that my Lord Cecil [not the lords] asked my
opinion concerning La Renzi'.[17]

That Cecil strongly suspected Cobham is without doubt because on 4 August,
in a letter to Sir Thomas Parry, the English ambassador in France (see appendix B), he states his reasons for detaining Ralegh at Windsor: 'first, he hath been
discontented *in conspectu omnium* ever since the King came ... Secondly ... his
governing of the Lord Cobham's spirit, made great suspicion that in these treasons he had a part.'[18] In other words, Ralegh was suspected because his close
confidante, Cobham, was under suspicion. Cecil was fully aware that both Ralegh
and Cobham were dangerously disaffected and that they met frequently together
(three times a week according to Brooke).

Under these circumstances, as a spymaster commanding the most extensive
intelligence network in Europe, he would certainly have put the two malcontents
under close surveillance. Indeed, that Cobham assumed as much is shown by the
fact that when he visited Aremberg he 'was brought up a back way at the night
time'.[19] Cecil's agents would, then, have seen Cobham being rowed from Durham
House across the river to St Mary Saviour's — possibly even from the vantage
point provided by Cecil's own mansion, Cecil House, which was conveniently
situated next door to Durham House and overlooked Ralegh's waterfront.

Furthermore, it is highly probable that after Cecil's suspicions were aroused
he intercepted correspondence between Cobham and Aremberg. In his letter to
Sir Thomas Parry dated 4 August, Cecil says that 'Not three days before his commitment he [Cobham] wrote to the Count' about raising money from Spain.[20]
Cobham was committed on 16 July, which would mean that if this last letter was

intercepted it would have been available to Cecil on 13 July – immediately before Ralegh's detention at Windsor. When Brooke was arrested on 14 July Cobham sent a verbal message to Aremberg via La Renzi: 'to tell him that my brother was committed, so I durst write no more'.[21] But it seems that this warning came too late to prevent a final letter from Aremberg being intercepted.

The evidence for this supposition is persuasive. Cobham in his examinations refers to three letters exchanged between him and Aremberg,[22] but La Renzi said that he carried over 'four several letters from Cobham to Aremberg and like letters from Aremberg to Cobham'.[23] The inference is that the last letters may have been seized. Cobham, in an undated letter to the Lords written after his imprisonment, pleads that the plans discussed with Aremberg were a passing conceit and never intended to be implemented. He then appears to make a reference to letters written but not received: 'How far this may be wrested in law, I am ignorant, and how likely this was to be a dangerous practice *when he could neither read mine nor I his letters* [Italics added].'[24] Finally, that Cecil was in possession of correspondence from Aremberg to Cobham is evidenced by de Beaumont, the French ambassador, who claimed to have seen it,[25] and by Sir Dudley Carleton who said at Cobham's meagrely reported trial: 'a letter was produced which he [Cobham] wrote to Aremberg for so much money; and Aremberg's answer consenting for the furnishing of that sum.'[26]

All this puts an entirely new gloss on Ralegh's detention at Windsor on or around 14 July. Cecil was by then almost certainly aware of an embryonic plot involving Cobham, Ralegh and Aremberg, although whether it was linked to the Bye Plot he would not have known at this stage. On the other hand, Cecil did not wish to reveal to the lords – or perhaps even to the king – his clandestine intelligence operations. The lords' remit at Windsor was therefore limited to questioning Ralegh on Copley's disclosures, and when this examination yielded nothing to implicate Ralegh, Cecil, knowing much more than he gave away, asked Ralegh about Cobham's dealings with Aremberg. The fact that Ralegh was questioned and detained before Cobham also shows that Cecil regarded him, and not Cobham, as the real danger man.

Ralegh, following his disconcerting interview with Cecil at Windsor, would have realised that the secretary had been put on alert by his powerful intelligence network. He may have thought that Brooke had already betrayed his brother, and he would certainly have suspected that Cobham's visit to Aremberg across the river had been observed and its potential significance noted. Ralegh was uncomfortably aware that Cecil now had the two collaborators in his sights, and this prompted him to write three letters.

The first note he managed to smuggle to Cobham through his trusty aide, Keymis. In it he said he had been examined by the lords but had cleared Cobham of any wrong doing. He also gave verbal instructions to Keymis to tell Cobham that he need fear nothing because one witness alone (presumably he was referring to Brooke) could not harm him. Ralegh requested the return of his letter which he then burned.[27] He was trying to strengthen his friend's resolve ahead of the interrogation that was bound to come, but this communication looked highly suspicious when it came to light at his trial.

Ralegh's second letter, written to the lords but seen first by Cecil who withheld it, deliberately pointed the finger at Cobham by expressing Ralegh's suspicion that his friend had had recent dealings with Aremberg. This letter has not survived but Ralegh referred to it at his trial:

> … I suspected [Cobham] visiting Aremberg from this; for after he departed from me at Durham House, I saw him pass by his own stairs [at Blackfriars] and go over to St Mary Saviour's, where I knew that La Renzi lay, who was a follower of the Count of Aremberg. I gave intimation thereof by letter to the Lords, but I was willed by my Lord Cecil not to speak of this, because the King, at the first coming out of Count Aremberg, would not give him occasion of suspicion.[28]

Believing that Cobham's movements had been detected, Ralegh felt impelled to acknowledge Cobham's cross-river trip from Durham House – while seeking to distance himself from whatever purpose Cobham had in mind. Ralegh knew how to handle himself in difficult situations and it should be obvious that he would not have written such a dangerous letter unless he felt that Cecil was already aware of Cobham's 'secret' movements. Cecil's unwillingness to share Ralegh's disclosure with his fellow privy councillors was no doubt due to sensitivities over peace negotiations with Spain, which might be derailed if it became known that Aremberg was implicated in scheming against the king. But Cecil also had private information about Aremberg which he preferred to keep to himself.

Finally, Ralegh followed up his letter to the Lords with another brief note – this time addressed discretely to Cecil since Cecil had intimated his sensitivity in matters relating to Aremberg. The precise wording of this cryptic message is important:

> If your honours apprehend the merchant of St Hellens the stranger will know all is discovered of him, which perchance you desire to conceal for some time. All the danger will be lest the merchant fly away. If any man know any more of the Lord Cobham, I think he trusted George Wyet of Kent.[29]

The 'merchant' is La Renzi and the 'stranger' (foreigner) is clearly Aremberg. What Ralegh is suggesting is that if Cecil wishes to get to the bottom of what is going on between Cobham and Aremberg he may wish to bide his time for a while, the only danger being that La Renzi (a small fish) might disappear. Worried that the net was closing in on Cobham and himself, Ralegh was trying to buy time by advising Cecil against any premature intervention. He needed the extra time to establish a common line of defence with Cobham, to get La Renzi out of the way and to ensure that Aremberg was warned about possible interception of his letters. As matters transpired, this last letter proved disastrous because it was later shown to Cobham as evidence of Ralegh's betrayal of his close friend and ally. Over two years later, while imprisoned in the Tower, Ralegh referred to this fateful correspondence when writing to the Privy Council in connection with the Gunpowder Plot: 'I sent your Lordships in the beginning of my troubles a letter from Sir John Bodle's [his place of detention] concerning La Renzi and others; and the same was my utter ruin. I did it to do the King's service'.[30]

Significantly, Ralegh at his trial put a different gloss on his correspondence with Cecil. He is reported as saying 'I wrote to the Lord Cecil that if La Renzi were not secured the matter would not be discovered for he would fly; yet if he were then apprehended it would give matter of suspicion to Lord Cobham'.[31] The inference here is that Ralegh had urged the early apprehension of La Renzi in order to unravel the plot, whereas the letter he actually wrote was clearly designed to delay any such move. The change of emphasis no doubt reflected Ralegh's embarrassment at his rather obvious ploy to buy time and to escape detection.

In any event, Cecil read his man and wasted no time in moving matters forward. On 19 July, La Renzi was detained and examined. The substance of his evidence was presented at Ralegh's trial – which La Renzi attended as a spectator:

> Within five days after the arrival of the Count Aremberg, [around 9 June] the Lord Cobham wrote a letter to him, and he to the Lord Cobham: the same night Sir W. Raleigh supped with the Lord Cobham, the Lord Cobham went with this Examinate to Count Aremberg; he was brought in by a privy way, and had two hours conference with him that night; and after this, further letters passed betwixt them. My Lord Cobham told La Rensy [sic], if Count Aremberg would procure the contents of that letter, he last wrote, no doubt his Master might have peace. At the time when La Rensy delivered a private letter to the Lord Cobham from Count Aremberg, promising the money, Sir W. Raleigh was below in the hall with Lord Cobham, at his house at Blackfriars; and afterwards the Lord Cobham took Sir. W. Raleigh up into his chamber with him in private, and left La Rensy in the hall.[32]

Armed with new evidence, the Council examined Cobham again on 20 July. The interrogation, like the previous day's examinations of both Cobham and Brooke, was held at Richmond and appears to have been carefully stage-managed by Cecil.[33] No doubt anticipating important disclosures, he had managed to assemble no less than eleven councillors (according to his own statement) which was well in excess of the handful that normally attended on these occasions. He had brought with him the letter from Ralegh referring to the suspicious dealings between Cobham, Aremberg 'the stranger' and La Renzi 'the merchant', and he now played his master card by presenting Cobham with this note written in

Ralegh's familiar hand. Although the examination record is missing, Cobham's reaction was documented both by the Lord Chief Justice and the Lords:[34] Cobham studied Ralegh's note twice – which he would need to do given its cryptic content – and then burst out with a denunciation of his friend and ally: 'Oh wretch, Oh traitor' he cried several times. He then said 'I will tell you all truly'. He went on to insist that everything he, Cobham, had done was by Ralegh's instigation and that Ralegh would 'never let him alone'. He and Ralegh had intended that Cobham should travel to Flanders under the pretext of visiting Spa to take the waters; to obtain (with Aremberg's help) a passport from the Archduke; to travel on to Spain; and once there, to negotiate with the king the terms of a loan of 500 or 600,000 crowns; then return via Jersey, where Ralegh was governor. He would meet in Jersey with Ralegh, who would decide how the money was to be distributed 'according to the occasions and opportunity which discontentments in England should have afforded'. There had also been talk of military action, presumably by Spain. According to Cobham, 'Ralegh spoke of plots and invasions of the particulars of which he can give no account, but sayth that he and Ralegh had conferred of them'.

In this angry outburst, Cobham had openly admitted to high treason involving financial and, possibly, military support from England's old enemy Spain, while also accusing Ralegh, a man of the sword, as the prime mover in a plot to overthrow Cecil and James. However, his anger having subsided, Cobham quickly thought better of it. He refused to put his name to his declaration and shortly afterwards he appears to have denied absolutely much of what he had said, particularly as it related to Ralegh. He did admit, in a letter to Cecil dated 23 July, that he may have contemplated backing Lady Arabella's claim to the Crown, although he insisted that 'God is my witness, when I saw her, I resolved never to hazard my estate for her'.[35]

Cobham was examined again towards the end of the month.[36] His answers to interrogatories, provided in a letter to the lords in his own hand and signed, are dated only 'July'[37] (at Ralegh's trial the date given is 29 July). In the letter, Cobham acknowledged his own role in the attempt to raise money from Spain but there is no mention of military action nor of any involvement by Ralegh. He claimed he had visited Aremberg between 10 and 11 at night a few days after the latter's arrival in London, and gave warning that the peace negotiations with Spain were likely to founder because of the opposition of some key councillors. Subsequently, there were three exchanges of letters, the first two of which were concerned with the prospects for peace and England's military support for the Low Countries. However, in his third letter to Aremberg, Cobham had broached his planned trip to Spain:

> The last letter I wrote him, was that he would procure me a pass for my safe going to Spain; that his master was at great charge; but if he should be advised

to deliver 400,000 or 500,000 crowns as I would direct, it should save his master millions. To this he returned this answer: 'that money should be procured'; but how it should be distributed, there was the difficulty; and prayed for my direction to satisfy the scruple which may arise, what should be done with these 400,000 or 500,000 crowns? I must say, and say truly, nothing was determined; but only we did expect the general discontentment which in my opinion I conceived must be; and so this sum of money was to be employed as time and occasion was offered.[38]

So far as the available trial materials and examination records are concerned, this is the sum of it. Cobham was trapped into a confession in which he blamed Ralegh as the lead conspirator in a plot to overthrow the king and his government; but then retracted his accusation against Ralegh while acknowledging his own role in a more limited but still potentially treasonable plan to raise money from Spain for unspecified, though highly questionable, purposes.

But the papers relating to Cobham's critical examination on 20 July are missing, suggesting that there may have been something on the record that Cecil and some of his fellow prosecutors wished to hide. If we look at the pattern of interrogations the general technique was to extract from the examinee a full account of the actions and words of others, and then confront those who had been accused with the charges against them. This, certainly, was the approach adopted in Cobham's early interrogations. When we come to 20 July the examiners would have been able to use Brooke's dramatic disclosures of 18–19 July, La Renzi's admissions of 19 July and, quite possibly, intercepted correspondence between Cobham and Aremberg. There was enough here to build a case against Cobham but the real target for Cecil was Ralegh, a much more dangerous and resourceful man.

If Cecil wanted to extract from Cobham an acknowledgement of Ralegh's involvement in the Spanish plan, he would presumably have wished, first of all, to break Cobham by confronting him with the extremely damaging evidence that had been gathered against him personally. Only then, when he had already confessed, would the examiners have presented him with the subtle imputation contained in Ralegh's letter, thereby inducing him to take revenge against his apparently treacherous friend and collaborator. To believe that the examiners would first have presented the Ralegh letter, before getting a substantive confession from Cobham, is to underestimate the interrogation skills of Cecil. It is also improbable that Cobham would have confessed all, and possibly thrown away his life, on the basis of a cryptic note that did not directly implicate him in anything.

This interpretation is confirmed by Cecil himself in his letter to Sir Thomas Parry, the English ambassador in France, dated 4 August 1603 (appendix B). In this correspondence, Cobham is said to have admitted writing to Aremberg requesting 400,000 or 500,000 crowns from Spain which, if provided, 'could show him a better way to prosper than by peace'.[39] Cecil is at pains to suggest – for public consumption – that Aremberg did not agree to this, so he tells an outright lie: he says 'to which letter, before the Count could make any direct answer, the Lord Cobham was apprehended'[40] (whereas Cobham himself, Brooke and La Renzi all agreed that Aremberg wrote to Cobham promising the money). Cecil then says that after Ralegh's examination at Windsor:

> the Lord Cobham being called in question, *he did first confess his own treasons as above said*: and *then* did absolutely, before eleven Councillors, accuse Ralegh to be privy to his Spanish course, with further addition and exclamation, that he had never dealt therein but by his own incessant provocation [Italics added].[41]

Cecil concluded by saying that although Cobham accused Ralegh in front of everyone, 'yet being newly examined [probably on 27 July] he seemeth now to clear Sir Walter in most things, and take all the burden to himself'.[42]

The sequence of events, as described above, is crucial to an understanding of Ralegh's trial, and of the lengths to which the prosecuting authorities were prepared to go in order to secure a conviction. For the time being, however, Cecil's attempt to ensnare Ralegh was derailed. As the Count of Beaumont, French ambassador to the English court, put it in a letter to Henry IV dated 3 August: 'Lord Cobham, having denied as he did what it is alleged he charged upon Sir Walter Ralegh, the Lords of the Council find it difficult to sustain Ralegh's prosecution.'[43] Cecil's attempt to nail Ralegh down had been frustrated. But he was a patient man and always prepared to play the long game. He knew Cobham's weaknesses and the pressures that could be brought to bear on a person of such fragile temperament. He had also acquired the services of a very resourceful attorney general who, when it came to matters of treason, understood how to make the most of an unpromising brief – even if it meant bending the rules.

8

HOLDING THE LINE

We have to distrust each other. It's our only defence against betrayal.

Tennessee Williams

When he trapped Cobham into an angry denunciation of Ralegh, Cecil must have felt that he had cornered his man and would be able to use Cobham's testimony to charge Ralegh with treason. But Cobham's subsequent retraction left the investigation in disarray, and if Ralegh could persuade his ally to stick to a common, innocent explanation of their conduct, there would be insufficient evidence against him to bring before a jury. Cecil, having initially outwitted his adversary, now found himself thwarted by Ralegh's manipulation of Cobham. Checkmate looked like becoming stalemate.

Cobham's behaviour, up to this point, can be explained as the response of a rational man to successive allegations made against him. First he denied everything, then when confronted with Brooke's early confession, he made a partial admission in respect of his dealings with Lady Arabella. After the further devastating testimony of his brother and the disclosures of La Renzi, he made a much fuller confession of his planned trip to raise money from Spain. At this point he was confronted with Ralegh's letter, which led him into a more dangerous elaboration of his Spanish project, and the admission of proposed uprisings and invasions drawing on the acknowledged expertise of the country's leading military strategist, Ralegh.

Cobham's immediate retraction of his heated accusations against Ralegh ('ere he came to the stair foot' according to Ralegh's own account),[1] is also understandable. By accusing Ralegh, Cobham was elevating his own treason to a higher level: he would be transforming his own transgression from an 'inward conceit', as he later described it, to an overt act of treachery involving a conspiracy with a renowned soldier.

The difficulty facing both Cobham and Ralegh, in deciding how to respond to the charges of their interrogators, can also be viewed as an example of the classical game theory conundrum known as 'The Prisoners' Dilemma' (see appendix A). It was entirely rational for Cobham to seek to blame Ralegh while attempting to minimise his own role in the hope of being treated leniently. It was equally rational for Ralegh to point the finger at Cobham (as he initially did) while denying his own involvement. However, by betraying one another the two suspects would very likely bring each other down, whereas if they could reassure themselves that they would not be betrayed by their co-accused, the optimal approach for each was to refrain from betraying the other.

Ralegh seems to have realised early on that the best hope for himself and Cobham was to formulate a common defence that was consistent, so far as possible, with the admissions Cobham had already made in response to Brooke's allegations. The first indication of such a co-operative approach came shortly after the 20 July examination. Cobham later admitted that, following his intemperate accusation of Ralegh, there was communication between the two men. Looking out of his window, Cobham saw the son of the lieutenant of the Tower talking to Ralegh. When this young gentleman came to visit him a little later, Cobham remarked: 'I saw you with Sir Walter Ralegh – God forgive him! He has accused me, but I cannot accuse him.' The young warder replied: 'He doth say the like of you: that you have accused him, but he cannot accuse you.'[2] This brief exchange appears to have been the opening move in a correspondence between the two prisoners, using the prison governor's son as an intermediary as well as Ralegh's own attendant, Edward Cotterell.[3] It also marked the beginning of a new phase of co-operation between Ralegh and Cobham as they drew back from mutual denunciation and sought to establish instead a united front against their common foe, Cecil.[4]

Significantly, when Ralegh and Cobham were examined separately on 13 August, their accounts were very similar. Cobham reconfirmed his intention of travelling to Spain to raise funds, but insisted that Aremberg had promised money, of which Ralegh was to receive part, only to help further the peace negotiations between England and Spain.[5] Ralegh's examination yielded the same response: 'he confesseth the Lord Cobham offered him 10,000 crowns of the money for the furthering of the peace between England and Spain.'[6] Furthermore, Ralegh accepted Cobham's statement that they were to meet in Jersey after the latter's return from Spain, though Ralegh said that as far as he was concerned the purpose of the get together was purely social (at his trial Ralegh insisted that he understood Cobham would be returning from France, not Spain).[7]

Why did Ralegh make the damaging admission that he had been offered money by Cobham for furthering the peace with Spain, when an absolute denial might have served his interests better? There are two possible reasons. First he may have suspected that correspondence between Cobham and Aremberg mentioning his, Ralegh's, name had been intercepted. But more importantly, by agreeing to a common line with Cobham which acknowledged a lesser offence (discussing Spanish money for the peace), rather than the high treason of an attempted coup against king and government, both Cobham and Ralegh might hope to escape the full force of the law. In other words, a co-operative solution to the prisoners' dilemma offered the best prospect of acquittal.

Cobham was, however, at a disadvantage. Unlike Ralegh he had already made a very damaging confession on 20 July, and he was implicated by Brooke's and La Renzi's evidence. Ralegh, therefore, sought to strengthen Cobham's resolve by invoking the so-called two witness rule (that a treason charge could only be sustained if there were at least two witnesses), arguing that since the only credible witness against him was Brooke, he could expect to escape conviction so long as he held firm and stuck to the 'money for peace' version of events. There was also an implied threat in Ralegh's reasoning: if Cobham decided to denounce him in the hope of obtaining the king's mercy, Ralegh could be a compelling witness against him.[8]

For his part, Ralegh had two major concerns. First that Cobham might waiver, confess all once more and throw himself on the king's mercy; and second, that the prosecution might consider Cobham's angry accusations of 20 July as sufficient to sustain a charge of treason against himself. He therefore pressed Cobham for an additional safeguard in the form of a letter that would formally acknowledge the falsity of his earlier accusation, and clear Ralegh of any involvement in a plot to overthrow the king.

Cobham was evidently prepared to go this far, presumably as a further induce-ment to Ralegh to support the innocent version of Cobham's admitted Spanish project. The intention appears to have been for Cobham to write a letter to the lords and accordingly, on 24 October, he requested the son of Sir George Harvey, the newly appointed lieutenant of the Tower, to pass on to his father a brief note:

> If that I might write unto the Lords I would, touching Sir Walter Ralegh; besides my letter to my Lord Cecil, God is my witness, it doth trouble my conscience: as you shall send me word so I will do, that my letter may be ready against your son's going: I would very fain have the words that the Lords used of my barberousness in accusing him falsely ...[9]

Harvey declined to accede to this request however. He suppressed the letter and only revealed its existence one month after Ralegh's trial, so it played no further part in the proceedings. However, about ten days later Ralegh did manage to extract from Cobham a letter of exoneration delivered to himself. The means of communication were graphically described in later testimony provided by Ralegh's personal servant, Edward Cotterell:

at the great entreaty of Sir Walter Ralegh he [Cotterell[took an apple from him to which a letter or writing was tied with a thread, and did throw the same in at the window in the Wardrobe Tower where the Lord Cobham was lodged, about eight o'clock on the evening: and he came again the next night about the same time, and took a letter which the Lord Cobham wrote that was put under the door of the prison, and brought the same to Sir Walter Ralegh and this was not past four or five days before Sir Walter Ralegh went to Winchester.[10]

The letter, which went through at least one draft before Ralegh was satisfied with it, was later to be read out at Ralegh's trial:

> Now that the arraignment draws near, not knowing which should be first, I or you, to clear my conscience, satisfy the world with truth, and free myself from the cry of blood, I protest upon my soul and before God and his angels, I never had conference with you in any treason, nor was ever moved by you to the things I heretofore accused you of; and for any thing I know, you are as innocent and as clear from any treasons against the king as is any subject living. Therefore I wash my hands, and pronounce with Daniel, *Purus sum a sanguine hujus;* and God so deal with me and have mercy on my soul, as this is true![11]

At about the same time that Ralegh was seeking cover against Cobham's earlier charges, Cobham was himself engaged in a secret correspondence with his steward, Richard Mellersh, with a view to undoing some of the damage inflicted by his own confession. In a letter to Mellersh dated 29 October he proposed two elaborate ploys to help his case.[12] First, Mellersh was to write to Cobham's wife, Lady Kildare, to say her husband was ill and wanted to speak to a minister of the church so that he might confess all. His wife was to propose the name of one of the king's intimate clerics in order that her husband's confession might carry the greatest possible weight with James. Cobham on the other hand would suggest to the lieutenant of the Tower the name of another confessor in case something should be suspected. The idea was that Cobham's confession, made while apparently contemplating death, would stress his innocence and incline the king towards mercy. The second ploy involved Sir Thomas Fane, Cobham's lieutenant at Dover Castle. Cobham had drafted a back-dated letter to Fane, saying that he intended to visit him at Dover on harbour business and had postponed his planned visit to the continent. Fane was asked to write a suitably back-dated response. This contrived correspondence, together with an undelivered letter to Cecil explaining Cobham's changed travel plans, was to be 'discovered' by Mellersh among his papers and then shown to the lords 'whereby he shall remove some doubts that he only intended to travel to practice against the King'.[13] It was later suggested by the prosecution that Ralegh had some hand in these subterfuges. But the impression conveyed by Cobham's lengthy correspondence with

Mellersh is that of a desperate man, driven by the long shadow of the axe to frantic manoeuvring. In any event, all came to nothing because Fane immediately informed the Council, the whole correspondence was discovered in Mellersh's possession, and Mellersh himself was sent to the Tower at the end of October.

As the day of the trial approached, and the prisoners in the Tower were being prepared for their journey to Winchester, Ralegh was no doubt aware that his life depended on Cobham's resolve to hold to the agreed common line. But Cobham, always intemperate and impulsive, was now a very fragile vessel. Unlike his brother Brooke, he was denied visits from his wife; his trusty steward Mellersh had been arrested; and he wrote bitterly to Cecil that he was now cut off from the outside world. He could no longer write to his wife and, critically, had no means to obtain legal advice ahead of his arraignment.[14] Cobham also suffered very poor health, and in late October he complained to Cecil that 'these three days I have neither ate nor drunk, sleep I cannot; pain in my legs is such extremity as I never had in my life …'[15] Moreover he felt humiliated because he had no money to buy everyday items he would need for his impending coach journey: 'They say that on the 5th November I must go towards Winchester. Money, God is my witness, I have not two pence. The ordinary necessaries that I want I am ashamed to write what they be.'[16]

Pressure on Cobham was building. Towards the end of October Lady Kildare had written to her husband saying that she had met Cecil at Nonsuch Palace but that 'he gives me small comfort'. She then offered Cobham some advice, which it may be presumed she was passing on from Cecil: 'but help yourself if it may be. I say no more, but draw not the yoke of others' burdens.'[17] Clearly, Cobham's continuing refusal to denounce Ralegh was displeasing to those in high places.

While Cobham showed signs of increasing mental stress during his four month detention in the Tower, Ralegh's state of mind appears to have followed a very different course. When he was transferred to the Tower in the aftermath of Cobham's 20 July denunciation, he immediately fell into a deep despair which led him into a botched suicide attempt. While he was at table, dining in the company of the lieutenant of the Tower, Sir John Peyton, he suddenly tore his vest open, seized an ordinary kitchen knife and plunged it into his breast. It struck a rib and glanced aside, and though at first the wound seemed dangerous it turned out to be relatively minor.[18] Cecil described the episode in his letter to Parry of 4 August:

> Although lodged and attended as well as in his own house, yet one afternoon, while divers of us were in the Tower examining these prisoners, Sir Walter Ralegh attempted to have murdered himself, whereof when were advertised we came to him and found him in some agony, seeming to be unable to endure his misfortunes, and protesting innocency with carelessness of life. In that humour he had wounded himself under the right pap but no way mortally; being in truth, rather a cut than a stab.[19]

That Ralegh's suicide attempt was premeditated rather than prompted by a sudden impulse is shown by a letter he wrote to his wife in anticipation of death.[20] In this farewell address, he first acknowledges the force of divine law: 'I know it is forbidden to destroy ourselves; but I trust it is forbidden in this sort – that we destroy not ourselves despairing of God's mercy.' As a proud man he is mortified by the ruin of his reputation: 'All my services, hazards and expenses for my country – plantings, discoveries, fights, councils, and whatever else – malice hath now covered over. I am now made an enemy and traitor by the word of an unworthy man.' He gives advice to his wife:

> thou art a young woman, and forbear not to marry again … To witness that thou didst love me once take care that thou marry not to please sense, but to avoid poverty and to preserve thy child. That thou didst also love me living, witness it to others – to my poor daughter [his illegitimate child in Ireland], to whom I have given nothing; for his sake who will be cruel to himself to preserve thee. Be charitable to her and teach thy son to love her for his father's sake.

And finally:

> I bless my poor child, and let him know his father was no traitor … let my son be thy beloved, for he is part of me and I live in him … and the Lord for ever keep thee and them and give thee comfort in both worlds.

On 23 July, a day or two after Ralegh's suicide attempt, Peyton wrote to Cecil describing his charge's agonised state of mind: 'I never saw so strange a dejected mind as in Sir Walter Ralegh. I am exceedingly cumbered with him. Five or six times in a day he sends for me in such passions as I see his fortitude is [not] competent to support his grief.'[21] As in other great crises of his life, Ralegh first plumbed the depths of despondency and then recovered his nerve, his cool, and his ability to scheme. Some two weeks after the attempted suicide Cecil was able to report to the English ambassador in Paris that 'he is very well cured both in body and mind'.[22] And within three weeks of the episode he was wholly focused on establishing a common line of defence with his former detractor, using every artifice available to a state prisoner under close surveillance. So as Cobham became increasingly abject, it fell to Ralegh to strengthen their joint resolve and to resume battle against their accusers.

The main body of prisoners in the Tower, including Cobham and those charged with the Priests' treason, left the Tower around 10 November and arrived in Winchester late in the evening of 12 November, their trunks coming after them. Most rode on horseback but the two noblemen, Gray and Cobham, were carried in coaches and accompanied by fifty horse. Because of the need for special security precautions it seems that Ralegh's coach travelled behind the others.

In any event he had a stopover at Bagshot, and from here he managed to send a letter on to Cobham on 10 or 11 November, presumably through his servant, Cotterell, who was allowed to accompany him to Winchester. The letter, which was carefully couched in terms that would minimise embarrassment if officially scrutinised, read as follows:

> I do not know whether your Lordship or myself shall be first arraigned. I think I shall be the first. I beseech your Lordship as you would have God should comfort you so deal with me in this matter. You know in your soul that you never acquainted me with your Spanish imaginations, and that you had really satisfied me of Copley. I never suspected you afterwards. You know that you offered me the money bona fide for the peace. I trust in God that you never spake those words of the King, [a reference to Cobham's alleged threat to destroy 'the King and all his cubs'] and if you be clear of it, your peers will never condemn you for your Spanish intent, seeing as you have changed your thoughts and discovered it to the King first. Your brother is no lawful witness against you, having sought to injure you as he have heretofore. Good my Lord, according to the truth, write accordingly and that effectually. And direct it to my Lord Chief Justice Popham and the rest of the Commission.
>
> From Bagshot and so I hope God will bless you for it in doing me right.
> Your poor and unfortunate friend,
>   W.R.[23]

Ralegh's thoughts, as he jolted along muddy roads towards his day of destiny in Winchester, were focused on the man who could make or break him. He wanted the letter of exculpation from Cobham which was to have been sent to the lords from the Tower, but which the Tower lieutenant had disallowed, to be addressed now, at this final hour, to the commission due to preside at his trial. Ralegh was using all his powers of persuasion and artifice to manipulate his pliant friend to his own advantage. But Cecil, now waiting in the wings, knew very well how to use the terror of the scaffold to bend a man to his will. The battle for Cobham's soul was yet to be won.

9

Preparing for the Trial

> Peruse over all our books, records, and histories, and you shall find a principle
> in law, a rule in reason and a trial in experience, that treason doth ever produce
> fatal and final destruction to the offender.
>
> Sir Edward Coke, *Third Institute*

Ralegh and his co-accused faced the charge of high treason. This offence was distinguished from petty treason which was the slaying of a master by his servant, a husband by his wife or a prelate by a lesser cleric. The classic definition of high treason embodied in the 1352 Act of Edward III was, 'to compass or imagine the death of a King, his Queen or the royal heir', but it also included levying war against the king; adhering to the king's enemies; killing a high official; and violating the king's consort, his eldest daughter or the wife of his eldest son. The scope of the law was broad because 'imagining the death of a King' could be construed to cover words and writings, while under common law failure to report knowledge of intended treason was treasonable itself, even though not mentioned in the statute.[1] The historian Samuel Gardiner has emphasised the breadth of the offence of high treason:

> In the case of ordinary crimes it was necessary to prove that the prisoner had actually taken part in the criminal action of which he was accused. In cases of treason it was sufficient if any one person had committed an overt act; all others to whom the treason had been confided, and who had consented to perpetration of the crime, although they might have taken no part whatever in any treasonable action, were held to be as much guilty as the man would have been who actually led an army against the King.[2]

A host of treason acts were passed during the Tudor period, mainly designed to deal with problems raised by the religious upheavals of the time. Some of these statutes, such as the Edwardian Treason Act of 1547, specified the need for 'two lawful and sufficient witnesses' against the accused. During the reign of Mary Tudor the two witness rule was repealed but then apparently restored, while Elizabeth incorporated a requirement for two witnesses in her treason act of 1571. Elizabeth's statute was, however, expressly limited to the natural life of the queen, the intention being to prevent any usurping successor such as Mary Queen of Scots from enjoying its protection. Through all these changes the original act of 1352 remained on the statute book. Since this legislation said nothing about procedural requirements, the prosecuting authorities could always get round the more exacting demands of subsequent legislation by framing the indictment under the old statute. The attitude of the state was, perhaps, reflected in a statement by the solicitor-general in a treason case of 1586 that 'no treason would ever be sufficiently proven if two lawful witnesses had to be produced every time'.[3]

Anyone charged with treason faced a formidable challenge when it came to organising a defence. Few knew precisely what charges were included in the indictment until it was read out to them in court. Access to legal advice (and sometimes even law books) was prohibited during the period between arrest and arraignment. This was to be demonstrated only too clearly when William Gosnall, a lawyer of the Middle Temple who had been discreetly advising Lord Cobham during his imprisonment, was himself detained and examined. The accused was allowed no legal representation at the trial itself and had to rely entirely on his own wits. The absence of legal representation was particularly disadvantageous in treason cases due to the complexity of the numerous overlapping treason statutes – a complexity which, it has been suggested, was deliberately fostered because it strengthened the hand of the judges and the serjeants.[4] The accused was not entitled to call witnesses in his favour, though any number could appear against him. When an accused applied to the court for leave to call a witness, the answer typically was that 'because their witness was against the King's Majesty, they could not be heard'.[5] Witnesses against the accused generally gave their evidence in the form of written depositions, and the accused had no right to demand that they appear face to face, still less to cross-examine them. Hearsay evidence was freely allowed, and a witness against the accused who had already confessed to treason could still be a valid witness. The commission presiding at the trial was far from being independent. It generally comprised senior government officials as well as judges, and might also include persons who had played a major part in planning the prosecution (such was the case in Ralegh's trial where Cecil in effect chaired the commission).

Finally, the jury itself was unlikely to find in the accused's favour, because to do so might be viewed as an affront to the sovereign, with possibly dangerous consequences. When Sir Nicholas Throckmorton was acquitted on a charge of treason in 1554, the jury members were required to appear before the Star Chamber, then imprisoned in the Tower and the Fleet, and subjected to hefty fines of between £60 and £250 each.[6] At the outset, therefore, the odds were very heavily stacked against the accused, and it is not perhaps surprising that only about one in twenty were acquitted.[7] Nevertheless, the Throckmorton case showed that if the prosecution failed to put together at least a prima facie case based on credible evidence, a conviction was not a foregone conclusion.

Cecil had played a dominant role in unravelling both the Bye and Main plots and extracting confessions from those involved. The commitment which he showed in pursuit of Ralegh's investigation in particular is suggested by the French ambassador, de Beaumont, who wrote in early August that 'he [Cecil] undertakes and conducts it with so much warmth, that it is said he acts more from interest and passion than for the good of the Kingdom'.[8] However, once Cecil had gathered together the various depositions, the task of drawing up indictments and formulating the prosecution's case against those charged was handed over to Sir Edward Coke, the Attorney General.

Coke was a man of considerable intellectual gifts who had risen from humble beginnings, partly through his own industry, but also helped by his political alignment with the Cecils. In 1594 there had been a bitter tussle between Essex, who favoured Francis Bacon for the vacant position of Attorney General, and the Cecil faction, who backed Coke. Elizabeth eventually came down in favour of Coke who was no doubt duly grateful to his powerful sponsors. When in 1598 he married the very wealthy widow of Sir William Hatton (nephew and heir to Sir Christopher), his links with the Cecil family became closer still, since Lady Hatton was the granddaughter of Lord Burghley and Sir Robert Cecil's niece.

Coke's indebtedness to the Cecil family is underlined by a letter he wrote to Cecil in early May 1603, which spoke of the knighthoods that had been conferred on previous holders of his office. He referred to the possibility of himself being similarly honoured and added: 'I thank God that I am not ambitious, but as all my good fortunes have come ... either by your honourable father or by you, I would account it the greater if it came by your honourable means.' Coke then asked for his letter to be burned but Cecil failed to do so – perhaps because he thought it might come in useful at some future date if Coke needed reminding where his loyalties lay. In any event, the request was granted and Coke was duly knighted at Greenwich Palace on 22 May.[9]

Coke was eventually to distinguish himself as a formidable legal scholar and a great upholder of English liberties. Indeed, he was to cause such offence to James as a defender of the Commons' privileges against the Crown that at the age of 70 he was forced to spend seven months in the Tower of London. But in the early months of James' reign, he was still making his way in the world and anxious to please his new sovereign. One of his main tasks, which he pursued with characteristic vigour, was to secure convictions against those who had allegedly conspired against the king, and above all, Ralegh.

The problem for the prosecution was that the only substantive evidence against Ralegh was Cobham's accusation of 20 July, which he had almost immediately retracted. It will be recalled that this outburst was made after Cobham had confessed his own treasonable actions in soliciting money from Spain. The examination of 20 July in which Cobham must have made his confession is now missing, but the fact that it took place is made clear by Cecil's letter to Parry dated 4 August, and also by an intervention by the Lord Chief Justice at Ralegh's trial:

> My Lords, when Cobham was first examined upon interrogatories, he denied everything, but he refused to sign his Examination, standing upon it as a matter of honour, that being a Baron of the Realm, his declaration was to be accepted without subscription. Notwithstanding he said at last, that if I would say he was compellable and ought to do it, then he would sign. Whereupon I, then lying at Richmond for fear of the plague, was sent for, and I came to the Lord Cobham, and told him he ought to subscribe, or it would be a contempt of a high nature; which presently after he did. Afterwards the Lords showed him a letter written by Sir W. Ralegh to My Lord Cecil, and on reading it he exclaimed 'That wretch! that traitor Ralegh! hath he used me thus? Nay, then I will tell you all'.[10]

The crucial question is: what was the examination that Cobham initially refused to sign but eventually did sign? It was not the examinations of 16 or 17 July because neither of these were subscribed. Cobham did sign his 19 July examination, but the events which the Lord Chief Justice is referring to occurred on 20 July. Besides, in the 19 July examination Cobham gave little away and continued to deny any wrong doing: presumably he was willing to subscribe, partly because his declarations were relatively innocuous, but also because he had already been warned by his examiners that failure to sign was a contempt.[11]

It seems clear that the examination which Cobham had to be persuaded to sign was the suppressed interrogation of 20 July, in which he confessed to his Spanish treason as described in Cecil's letter to Parry ('… the Lord Cobham, being called in question, he did first confess his own treasons … and then did absolutely accuse Ralegh'). Cobham might well have been reluctant to subscribe to this confession, since to do so could amount to signing his own death warrant. On the other hand, Cobham's examiners, for the very same reason, would have wished to apply every possible pressure to get him to sign, which is why they took the unusual step of sending for the Lord Chief Justice to bully him into submission. The irony is that after going to such lengths to obtain this confession, the prosecution decided to bury it because it weakened the evidential value of Cobham's subsequent outburst against Ralegh. Six weeks later, Cobham, then a prisoner in the Tower, dwelt ruefully on this episode. Commissioner Sir William Waad reported that he was 'very much distempered, and very penitent he kept not his first resolutions from which the opinion of the Lord Chief Justice did remove him, and protesteth hereafter he will set his hand to nothing'.[12]

The problem then, for Coke and the prosecution team, was that Cobham had already admitted to treasonable conduct *before* he accused Ralegh. This was a problem because to secure a conviction against Ralegh it would be necessary to show that in accusing him, Cobham had for the first time confessed to his own treason. Only then could Coke argue that the accusation of Ralegh was conclusive evidence because the accuser had simultaneously implicated himself.

The solution to this problem, as it turned out, was quite simple. Coke conspired with Cecil to have Cobham's confessional examination of 20 July removed from the record. When the depositions were read out at the trial it would therefore appear that Cobham had first incriminated himself when he accused Ralegh. The approach is reflected in a draft of the prosecution case against Cobham and Ralegh drawn up by Coke. This 'prosecution document' (see appendix D) was recently discovered in the Bodleian Library by the historian, Mark Nicholls.[13] In the document Coke stresses the force of Cobham's accusation against Ralegh. The evidential weight of such a confession is especially heavy because, according to Coke, 'the law alloweth the approvement or accusation of a co-offender to be as strong as an indictment by the oath of twelve jurors'.[14] His argument here is that the statement of an accomplice who accuses himself is of such weight in law as to be considered equivalent to the presentment of a grand jury. Elsewhere Coke asks: '… what colour of cause should move Cobham jointly to accuse himself and Ralegh of high treason, ruinating thereby his own honour, life and estate, except they thereof were guilty, against whom before that his confession nothing was proved?'[15] How this line of reasoning was further developed at the trial remains to be seen, but it is clear that in the absence of any other convincing direct evidence against Ralegh the prosecution, at an early stage, felt obliged to play up for all it was worth Cobham's outburst of 20 July – even if it meant suppressing evidence that might point in another direction.

While giving centre stage to Cobham's accusation, the prosecution document also suggests that in cases of treason a lower standard of proof is required than for other offences. The reasons given are, first, that honest witnesses are not to be found in such cases; second, that treason is necessarily cloaked in secrecy; and third, that because the offence is so horrible and vile in the eyes of men and carries such severe penalties, the guilty parties use every device to conceal their treason and so 'both law and reason alloweth violent concurring presumptions for concluding proof'.[16] Finally in the document, Coke draws attention to the character of the man against whom a conviction is sought:

Who is Sir Walter Ralegh? A man by nature of an extraordinary wit, and thereby the better furnished to shadow his misdoings. Secondly, a man of too much more than ordinary policy [political guile] and thereby the better provided to prevent the discovery of his secret unlawful purposes.[17]

Since the nature of the planned treason is violent and bloody, and Cobham is a man neither of the sword nor of arms, Coke saw it was probable 'that Ralegh being a man of both was the inciter of him thereunto'.[18] Furthermore Coke alleged that:

> these treasons could not be either plotted or performed but out of an extraordinary wit and policy, but Cobham of himself is far from them, but Ralegh owner of them all, and therefore more probable that these treasons as Cobham affirmeth are arrows drawn out of Ralegh's quiver than of his own ...[19]

So what we have here in Coke's preparatory notes for the trial are, first, an assertion that Cobham's retracted accusation of Ralegh is equivalent to the testimony of twelve men; second, a view of the law which demands a lower standard of proof for cases of high treason; and third, a presumption that because Ralegh, in contrast to Cobham, is extremely clever and has also performed distinguished military service, he is likely to have been the instigator of any treasonable activity that Cobham may have had in mind. If the jury were to accept the attorney general's conception of the law and its application to the charges against Ralegh, what chance was there for the accused?

While the prosecution case was based on a single (retracted) witness statement, Ralegh set out to rebut the argument that this was sufficient evidence to convict him. Under a fairly permissive regime in the Tower he had clearly been allowed access to law books and, above all, to the detailed account of Sir Nicholas Throckmorton's celebrated acquittal on a charge of treason in 1554. This apparently verbatim transcript was widely available, having been published in 1577 and reprinted ten years later. Throckmorton's alleged offence, as a prominent protestant, was complicity in the failed rebellion of Sir Thomas Wyatt against Mary Tudor in 1553. He was sent to the Tower and indicted for treason on the testimony of one of Wyatt's followers, Cuthbert Vaughan. After his acquittal he was eventually released from the Tower and later prospered under Elizabeth, dying in 1571 at the age of 56.

Throckmorton had married Anne, daughter of Sir Nicholas Carew, and it was one of his daughters, Elizabeth, whom Ralegh had married in 1591. Ralegh would have been familiar with his father-in-law's case and indeed he was to refer to it during his trial. It may be said, therefore, that Throckmorton's success in clearing his name provided a model for Ralegh's own defence. Throckmorton's central argument was that a single witness was insufficient to sustain a charge of treason. From memory he was able to cite key passages from the Edwardian treason acts of 1547 and 1552, including in particular the later statute's reaffirmation of the need for at least two accusers, 'who shall be brought in person before the said party accused, and avow and maintain that they have to say against the said party ...'[20]

Throckmorton claimed that the law required two lawful witnesses to be brought before him face to face, whereas Vaughan, who appeared in court to testify against him, was but one. Furthermore Vaughan was, according to Throckmorton, an unlawful witness, being already condemned and therefore knowing that the only way of saving his life was to accuse others. Throckmorton then requested that the first Marian treason act of 1553 be read out in court. This demand was met with a remarkable display of judicial stone-walling that cannot have impressed the jury or others present:

> *Commissioner Bromley*: No sir, there shall be no books brought at your desire. We do all know the law sufficiently without book.
>
> *Throckmorton*: Do you bring me hither to try me by the law, and will not show me the law. What is your knowledge of the law to these men's [the jurors] satisfactions, which have my trial in hand? I pray you my lords, and my lords all, let the statutes be read as well for the Queen as for me.
>
> *Commissioner Hare*: You know not what belongeth to your case, and therefore we must teach you. It appertaineth not for us to provide books for you, neither sit we here to be taught of you. You should have taken better heed of the law before you had come hither.[21]

Throckmorton then astonished the court by quoting from memory the precise wording of the statute concerned. This act repealed all treason legislation which had been enacted since the original treason act of 1352, thereby restoring the law to the position prevailing 200 years earlier. Throckmorton pointed out that the 1352 act required proof of an 'open deed' by the accused and since he was not charged with any overt treasonable act he could not be convicted as a traitor. The judges' response to this line of argument was unequivocal:

> *Commissioner Bromley*: If three or four do talk, devise and conspire together of a traitorous act to be done, and afterwards one of them doth commit treason, as Wyatt did, then the law doth impute them, and everyone of them as their acts ...[22]
>
> *Commissioner Sanders* [equally emphatic on this point]: The law always in cases of treason doth account all principals and no accessories as in other offences; and therefore a man offending in treason, either by covert act or procurement, whereupon an open deed have ensued as in this case, is adjudged by the law a principal traitor.[23]

We do not know on what grounds the jury found Throckmorton not guilty, but Ralegh was to follow his father-in-law's example by citing the Edwardian statutes requiring two witnesses. He would also cite the second Marian treason act of 1554, passed shortly after Throckmorton's acquittal, which made it obligatory once more for two accusers to appear before the party arraigned. Ralegh would quote from Clause 11 which reads:

... at the arraignment of any man for treason every person who shall declare,
confess, or depose anything against him, shall, if living, and within the realm,
be brought forth in person, before the party arraigned, if he require it, and
object and say openly in his hearing what he can against him unless the party
arraigned shall willingly confess the same.[24]

These procedural requirements seemed straight forward enough, as well as equi-
table and in conformity with natural justice. Certainly Ralegh relied heavily on
their efficacy for his own defence, and he had also managed to persuade Cobham
that the two witness rule could be used in his case to neutralise Brooke's allegations against him. A great deal was therefore riding on a literal interpretation of
the Marian statute, since it underpinned a joint defence that shielded Ralegh
from the former accusations of his one time friend and collaborator.

However, there was an internal contradiction within the act. On the one hand
Clause 11 reaffirmed the need for two witness-accusers, but at the same time
Clause 6 said treason trials were henceforth to be by 'the common law' which did
not require such accusers. Even today, legal historians are divided as to the true
intent and meaning of the second Marian treason statute and how it affected the
two witness rule.[25] The legal ambiguity was doubly dangerous for the accused
because it gave considerable discretion to judges to interpret the law to suit the
occasion. In 1556 a meeting of judges and law officers of the Crown tried to
clarify the issue,[26] but who was to say how the commission sitting at Winchester
would now apply the law?

Apart from his technical legal defence based on insufficiency of proof, Ralegh
also relied heavily on what he claimed was the implausibility of the charges
against him. For this purpose he prepared a statement, to be delivered at his trial,
which focused on several circumstances in his favour. First, he said it was inconceivable that he would collude with Spain, given his own record of consistent
opposition to that country. He had only a few months before presented a treatise
to the king's majesty on the present state of Spain and the reasons for opposing
peace. He had himself served his country at sea against Spain on three separate
occasions, and he had sunk some £40,000 of his own money in these campaigns.
Furthermore, Spain was in decline and England never stronger:

Moreover, I was not so bare of sense but I saw, that if ever this State [England]
was strong and able to defend itself, it was now. The kingdom of Scotland
united, whence we were wont to fear all our troubles; Ireland quieted, where
our forces were wont to be divided; Denmark assured, whom before we were
wont to have in jealousy; the Low Countries, our nearest neighbours at peace
with us; and instead of a Lady, whom time had surprised, we had now an active
king, a lawful successor to the Crown, who was able to attend to his own business. I was not such a madman as to make myself in this time a Robin Hood, a

1 Ralegh as the victor of Cadiz. He was lauded for his role in the naval assault but received a serious leg wound and complained that he had 'possession of nought but poverty and pain'.

SERO, SED SERIO

2 Robert Cecil in 1602. Francis Bacon observed that he was a man who played both sides and whose face could turn two ways – like a boatman rowing up the Thames who 'looketh toward London Bridge when he pulleth toward Westminster'.

3 Edward Coke aged 41.
A formidable lawyer but at
Winchester he 'reviled and insulted
Ralegh in a manner never imitated
… before or since in any English
court of justice' (James Stephen,
legal historian).

4 Henry Howard, later Earl of
Northampton. Described by Lady
Bacon as a 'subtle serpent', he
predicted that after Queen Elizabeth's
death, Cecil could deliver Ralegh 'to
the judge, and the judge to prison'.

5 A Hilliard miniature of Ralegh as the dazzling young courtier. He was a man whom 'a Prince would rather be afraid of than ashamed of' (John Aubrey).

6 Durham House and Salisbury House c. 1630. 'Durham House was a noble palace … I well remember [Ralegh's] study, which was a little turret that looked into and over the Thames' (John Aubrey).

7 Twin portrait of Lord Burghley and Robert Cecil. 'The father and son are affectionate[ly] joined in power and policy' (Lady Bacon).

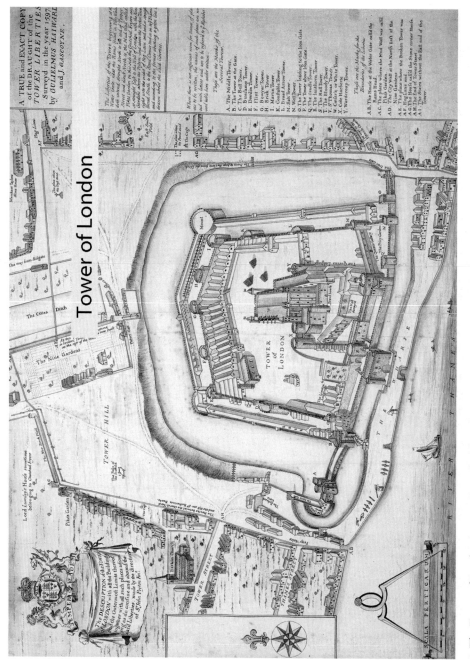

Tower of London

A. The Middle Tower.
B. The Tower at the Gate.
C. The Bell Tower.
D. Beauchamp Tower.
E. Devlin Tower.
F. Flint Tower.
G. Bowyer Tower.
H. Brick Tower.
I. Martin Tower.
K. Constable Tower.
L. Broad Arrow Tower.
M. Salt Tower.
N. Well Tower.
O. The Tower leading to the Iron Gate.
P. The Tower above Iron Gate.
Q. The Cradle Tower.
R. The Lanthorn Tower.
S. The Hall Tower.
T. The Bloody Tower.
V. S. Thomas's Tower.
W. Carleck, or White Tower.
X. Cole Harberte.
Y. Wardemrop Tower.

A.B. The House at the Water Gate call'd the Rams Head.
A.C. The place where the Mud Wall was call'd.
A.D. The City Wall at the North end of the Nine Gardens.
A.E. The place where the Broken Tower was.
A.F. Hog Lane end.
A.G. The House call'd the Stone corner House.
A.H. The End of Tower Street.
A.I. The Stairs without the East end of the Tower.

8 The Tower of London in 1597. Described by John Stow as 'a prison of state for the most dangerous offenders'. Ralegh spent thirteen years in the Bloody Tower (T), while Cobham was imprisoned in the Beauchamp Tower (D).

9 The Spanish Treaty commissioners at Somerset House, 1604. Lord Cecil of Essendon and Henry Howard, Earl of Northampton, sit next to each other on the right. Charles de Ligne, Count of Aremberg, sits with the Spanish delegation on the opposite side, fourth from the window.

10 & 11 Robert Cecil's tomb in St Ethelred's, Hatfield, magnificently sculpted by Maximilian Colt (top). In contrast to this opulent memorial, Ralegh's decapitated body was buried in an unmarked grave beneath the chancel of St Margaret's, Westminster (above).

Wat Tyler, or a Jack Cade. I knew also the state of Spain well; his weakness, and poorness, and humbleness, at this time. I knew he was discouraged and dishonoured. I knew that six times we had repulsed his forces, thrice in Ireland, thrice at sea, and once at Cadiz on his own coast ... I knew that where before-time he was wont to have forty great sails at the least in his ports, now he hath not past six or seven; ... I knew that of five and twenty millions had had from his Indies, he had scarce any left; ... his pride so abated, as, notwithstanding his former high terms, he was glad to congratulate the King, my master, on his accession, and now cometh creeping unto him for peace. [27]

Furthermore, it was surely beyond belief that Spain would freely disburse 600,000 crowns to Cobham without any kind of security, particularly as the country was now impoverished. When Elizabeth lent money to the Netherlands she was given Flushing and Brill by way of security, and even the city merchants, when lending to the queen, were given a lien on her lands. So if he and Cobham had tried to raise money 'what pawn had we to give the King of Spain?'[28]

Finally, Ralegh asked, was it likely that he would choose Cobham as his co-conspirator in a plot to overthrow the king? Cobham was a baron of the realm on whom his family's honour rested, and his property was worth over £5,000 per annum. Was it probable that such a man upon an idle humour would risk all this and 'is it likely that I should employ a man of these fortunes to enter into such gross treasons, when I knew that [others] of better understanding than Cobham were ready to beg their bread?'[29]

This, then, was Ralegh's defence. He would argue for the need for two witnesses; when confronted with Cobham's retracted accusation he would demand that Cobham be brought before him to repeat the charges face to face; and he would ridicule the idea that he had employed Cobham to seek large sums of money from Spain to stir up rebellion. As a final trump card he had in his possession the letter of exculpation that he had managed to obtain from Cobham when in the Tower, which he hoped to be able to read out in court.

Ralegh's defence was inextricably linked to that of Cobham – whom he had persuaded to retract his original accusation and to agree a common version of events. But Cobham was not Ralegh's puppet: he was an educated man who was capable of taking an independent view of his own predicament. Agonised by the very real prospect of losing his head, he cast around for a way out. He obtained an independent legal opinion from William Gosnall of the Middle Temple, who at his instigation met Cobham's steward, Mellersh, at his house in Blackfriars in mid-October. Mellersh gave Gosnall instructions and later took a case report from Gosnall to his master in the Tower.[30] It seems that Gosnall presented a bleak view of his client's situation, because in his letter to Mellersh towards the end of October, Cobham revealed strong doubts about the common defence he had agreed with Ralegh based on the two witness rule: 'I remember you told me that mine own confession of itself was not treason nor my brother's accusation of me, but both together doth make it treason. This I would gladly know because it is very material for me to remember it at my arraignment.'[31]

Cobham's access to further legal advice was abruptly cut off on 27 October when the Lord Chancellor, Ellesmere, arrested both Gosnall and Mellersh – having been tipped off by another lawyer whose opinion Gosnall had sought on the Cobham case. The Lord Chancellor wrote obsequiously to Cecil expressing his outrage at this breach of security which, if not severely dealt with, 'all your former great and honourable travails in discovering these treasons will prove illusory, and the proceeding in the trial not free from some aspersion of dishonour'.[32]

Recognising the weakness of his legal case, Cobham tried to deal with the two main pieces of evidence against him, namely his brother's accusations and his own earlier confession. So far as Brooke was concerned, there were two grounds on which his independence as a witness might be challenged. First, it could be argued that Brooke was an unlawful witness because he had been promised his life as a reward for his accusation. In notes for his defence made before the trial, Cobham quoted from Corinthians to the effect that 'one who accuses another in order to save his own life is a false witness', so clearly this explanation for his brother's conduct was very much in mind.[33] However, it would have been impossible to prove such a claim and Cobham focused instead on his brother's enmity towards him. He asked Mellersh to obtain a sworn statement from one of his friends certifying that Brooke hated him. This request appears to be related to an assertion in Gosnall's case report, that Brooke 'had practised, wished and desired his lordship's death'.[34] Later, at his trial, Cobham was to claim that his brother was jealous of his wealth and wanted to be rid of him so that he could inherit the family estate. He even went so far as to suggest that Brooke had tried to poison him – and added for good measure that Brooke was guilty of incest (his wife's sister then being with child).[35] In any event Brooke's true motive for accusing his brother of treason was, according to Cobham, 'covetousness of his estate'.

Cobham then had to address the difficulty presented by his own earlier admission that he had sought Spanish money to distribute to 'discontented persons'. Here, like Ralegh, he appears to have studied the Throckmorton case, although whereas Ralegh focused on the two witness rule, Cobham began to favour an alternative line of defence based on the distinction between thoughts, or 'imaginings', and deeds. In his pre-trial memorandum he noted the distinction in the sixteenth-century Edwardian legislation between treasonable acts and treasonable words, for which the respective penalties were death and imprisonment. Also, like Throckmorton, he noted that under the 1352 treason statute there must be an 'open deed' to secure a conviction. He asks 'where doth appear my open deed of any compassing or imagining the King's death?'[36] His thoughts on this matter were further revealed in his letter to Mellersh: 'I am the first peer in England that is or shall be called in question upon conceit which was never intended to put in execution.'[37]

In an undated letter to the lords, Cobham developed further the idea that his so-called treason was merely an inward conceit:

> But the matter which has most touched me is that of Aremberg of which I can make no better comparison than this, that as if a man thinking to do a robbery never did it, nor never prosecuted it with means for so is the truth of my cause … being before my apprehension the concept of it was gone … my offence being but a conceit acquainting nobody with it …'[38]

In the same letter he pleaded for a punishment other than death:'that my offence may be redeemed with fine and ransom; in that kind more profit will redound unto his Majesty than if with extremity I be proceeded withal …'[39] At his trial Cobham stood by his defence that he had committed no open deed. In one report of the proceedings he challenged his peers to 'find by the sense of any statute in force that I have compassed or imagined the death of the King or his royal issue, and conspired the same by any fact, consultation or deed, and therefore provably attainted by lawful witnesses or my own confession …'[40]

How did this late shift in Cobham's defence affect his co-operation with Ralegh? In one sense it was fortunate for Ralegh because any admission that the two men had conspired or conferred together would expose Cobham to the charge of having committed an open deed. Hence Cobham had every interest in continuing to deny Ralegh's involvement in his Spanish plans which, he insisted, were no more than idle thoughts confided to no-one. However, Cobham faced an acute dilemma here. He well knew that Cecil wanted him to renew his accusations against Ralegh and that such a move on his part could open the way to the king's mercy. But how could he accuse Ralegh without at the same time undermining his own legal defence?

Cobham had, it seemed, a clear choice: he could either confess openly to his conspiracy with Ralegh and thereby admit to treason by open deed, hoping to obtain the king's favour; or he could risk the king's wrath by insisting that his 'treason' was an inward conceit only, pinning all his hopes on securing an acquittal at his arraignment. It seems that Ralegh was well aware of this inner conflict because according to Cobham, 'in his last letter he advised me that I should not be overtaken by confessing to any particular. For the King would better allow my constant denial than my after-appealing [throwing himself on the King's mercy after conviction]'.[41]

After his arrival in Winchester on the evening of 12 November, Cobham was left alone to agonise over his predicament. Racked with indecision and tormented by thoughts of the scaffold he at last decided, two days later, to seek an urgent meeting with the lords of the Council. This move, by a man now in panic, was to have far reaching consequences for the prosecution's case against Ralegh, Ralegh's defence against his accusers and Cobham's own fate.

10

THE TRIAL

In deciding Crawford v. Washington [2004] the United States Supreme Court demonstrated that Sir Walter Ralegh's Case is not merely a bleak episode of legal history, but rather that it remains a vital legal precedent, one from which a redeeming lesson may be drawn: Crawford requires, in any case where a witness is not present for trial, that the witnesses' prior testimonial statements ... may not be used unless the witness is unavailable and the defendant had the prior opportunity to cross-examine the witness.

Allen Boyer, Trial Counsel, New York Stock Exchange

On the morning of 17 November 1603, Ralegh faced his accusers in the Great Hall of Winchester Castle on a charge of treason. There was a well-established procedure in such cases which began with the reading of the indictment by the Clerk to the court and a short address by the king's Sarjeant at Law. The Attorney General would then outline the case against the accused and proceed to read the proofs, which typically took the form of sworn depositions made by witnesses who might or might not be called to testify in person. It was usual for the court to agree to a request from the accused that he be allowed to respond to each separate proof against him as it was presented, rather than have to await the completion of the prosecution's case before replying. The inevitable result of this concession was to break the trial up into a series of confrontational exchanges which tested the temperament as much as the forensic skill of the protagonists.

In all treason trials of the time the rules on evidence and procedure overwhelmingly favoured the prosecution. But there were two particular features of the Winchester proceedings that added to Ralegh's difficulties. First, no statute was cited in the indictment against him, which meant that the prosecution could fall back on the still extant 1352 treason act if challenged on the basis of more recent statutory requirements. Second, the one key witness against him, Cobham, was not to be produced in court. Furthermore, since Cobham's crucial testimony was not only unsubscribed but also quickly retracted, it was, unusually, to be verified by certificates from the lords and the Lord Chief Justice who had been present at the examination.

Once the court was settled and Ralegh had pleaded not guilty to the indictment, Sarjeant Hale gave a brief address. He outlined the charges and stressed the importance of the Spanish money that Ralegh and Cobham had allegedly sought, 'for money is the sinew of war'. He told the court that 'Cobham took Ralegh to be either a God or an idol', and contrasted Ralegh's military experience and 'great wit' with Cobham's callowness. He concluded: 'now whether these things were bred in a hollow tree [a reference to Cobham] I leave them to speak of, who can speak far better than myself.'[1]

The Attorney General, Sir Edward Coke, then introduced the case against Ralegh. His problem was that the evidence was very thin, so he started by describing in detail the Bye Plot where there was little room for doubting the facts, and where convictions against the accused had been secured only two days before. When Ralegh intervened to point out the obvious, which was that he was not charged with the Bye Plot, Coke asserted obscurely that these treasons were 'like Sampson's foxes, which were joined at the tails, though their heads were severed'.[2]

Coke then anticipated Ralegh's two witness legal defence by citing a previous case where the Lord Chief Justice had determined that the statute of Edward VI requiring two witnesses had been repealed. That this was an argument to suit the occasion is suggested by the fact that in his great work, 'Institutes of the Laws of England', Coke later asserted without qualification that two witnesses were needed to prove treason.[3] Apparently, the Attorney General was adapting his own conception of the law to obtain a conviction that would ingratiate him with his new sovereign. Coke sought to strengthen his argument by asserting that he could, in any case, give proof that was better than two witnesses:

> But in our case in hand, we have more than two witnesses; for when a man, by his accusation of another, shall by the same accusation, also condemn himself, and make himself liable to the same punishment, this is, by our law, more forcible than many witnesses, and is as the inquest of twelve men; for the law presumes that a man will not accuse himself in order to accuse another.[4]

This was the key prosecution argument against Ralegh but, as we now know, it was based on a subterfuge that involved the suppression of an examination in which Cobham had confessed to his own treason *prior* to his accusation of Ralegh.

Finally, Coke described the correspondence between Cobham and his steward, Mellersh. In his letters, Cobham had sought to contrive backdated correspondence with the lieutenant of Dover Castle in order to give the impression that

he had resolved not to travel to Spain. Coke now attributed this stratagem to
Ralegh's 'devilish and machiavelian policy [sic]', although he offered no evidence
linking Ralegh to the correspondence. This unsupported allegation prompted a
preliminary skirmish between the accused and his accuser:

> *Sir Walter Ralegh*: What is that to me? I do not hear yet that you have spoken
> one word against me; here is no treason of mine done; if my Lord Cobham be a
> traitor, what is that to me?
>
> *Attorney General*: All that he did was by thy instigation, thou viper, for I thou
> thee, thou traitor! I will prove thee the rankest traitor in all England.
>
> *Sir Walter Ralegh*: No, no, Mr Attorney, I am no traitor. Whether I live or die,
> I shall stand as true a subject as any the King hath; you may call me traitor at
> your pleasure; yet it becomes not a man of quality and virtue to do so; but I take
> comfort in it, if it is all that you can do, for I do not yet hear that you charge me
> with any treason.
>
> *Lord Chief Justice*: Sir Walter Ralegh, Mr Attorney speaks out of the zeal of his
> duty for the service of the King; and you for your life; be patient on both sides.[5]

Coke then read out his first proof. This was a report of Cobham's angry outburst
of 20 July. According to Howell's *State Trials*, this began with Cobham breathing
out oaths and exclamations against Ralegh and was then followed by allegations
of his conspiracy including the statement (slowly repeated by the clerk to the
court at the request of Coke), that 'he [Ralegh] would never let him alone'.[6] The
source of this passage, which is both garbled and compressed in the trial reports,
has been the cause of some confusion among historians.[7] But it is clear that it
is the same unsubscribed denunciation of Ralegh, certified by the lords, that is
repeatedly quoted in Coke's prosecution document.[8]

Ralegh was allowed to respond to Cobham's accusation, and he took the
opportunity to present his prepared defence based on his service for his country
against Spain. It was immediately after this address that the Lord Chief Justice,
Sir John Popham, made his own important contribution to the proceedings.
Popham, now aged 72, had had a long and successful career as a lawyer during
the course of which he had accumulated a huge fortune – including three great
estates in Wiltshire, Somerset and Devon – the precise source of which is a little
unclear. He had presided over the trials of the Jesuit Robert Southwell in 1595,
where he pronounced the sentence of hanging, drawing and quartering, and of
Mary Queen of Scots in 1587. Although a respected jurist, he had a well-earned
reputation for severity.

Commenting on Cobham's outburst against Ralegh, which he had witnessed
along with the lords at first hand, Popham stated 'surely the countenance and action
of my Lord Cobham much satisfied me that what he confessed was true and that
he surely thought Sir Walter Ralegh had betrayed him'.[9] This could have no other

meaning than that, as far as he was concerned, Cobham's assertion that Ralegh was the prime mover in a plot against the king was the truth. For such an eminent legal figure to announce to the jury at the outset of a trial that he was totally persuaded of the accused's guilt, was, of course, to subvert the course of justice – but then it was state interest, rather than justice, that had to be served that day.

Coke then asked the clerk to the court to read out his second proof (misleadingly described in various trial reports as Cobham's 'second examination'). The original intention, it seems, was to present this evidence immediately after the first proof, since its subject matter was again Cobham's outburst against Ralegh – although this time testified by the Lord Chief Justice rather than the lords. The disjointed nature of the proceedings has misled some historians into believing that the two versions of Cobham's 20 July confession arose from two separate examinations. However, the prosecution document makes it quite clear that Coke cited first the lords' account of Cobham's accusation, and then Popham's. It may be added that the separate recital of these two versions of the same incident, together with the Lord Chief Justice's further intervention on the subject, was calculated to lend maximum force to Cobham's allegations against Ralegh.

At this point in the proceedings the foreman of the jury, Sir Thomas Fowler, asked a very pertinent question – although there is disagreement between the trial reports as to its precise terms.[10] The most coherent account is given in *State Trials*, according to which the juror asked: 'Did Sir Walter Ralegh write a letter to my Lord [Cobham] before he was examined concerning him or not?' The Attorney General straight away answered 'yes', but the more interesting response was from Cecil who took it upon himself to provide a long and tortuous explanation which ended up by answering a different question.

Cecil began by admitting to a 'former dearness' between himself and Ralegh, 'now broken by a discovery of his imperfections' (surely another intimation at the highest level of his guilt). He went on to describe how he had detained Ralegh at Windsor, and expressed the hope that it should not be thought that he had greater judgement than the rest of the lords in making this haste to have him examined. He said that Ralegh was then examined by the lords 'but not concerning my Lord Cobham, but of the surprising treason'. Cobham was later interrogated at Richmond 'but that Ralegh knew that Cobham was examined is more than I know'.[11] The juror's question, however, was not whether Ralegh knew if Cobham had been examined, but whether Ralegh himself had been asked about him – Cecil well knowing that he himself had done so at Windsor outside the Council Chamber. Cecil's dissimulation on this point was highly damaging to Ralegh's cause, as shown by an unnamed observer's account of the trial:

But that which weighed most with me was that so soon as Ralegh had been questioned ... when Cobham was not so much as named, he speedily despatched a letter to Cobham to this effect – 'I have been examined of divers points touching you, before the Lords of the Council; but I have cleared you in all: be firm, and know that one witness cannot hurt you'. Which letter seems to have been written by Ralegh rather to arm Cobham for that which might be to come, than to instruct him for that which passed.[12]

Ralegh was clearly embarrassed by the warning he had allegedly given to his friend via his servant, Kemys. The explanation he offered was that his exchange of letters with Cobham related to some jewels which Cobham had entrusted to him, and that Kemys' confession – that he had taken a verbal message to Cobham – had been extracted by the threat of the rack. The same spectator's account of the trial pointed to the weakness of Ralegh's version of events: 'for he denied it improbably'.[13]

The Attorney General at this point took up the argument presented by Ralegh that Cobham's accusation against him was made in a vengeful and passionate rage provoked by the letter he had written to Cecil. Coke said that Cobham had twice called for the letter, and twice paused a good while on it, before making his allegations. But in order to dispel any doubts, he said he would prove through compelling circumstantial evidence that Cobham's claims were true.

Before Coke could proceed further, Ralegh intervened to ask that Cobham be brought to him face to face, citing the treason statutes of Edward VI and Philip and Mary. He said he did not know whether these laws were still in force but 'if the wisdom of former times, the assemblies of all the three estates in several parliaments, thought it just to have the accusers produced, surely you will not withhold my accuser?'[14] He went on: 'If you proceed to condemn me by bare inferences, without an oath, without a subscription, without witnesses, upon a paper accusation, you try me by the Spanish Inquisition. If my accuser were dead or abroad, it were something; but he liveth, and is in this very house.'[15]

Ralegh supported his demand by quoting from Deuteronomy: 'at the mouth of two or three witnesses shall he that is worthy of death be put to death; but at the mouth of one witness he shall not be put to death.'[16] And he concluded: 'If, then, by the statute law, by the civil law, and by God's word, it be required that there be two witnesses at least, bear with me if I desire one; prove me guilty of these things by one witness only, and I will confess the indictment.'[17]

The Lord Chief Justice was quick to dismiss this line of argument. The Edwardian statutes Ralegh had referred to 'were found to be inconvenient' and were repealed; the Marian statute he cited had reinstated the common law as the only governing law in treason cases and by the common law one witness was sufficient; the subscription of a witness was not necessary if other credible persons had testified to his confession; and 'of all other proofs, the accusation of one, who by his accusation accuseth first himself is the strongest for that hath the force of the verdict of twelve men.'[18] When Justice Warburton weighed in with the assertion that 'by law a man may be condemned upon presumption and circumstances, without any witness to the main fact',[19] this gave rise to a sharp exchange:

Sir Walter Ralegh: Yet by your favour, my Lord, the trial of fact at the common law is by jury and witnesses.

Popham, C.J.: No, the trial at the common law is by examination; if three conspire a treason, and they all confess it, here is never a witness, and yet they may all be condemned of treason.

Sir Walter Ralegh: I know not, my Lord, how you conceive the law; but if you affirm it, it must be a law to all posterity.

Popham, C.J.: Nay, we do not conceive the law, we know the law.

Sir Walter Ralegh: Notwithstanding, my Lords, let me have thus much for my life; for though the law may be as your Lordships have stated it, yet is it a strict and rigorous interpretation of the law. Now the King of England at his coronation swears to observe the equity, and not the rigour of the law; and if ever we had a just and good King, it is his Majesty; and such doth he wish his ministers and judges to be. Though, therefore, by the rigour and severity of the law, this may be sufficient evidence, without producing the witness, yet your Lordships, as Ministers of the King, are bound to adminster the law in equity.

Popham, C.J.: Equity must proceed from the King; you can only have justice from us.[20]

After this put-down, the Attorney General read proofs that were intended to corroborate Cobham's allegations against Ralegh. These included declarations of Copley and Watson as well as examinations of La Renzi and Brooke. Ralegh was allowed a table, pen and ink so that he could take notes while this lengthy evidence was presented. When Coke had finished Ralegh's response was that what the court had heard was mere hearsay evidence: 'You say that Brooke told Watson what Cobham told Brooke, that I had said to him – what proof is this?' He added, 'By this means you may have any man's life in a week'.[21] But the judges here advised the jury to observe that all this evidence was intended to support Cobham's accusations – by proof of speeches uttered by Cobham about his involvement with Ralegh before his apprehension, and before he had been provoked by Ralegh's apparent betrayal.

There then followed a curious digression in the proceedings which focused on a book which Ralegh had lent to Cobham. The book was a manuscript by one Robert Snagge which allegedly disputed the king's right of succession. It was evidently given to Cobham just after he had returned from the king in a resentful frame of mind, and Cobham had subsequently given it to Brooke who had burnt it. The evidence was intended to show how Ralegh had deliberately stirred up Cobham's dissatisfaction, but the emphasis given to all this by the prosecution was clearly considered, by some of those present, to be misplaced. Sir Robert Wroth, one of James' followers, was overheard whispering that the evidence being presented was not material, which led to a heated altercation with the Attorney General who, not for the first or last time in the trial, had to be placated.

Henry Howard, however, seized the opportunity to make a damaging point against Ralegh. He related that Cobham, when first examined about the book, admitted to having received it from Ralegh who allegedly said it was against the king's title. But Ralegh at his examination said that the book was concerned only with justifying Elizabeth's charges against Mary Queen of Scots, and, furthermore, that Cobham had taken it from his table without his knowledge. When re-examined Cobham retracted his previous account, and now said the book contained nothing against the king's title and that he had taken it from Ralegh's table while he was sleeping. The obvious conclusion was that the two accused were in close concert devising their common defence, and that Ralegh was manipulating Cobham. When the Attorney General remarked that this episode showed Ralegh's 'cunning' Ralegh replied: 'Everything that doth make for me is cunning and everything that maketh against me is probable.'[22]

Ralegh now pressed hard to have Cobham brought before him, arguing that it was he rather than his prosecutors who should be nervous about Cobham's presence in court:

> And if that be true which hath been so laboured all this day, that I have been the setter-on of my Lord Cobham, his instigator, and have *infused* these treasons into him, as hath been said, then have I been the efficient cause of his destruction; all his honours, houses, lands, and goods, and all he hath, are lost by me; against whom, then, should he seek revenge but upon me? And the world knoweth him as revengeful of nature as any man living. Besides, a dying man is ever presumed to speak truth: now Cobham is absolutely in the King's mercy; to excuse me cannot avail him; by accusing me he may hope for favour. It is you, then, Mr Attorney, that should press his testimony, and I ought to fear his producing, if all that be true which you have alleged.[23]

When Henry Howard told Ralegh he knew perfectly well that his request could not be granted and that he should waste no more of the court's time on the matter, Ralegh was swift to retaliate: 'Nay, my Lord, it toucheth my life, which I value at as high a rate as your Lordship.'[24]

Cecil here intervened to ask the judges whether it would be in order for proceedings to be stayed while the king's wishes were made known on the calling of Cobham. The answer was that the trial must continue uninterrupted to its conclusion. After this gesture of apparent generosity, Cecil then turned to Ralegh, and as a raptor might circle its prey, asked him whether he would acknowledge his guilt if Cobham were now to confirm his earlier accusations. To which Ralegh answered that he would 'put myself upon it'. Cecil's response as he swooped on his victim was almost exultant: 'Then, Sir Walter, call upon God to help you, for I do verily believe my Lords will prove this.'[25]

It may be asked why Ralegh was so confident that Cobham, if brought before the court, would continue to vouch for his innocence, and also why the prosecution were so reluctant to accede to Ralegh's request. From Ralegh's standpoint, the answer is clear: he was convinced that Cobham was still holding to the joint defence agreed between them ('money for the peace') and would not wish to expose himself to the charge of conspiring with Ralegh to overthrow the king. Furthermore, Ralegh had Cobham in an arm-lock: if he were to come before the court and accuse Ralegh to his face, Ralegh could be expected to confess all and expose Cobham as a traitor. If Cobham valued his life, which he clearly did, he would not accuse his friend – or so Ralegh thought.

From the prosecution's point of view the reverse applied. No doubt the Commissioners were aware that Cobham would not wish to incur Ralegh's wrath and thereby risk his own incrimination. However, their refusal to allow Cobham to appear posed serious presentational difficulties and the various explanations offered were less than convincing. When first pressed by Ralegh the Lord Chief Justice said:

> the accuser is not to be produced; for having first confessed against himself voluntarily and so charged another person, if we shall now hear him again in person, he may for favour or fear retract what formerly he hath said, and the jury may, by that means, be inveigled.[26]

When Cecil asked the judges whether as a matter of law (as distinct from the king's grace and favour) Cobham could be called they answered that 'it might be the means to cover many with treasons, and might be prejudicial to the King',[27] so it could not be allowed. The implication seems to have been that Aremberg, among others, could be incriminated by Cobham which would of course damage relations with Spain at a particularly delicate time.

At the end of the trial the Lord Chief Justice provided a third and highly improbable explanation for keeping Cobham out of court. With remarkable casualness he remarked, as if it were an afterthought:

> It now comes in my mind why you may not have your accuser come face to face … when [traitors] see themselves must die, they will think it best to have their fellow live, that he may commit the like treason again, and so in some sort seek revenge.[28]

The idea that Cobham, who was still hoping desperately for his life, would try to get Ralegh off the hook so that he, Ralegh, could engage in further treasons on Cobham's behalf is too far fetched to deserve further comment.

With the completion of the prosecution evidence it seemed that Ralegh had a good chance of emulating his father-in-law, Sir Nicholas Throckmorton, by securing an acquittal. True, the judges had ruled against him on his legal defence – that two witnesses were required and that his accuser should have to face him in court. But on grounds of natural justice and equity his arguments must have carried weight with the jury. Furthermore, the prosecution's proofs relied heavily on flimsy hearsay and circumstantial evidence – so much so that the Attorney General felt obliged to produce one witness in court. This was a ship's pilot named Dyer who testified that when he was in Lisbon in mid-July, a Portuguese gentleman told him that 'your King shall never be crowned, for Don Cobham and Don Ralegh will cut his throat before he come to be crowned'. When Ralegh asked what proof this tittle-tattle could conceivably be against him, Coke replied that it 'shows that your treason had wings'.[29]

In the gladiatorial contest between Ralegh and Coke, Ralegh had clearly scored heavily against his opponent. The Attorney General, too fired up in pursuit of his quarry and too anxious to demonstrate passionate loyalty to his new sovereign, had resorted to venomous personal attacks that were not calculated to endear him to the jury. At various times during the trial Ralegh had been described as a monster with an English face but a Spanish heart; a vile viper; a spider of hell; the most notorious traitor that ever came to the bar; and a damnable atheist. Even allowing for the more robust court proceedings of the times, Coke went so far beyond the bounds of judicial decorum that at one point, so we are told, 'the standers-by began to hiss and Mr Attorney to be something daunted'.[30] Nearly three centuries later an eminent legal historian gave his own verdict on Coke's conduct that day: 'The extreme weakness of the evidence was made up for by the rancorous ferocity of Coke who reviled and insulted Ralegh in a manner never imitated, so far as I know, before or since in any English court of justice, except perhaps those in which Jeffries presided.'[31]

Ralegh, on the other hand, had conducted himself with great restraint and dignity, as those present were subsequently to testify. According to the foreign observer, La Renzi, 'he suffered all [Coke's barbs] with so great modesty, universal learning, eloquence, judgement and wisdom, that all his speeches were applauded by general consent of all the auditory'.[32] Sir Dudley Carleton reported that Ralegh 'answered with that temper, wit, learning, courage and judgement, that, save that it went with the hazard of his life, it was the happiest day he ever spent'.[33] Sir Thomas Overbury, in his report of the trial, commended Ralegh's manner: 'First to the Lords, humble yet not prostrate'; 'towards the jury, affable but not fawning'; 'towards the King's counsel patient, but not … yielding to imputations laid against him by words.'[34] The two courtiers sent by the king to report the proceedings to him at Wilton were similarly moved. According to one, 'never any man spoke so well in times past nor would do in the world to come'; and the other concluded '… in one word, never was a man so hated and so popular in so short a time.'[35] Even Cecil's own secretary, Levinus Munck, made a diary entry for

17 November 1603 in the same vein: 'notwithstanding that Sir Walter, to all men's admiration, did as much as the wit of man could devise to clear an offender.'[36]

As he addressed the jury in his concluding speech, Ralegh, along with most of those present in the Great Hall, may well have thought that he had won the day. He knew that he still had in his pocket Cobham's letter which he planned now to reveal as a triumphant finale to his powerful defence. Before that could happen, however, there was a last altercation between accused and accuser as Ralegh asked whether he could say one more thing if the Attorney General himself had nothing else to add:

> *Sir Walter Ralegh*: If you have done, then I have somewhat more to say.
>
> *Attorney General*: Nay, I will have the last word for the King.
>
> *Sir Walter Ralegh*: Nay, I will have the last word for my life.
>
> *Attorney General*: Go to, I will lay thee upon thy back for the confidentest traitor that ever came to the bar.
>
> *Lord Cecil*: Be not so impatient, good Mr Attorney, give him leave to speak.
>
> *Attorney General*: I am the King's sworn servant, and must speak; if I may not be patiently heard, you discourage the King's Counsel, and encourage traitors.

Here, 'Mr Attorney sat down in a chafe, and would speak no more until the commissioners urged and entreated him'.[37]

After the Attorney General's tantrum came the bombshell that Cecil had already hinted at. Coke announced that Cobham, being unable to sleep until he had revealed the truth to the lords, had only the previous night written in his own hand a full account of his dealings with Ralegh. The Attorney General proceeded to read Cobham's statement in as loud a voice as he could manage. This confession described how Ralegh had allegedly tricked Cobham into writing a letter of exculpation in the Tower, and how Ralegh had done this only to clear his name by betraying his friend. Cobham now wished to retract what he had said in the letter and to set down the truth 'craving humble pardon of his Majesty and your Lordships for my double-dealing'.[38] There followed a new version of Cobham's allegations against Ralegh:

> At the first coming of Count Aremberg, Ralegh persuaded me to deal with him, to get him a pension of £1500 from Spain, for intelligence, and he would always tell and advertise what was intended by England against Spain, the Low Countries, or the Indies. And, coming from Greenwich one night, he told me what was agreed betwixt the King and the Low Countrymen, that I should impart it to Count Aremberg. But for this motion for £1500 for intelligence, I never dealt with the Count Aremberg. So also hath he been the only cause of my discontentment, – I never coming from the Court but still he filled and possessed me with new causes of discontentments.[39]

According to the trial reports, Ralegh was visibly stunned by this latest turn of events, but then seemed to regain his composure: 'I pray you hear me a word: you have heard a strange tale of a strange man; you shall see how many souls this Cobham hath, and the King shall judge by our deaths which of us is the perfidious man'.[40]

Ralegh now asked if he could read out the letter he had obtained from Cobham which cleared him of all treasonable conduct and retracted Cobham's former accusations. Coke objected but Cecil, much to the Attorney General's chagrin, overruled him and allowed Ralegh to go ahead. Cecil no doubt calculated that since the prosecution had now played the ace of spades it no longer mattered what card Ralegh had up his sleeve. In any event, the letter that Ralegh presented to the court had a very different impact from that originally intended, given that its author had issued a formal retraction only the night before.

Ralegh must have realised that with his defence blown apart, he was now a dead man. After the Earl of Devonshire had assured the court that Cobham's letter had not been extracted by any favour or hope of pardon, the jury left the hall to consider their verdict. Within a quarter of an hour they were back to announce their finding – that the accused was guilty of treason.

Asked if there were any reason why judgement should not be given against him, Ralegh said that he knew well that the jury having found him guilty, sentence must be pronounced. He protested that he was innocent of conspiring any treason against the king, but he acknowledged that Cobham had offered him a pension of £1,500 a year for intelligence, which he had never intended to accept, and that he was at fault for not disclosing the fact: 'If the King's mercy be greater than my offence, I shall take it thankfully; and if I die, I recommend my poor wife and child of tender years to his Majesty's compassion.'[41]

The Lord Chief Justice, a man renowned for his acquisitiveness, then gave what amounted to a lengthy sermon on the vices of over-eager ambition and covetousness which had, he said, led to Ralegh's downfall. He also dwelt on Ralegh's reputation for having 'heathenish, blasphemous, atheistical and profane opinions' and said that since those who held such opinions 'could not be suffered to live in any Christian Commonwealth' Ralegh would do well, before he left the world, to renounce such views.[42] But even Popham found it difficult to condemn to a traitor's death the man standing before him, concluding his address with the words: 'I never saw the like trial, and hope I shall never see the like again'.[43] He then pronounced sentence in the customary manner:

Sir Walter Ralegh, since you have been found guilty of these horrible treasons, the judgement of this court is, That you shall be had from hence to the place whence you came, there to remain until the day of execution. And from thence you shall be drawn upon a hurdle through the open streets to the place of execution, there to be hanged and cut down alive, and your body shall be opened,

your heart and bowels plucked out, and your privy members cut off and thrown
into the fire before your eyes. Then your head to be stricken off from your body,
and your body shall be divided into four quarters, to be disposed of at the King's
pleasure. And God have mercy upon your soul.[44]

How had this happened? Why had Cobham decided to destroy Ralegh at the
very last, and how did his new allegation – a pension for spying – tie up with the
original accusation of conspiring to overthrow the king? The answer to these
questions lies in the dilemma that had been pre-occupying Cobham since his
arrival in Winchester on 12 November: he knew that his best chance of obtaining
the king's mercy was to implicate Ralegh, but he wanted to argue at his arraignment that his so-called treason was merely a passing thought, without any 'open
deed' on his part. If he were to confirm his original accusation that Ralegh and
he were involved in a plot to obtain Spanish money for discontented persons, he
would bring himself within the 1352 treason statute and face certain conviction.
After all, Cobham had two chances for his life: acquittal at his trial and, if not,
royal clemency after it, and he did not wish to throw one of these away.

On 14 November Cobham had written to the lords of the Council to seek an
urgent meeting, suggesting he could come to them by coach to Wilton where the
king and court were now based. Evidently this prompted an immediate reaction
because we learn from Levinus Munck's diary that on 16 November, 'the Lords
Commissioners went to Winchester Castle to speak with the prisoners'.[45] Cecil,
whether or not accompanied by his fellow commissioners, must have talked at
length with Cobham that day and as a direct result of that interview, Cobham
wrote his letter re-accusing Ralegh.

The new allegations were carefully formulated in a way that did not expose
Cobham to the charge of conspiracy with Ralegh, nor involve him in any 'open
deed'. It was allegedly Ralegh who had sought the pension for intelligence, and
there was now no mention of going to Spain or raising funds to stir up rebellion in England. The confession had been recast to enable Cobham to offer a
legal defence (however flimsy) at his own trial – although whether this stratagem
was devised at Cobham's initiative or Cecil's we shall never know. Following this
agreed compromise, Cecil would not want Cobham brought into court because
he knew only too well that Cobham was not prepared to renew his original
accusations against Ralegh and thereby incriminate himself.

This puts an interesting gloss on Cecil's apparently helpful interventions on
Ralegh's behalf during the trial when he asked the judges whether, either in law
or by the king's favour, Cobham could be brought before the court. Cecil knew
very well what the judges' answer would be, because he would not have wanted
such a crucial matter left to chance. But Cecil went out of his way to appear to
be offering what support and comfort he could to a man whose conviction was
already determined.

Cobham's last minute volte-face sealed his friend's fate. Ralegh's only hope of reprieve was through the king's favour, but this seemed a remote prospect. Immediately after the verdict against him he had spoken privately in court with a number of the lords, including Henry Howard and Cecil. He had asked them to be his suitors with the king to request that, bearing in mind the positions of honour that he had held, his execution might be 'honourable and not ignomini-ous' – a plea for the clean blow of the axe rather than the traitor's noose and all its macabre accompaniments.[46]

That Ralegh had reconciled himself to his own death is shown by the letter of farewell that he wrote to his wife some days after the trial, and which is today remembered in anthologies of English literature:

> You shall now receive, my dear wife, my last words in these my last lines. My love I send you, that you may keep it when I am dead, and my counsel that you may remember it when I am no more. I would not by my will present you with sorrows, dear Besse; let them go into the grave with me, and be buried in the dust. And seeing that it is not God's will that I should see you any more in this life, bear it patiently, and with a heart like thyself.
>
> First, I send you all the thanks that my heart can conceive, or my words can rehearse, for your many travails, and care taken for me; which though they have not taken effect as you wished, yet my debt to you is not the less; but pay it I never shall in this world. Secondly, I beseech you for the love you bare me living, do not hide yourself many days; but by your travails seek to help your miserable fortunes, and the right of your poor child. Thy mourning cannot avail me – I am but dust … As for me, I am no more yours, nor you mine, death hath cut us asunder; and God hath divided me from the world, and you from me. Remember your poor child for his father's sake, who chose you, and loved you in his happiest times. … For know it, my dear wife, that your son is the son of a true man, and who, in his own respect, despiseth death, and all his mis-shapen and ugly forms. I cannot write much, God he knows how hardly I steal this time while others sleep, and it is also time that I should separate my thoughts from the world. Beg my dead body, which living was denied thee; and either lay it at Sherburne (if the land continue) or in Exeter Church by my father and mother. I can say no more; time and death call me away. … Written with the dying hand of sometime thy husband, but now, alas! over-thrown.
> Walter Ralegh[47]

11

Was he Guilty?

Twas a dark kind of treason and the veil is still upon it.

Rushworth, *Historical Collections*, 1659

On 1 December 1603 Cecil wrote a letter from the court at Wilton to Sir Thomas Parry, the English ambassador in Paris (see appendix C). This was intended to provide the official line on Ralegh's trial and conviction, which Parry was urged to make use of 'for his Majesty's service as you shall think convenient in your own discretion'.[1] In this letter Cecil identified and elaborated on the three main grounds for supposing Ralegh to be guilty. First, there was the retracted confession of Cobham which 'being of that nature, as it implied the accusing of his own self withal (than which kind of proof the law regardeth none greater) he was found guilty upon that accusation'.[2] But here Cecil contradicted himself, because in his earlier letter to Parry of 4 August he had stated unequivocally that Cobham had confessed his Spanish treasons *before* he was shown Ralegh's letter, and *before* his angry accusation of Ralegh.[3] The main plank of the prosecution's case against Ralegh – based on Cobham's alleged self-incrimination at the time he made his accusation – was an elaborate sham orchestrated by Cecil and his protégé, Coke, involving the suppression of an examination of Cobham in which he had already confessed to his Spanish treasons.

Second, Cecil placed heavy emphasis on the fact that Ralegh had contacted Cobham before Cobham was even suspected: 'You shall also understand that, at the first beginning, before ever the Lord Cobham was suspected, Sir Walter having been examined only about himself, immediately wrote a letter to the Lord Cobham, that he had been examined upon him.'[4] According to Cecil, Ralegh's false denial that he had sent such a letter undermined the credibility of his other testimony. However, Cecil once again contradicted himself. In his letter to Parry of 4 August he said that he had detained Ralegh because of his closeness to Cobham; and at Ralegh's trial he is reported as saying of the discovery of the Priests' treason 'When I found that Brooke was in it I suspected Lord Cobham'.[5] It was only because Cobham was a suspect that the finger of suspicion pointed also at Ralegh, prompting Cecil to have him examined. In other words, Cecil suspected Cobham at the outset and, on his own admission, this led him to have doubts about Ralegh. His assertion that Ralegh wrote to Cobham before the latter was suspected was therefore made in bad faith. Furthermore, Cecil suppressed the fact that, although Ralegh was not asked questions about Cobham by the lords, he and Ralegh had at Windsor discussed Cobham's 'discontentedness' privately outside the council chamber.

Finally, Cecil acknowledged that the letter of exculpation that Ralegh had obtained from Cobham in the Tower 'would have swayed the jury much', were it not for Cobham's further accusation made the night before Ralegh's trial.[6] But this last minute change of mind raises more questions than it answers. In particular, did the new accusation – that Ralegh sought a pension for intelligence – replace the previous allegation of conspiring to raise money from Spain, or was it an additional charge to add to the others? Ralegh, in a letter to the lords written after the trial, claimed that Cobham's new accusation in effect absolved him from participating in the Spanish treason, and that his admitted offence regarding the pension was merely that of listening to the offer of money.[7] What we can say is that the apparently bewildering sequence of Cobham's changing testimony – total denial followed by a partial confession, then a full confession involving allegations against Ralegh, a subsequent retraction and now finally a re-accusation against Ralegh – should have made Cobham's evidence worthless in any court of law. As one spectator at the trial expressed it, his evidence 'was no more to be weighed than the barking of a dog'.[8]

Each of the three pieces of evidence that Cecil cites as the basis for Ralegh's conviction can therefore be shown to be flawed. If one adds to this the procedural shortcomings of the trial – notably the refusal to allow Cobham to be brought before the accused, the intervention of the Lord Chief Justice in support of the prosecution case, and the reliance on remote hearsay evidence – one can safely argue that, from a strictly legal point of view, Ralegh's conviction was a gross miscarriage of justice. We can also concur with the historian William Stebbing, who over a century ago gave his view of the proceedings against Ralegh:

> Against the Court of James and its obsequious lawyers he was struggling for bare life, for no sublime cause, for no impersonal ideal. Yet so high was his spirit, and his bearing so undaunted, that he has ever appeared to subsequent generations a martyr on the altar of English liberties.[9]

Nevertheless, we should also ask the question whether Ralegh was guilty, if not in law, then in fact. It is almost impossible to avoid the conclusion that he was.

As a close confidant of Cobham, he must surely, at the very least, have known what Cobham was up to: he was with Cobham when the latter first sought to make contact with Aremberg through his servant Questor; he was with Cobham again the night he crossed the Thames to visit Aremberg with La Renzi; and he was with him also at Blackfriars when La Renzi brought back the letter from Aremberg agreeing to provide money. Ralegh lied about sending a letter to Cobham warning him that he, Ralegh, had been examined and detained; and he was clearly involved in a joint cover-up with Cobham when in the Tower devising a common resolution of 'the prisoners' dilemma'. As for Ralegh's admissions, he acknowledged that he was offered 10,000 crowns (£2,500) ostensibly 'for the peace'; he acknowledged that he had arranged to meet Cobham in Jersey on the latter's return from the continent; and he admitted to being offered £1,500 per annum as a pension in return for intelligence.

Strongly suggestive though they are, none of these things, individually or taken together, amount to a totally convincing case that Ralegh was planning a coup. But there are three other considerations which no court could take full account of, but which have a direct bearing on the issue.

First, there were the personal characteristics of the two alleged conspirators. The lords of the Council would be intimately familiar with the personalities of both Ralegh and Cobham, since courtiers observed each other at close quarters, month in month out, both socially and in the conduct of the government's business. The 'inside' view of Cobham comes across at Ralegh's trial: to his peers he was politically naïve, easily led, and lacking in 'wit' or intellectual sharpness – in Sarjeant Hale's words 'a hollow tree'. Though he was an educated man, his writing is disjointed and often incoherent, and it seems his performance at his own trial was disorganised and at times shambolic. Nor was Cobham noted for his martial qualities or his courage, though his obvious terror of the scaffold showed that he was an ordinary mortal rather than a coward as some would have it.

Ralegh was the very opposite. He was politically astute, 'the father of wiles' according to Coke,[10] and a natural leader who, as Northumberland said, 'desires to seem to be able to sway all men's courses'.[11] He was as well versed in the art of war as any man in England, and nobody doubted his courage or his willingness to play for high stakes. He was also capable of brazen mendacity as well as more subtle deception when it suited his purpose. It was obvious to all that he totally dominated Cobham who, according to Sarjeant Hale, idolised him.

The disparate personalities of Cobham and Ralegh appear to have weighed heavily with Cecil and his fellow commissioners – as well perhaps as the jury – in convincing them of Ralegh's guilt. They clearly found it impossible to believe that Cobham, on his own, would have had the inclination, nerve or capacity to devise a plot against the Crown involving the use of force; and they also found it inconceivable that Ralegh was not the driving force and mastermind behind Cobham's Spanish treasons.

A second consideration which has a direct bearing on Ralegh's guilt, is the extent to which he had been provoked and humiliated in the early months of James' reign. For a man who had enjoyed royal favour, great wealth and military command to be stripped of his income, his position at court and his house, was to invite some kind of retaliatory move. At his trial, Popham had suggested that Ralegh should have been content to live on a reduced income after his fall from grace under James. According to the Lord Chief Justice, he had been lifted up by the wheel of fortune and then cast down and he could not reconcile himself to a more lowly station in life. There was also a suggestion from Popham that Ralegh should have been more respectful of his humble origins: 'And sure had you remembered what you were, or in the times of good fortune contented yourself in your own rank, you could not then have fallen.'[12] There is a strong implication here that Ralegh had strayed too far from his modest roots in the West Country. In doing so, he had no doubt upset men of greater birth and entitlement, and when the queen on whose favour he depended was no longer, those who had been made jealous by his good fortune were happy to see him brought down. But Ralegh himself was not prepared to be humbled, and his conspiracy with Cobham may be viewed as a last roll of the dice in a desperate attempt to restore the status quo ante.

The final and most important pointer to Ralegh's guilt relates to the new interpretation presented here, of Cobham's apparently self-contradictory and incomprehensible confessions. We can now see that Cobham's testimony followed a consistent and intelligible pattern. First he denied everything; then, following Brooke's allegations, he confessed to his Spanish treason in an examination that was suppressed – though he kept Ralegh's involvement out of it because this could only make things worse for him. When he saw Ralegh's letter he angrily revealed his confederate's leading role in the conspiracy; then on reflection, and after consultation with Ralegh, he was persuaded that his best response to the 'prisoners' dilemma' was a common defence with his co-accused. Having held out for over three months, he eventually surrendered to Ralegh's enemies: tormented by the prospect of the axe and desperate to secure royal favour, he came up with a new accusation of his former friend and ally that still enabled him to maintain the argument that he himself had committed no overt act of treason.

When viewed in this light, Cobham's accusation against Ralegh becomes compelling. We know why he retracted his original accusation; we know also the reason for his re-accusation; and, most importantly, we know why the re-accusation took the form of a fresh allegation rather than a re-statement of his original charges. Instead of the rambling incoherence of a totally discredited witness, we have the convincing evidence of a rational but weak man buffeted by conflicting pressures.

There can be little doubt, then, that Ralegh was involved in a treasonable conspiracy with Cobham. However, he was so careful to limit his own direct involvement and to leave all the risky business to his partner, and so careful, too, to deal with no-one else but Cobham, that there was insufficient evidence of his guilt to bring before a jury. And it was because Ralegh was so adept at covering his tracks that Cecil and the prosecution resorted to dirty tricks to get him convicted, above all by fabricating a case based upon the false supposition that Cobham had, in his angry accusation of Ralegh, at the same time incriminated himself.

On the assumption that Ralegh was guilty it is possible to reconstruct the chain of events that led to his detention at Windsor in mid-July. In the first week of May, before he had reached London on his journey south, James held a Council meeting at Theobalds. It was here that the decision was taken to suspend the wine monopoly, immediately cutting off Ralegh's income. Ralegh knew that he was in deep financial trouble and began to cast around for an alternative source of revenue. It was very likely at this time that he asked Cobham to write to his friend Aremberg in Brussels to provide a pension for himself in return for military and political intelligence. Significantly, when at his trial Ralegh admitted to being offered money by Cobham he said the offer was made before Aremberg came over to England.[13] It is worth noting that Cobham was already conducting a clandestine correspondence with Aremberg through a Scottish courier named Penycuik. When detained in Dover on 7 May, Penycuik was found to have a letter from Cobham addressed to Aremberg concealed in the cape of his mantle, though he was allowed to proceed with his post unopened.[14]

First, then, came the request for a pension. But this was not a reliable source of income because, as Cecil himself pointed out, Ralegh could only be a spy for Spain 'if the peace went not forward'.[15] If Cecil's peace policy eventually succeeded, there would be no call for Ralegh's intelligence services. Ralegh was, of course, fully aware of this and when he was further riled by his dismissal as Captain of the Guard and exclusion from the enlarged Privy Council, he realised that there was no future for him under the new regime. Then came the ultimate humiliation, the order to quit Durham House where he had resided for nearly twenty years, with only two weeks to vacate. He must have known at this point that he was being deliberately targeted and very significantly, it was on the day following receipt of this eviction warrant (9 June) that he was alleged to have held a meeting with Cobham at which the overthrow of the king was discussed.

So it was that in the first days of June Ralegh, rather than face personal ruin and political oblivion, decided to explore the possibility of regime change using his faithful ally Cobham to engage in a highly risky project to raise money from Spain. Only when the money was assured would Ralegh use his contacts to stir rebellion among the disaffected. Until then he himself would be a sleeping partner in the enterprise: he would wait and see how Cobham got on; he would disclose his hand to no third party; and if Cobham was caught out on his planned visit to Spain, Ralegh could always turn him in (as Cobham himself suspected he might do).[16] In short, Ralegh played the role of inciter and puppet master while Cobham was to carry all the operational risks.

By the time Aremberg arrived in London in early June, Ralegh's ambition was no longer limited to a precarious pension of £1,500 per annum. He was now contemplating a full-blooded rebellion using Spanish money and, conceivably, Spanish military assistance to overthrow those who had tried to destroy him. Ralegh's claim at his trial that 600,000 crowns (£150,000) was an unrealistic sum to expect to raise from Spain was ingenuous: to put the figure in perspective, the capture of the Spanish carrack *Madre de Dios* alone had yielded around this sum while the annual cost of Elizabeth's military operations on the continent – presumably matched by Spain – had exceeded £150,000.[17] Nor would Spain expect 'security' for financing a coup, as Ralegh had maintained at his trial: the benefit would come with the change of regime and the huge financial savings that would flow from a favourable peace (roughly a one year pay-back in modern financial parlance).

Of course, if money was to be raised from Spain it was necessary to convince Aremberg that there was no present prospect of peace. Cobham admitted that during the two hours or so he spent with Aremberg on or around 9 June he dwelt on the obstacles to peace, and reported the fact that the French had persuaded James to provide further military support to the Dutch.[18] It was after this meeting that there was an exchange of correspondence, in which Cobham said that if some hundreds of thousands of crowns could be delivered to him and Ralegh it would save Aremberg's masters 'millions'. The outcome was that Aremberg agreed in principle to find the money, of which Ralegh was to receive between £2,000 and £2,500.

Where did Ralegh's plotting go wrong? First, he underestimated the danger posed by Cecil's omnipresent intelligence network, which picked up on Cobham's 'secret' visit to Aremberg after visiting Durham House. From that point on, Cecil was on his trail. Second, Ralegh allowed Cobham to confide in and enlist the support of Brooke who was garrulous, undisciplined, disloyal and thoroughly dangerous – particularly bearing in mind his close links with the ill-conceived Priests' Plot. Finally, Cobham was a weak man and no good in a crisis; he could not withstand aggressive interrogation and he was bound, in the end, to betray his confederate in order to save his life – just as Brooke betrayed his brother in an attempt to save his.

Ironically, the plot was in any case destined to fail because it depended for its success on continuing conflict with Spain. But both Ralegh and Cobham appeared to have misjudged Cecil's determination to drive through a formal peace treaty with England's great enemy. On 10 July 1603 Aremberg, having recovered from his gout, had his first audience at Windsor with the king who was himself pre-disposed towards peace. Then on 29 July Cecil and Henry Howard conferred with Aremberg at Staines, leaving the ambassador in no doubt about their interest in his peace overtures. All this was a favourable prelude to the Spanish ambassador's later arrival in August and his private audience with the king towards the end of September. Negotiations for the Spanish peace were now in train and would be triumphantly concluded by Cecil in August the following year amid great festivities.

Finally, if we accept, despite the travesty of his trial, that Ralegh was guilty of treason, how far should we go in condemning his conduct? The answer must be that the story of Ralegh's fall and Cecil's seamless rise under James does not provide material for a morality tale. Cecil had risked all on a secret correspondence with Elizabeth's unnamed successor behind his sovereign's back. That in itself was a form of treachery. Furthermore, he had used this illicit channel of communication to promote his own interests and to undermine his rivals. And while Cecil was quick to denounce Ralegh for soliciting a pension from Spain, he himself received a Spanish pension of similar magnitude as an expression of gratitude for his role in securing the peace treaty.[19] He also received a lump sum of no less than £12,500 from Spain in 1608 to ensure English neutrality over the Dutch/Hamburg peace treaty, and further Spanish bribes were apparently channelled through his confidante, the Countess of Suffolk.[20] In the words of a modern scholar: 'We can now be certain that an irregular but very substantial quantity of gold passed into Salisbury's [Cecil's] private treasure chest in the form of bribes from Philip III of Spain.'[21]

The reality is that both Ralegh and Cecil were men playing for extremely high stakes, and neither of them recognised any boundaries to the game. Behind a veneer of politeness and moral sensitivity they were engaged in a raw struggle for power, money and status. The methods that they were prepared to employ involved deception, bribery, personal betrayal and a readiness to eliminate anyone who got in the way. It was Ralegh's misfortune that Cecil found the former favourite's ambitions to be in conflict with his own, and had fully prepared himself for Ralegh's response once he had humbled him and fulfilled the promise 'to heap coals upon his head'.

12

THE AFTERMATH

What the Lord Cobham hath confessed, and how much it differeth from the
received opinion, I leave to their reports who know it. I will not in charity condemn his faith; because he was nearer death, though not nearer the expectation,
than I was.

Ralegh on Cobham's scaffold speech

The date of Ralegh's execution was set for 13 December, but Cecil had much
to attend to in the meantime. He shuttled back and forth between the king and
court at Wilton and the prisoners at Winchester Castle. This involved an uncomfortable coach journey of some 27 miles which, on the muddy roads of early
winter, would have taken around five hours each way. Cecil had also to ensure
that the trials of the two nobles, Cobham and Grey, went ahead smoothly and that
practical arrangements were made for the executions of those convicted – a particular difficulty because Sir Benjamin Tichborne, the High Sheriff of Hampshire,
had no previous experience of handling beheadings or constructing scaffolds.

While Cecil was naturally anxious that his first major challenge in the service
of the king should be successfully concluded, he had also to fulfil the day to
day administrative responsibilities of his office. Furthermore, the formalities of
court life were not to be ignored: the Venetian ambassadors had a public audience at Wilton on 20 November and feasted with the king nine days later. On
2 December thirty players came to Wilton to perform *As You Like It* for the
king and Council, apparently at the behest of the Countess of Pembroke who is
reported to have said that 'we have the man Shakespeare with us'.[1] Whether Cecil
had time to attend such entertainments we do not know.

Cecil was preoccupied with several other matters during late November and
early December. First, of those convicted of treason, who should live and who

should die? Formally this was a matter for the king, but it is hardly credible that his First Secretary, who had been so intimately involved in all stages of the investigations, indictments and trials of the accused, should not also be consulted in the final decisions as to their fate. Second, while the prosecution case against Ralegh had been upheld by the jury, the prisoner had emerged from his trial with his reputation greatly enhanced – as James' own observers at Winchester had reported back to him. This was politically damaging both for Cecil and the king, and it was therefore incumbent on Cecil to ferret out more material that could be used against Ralegh to neutralise his new-found popularity and further justify his conviction in the eyes of the world.

Finally, now that peace negotiations with Spain were proceeding, it was necessary to minimise the adverse publicity surrounding Aremberg and his alleged role in Cobham's Spanish treason. The Spanish ambassador had made representations to Cecil about the damage done to the reputation of his master and the Archduke, and the First Secretary was now determined to smooth ruffled feathers on the Spanish side by publicly clearing Aremberg of any wrong doing.

Cobham's trial, which was originally scheduled to take place on 19 November, was postponed to allow further questioning of the prisoner. Levinus Munck records that Cecil travelled from Wilton to Winchester on 19 November and again on 21 November, no doubt preparing the way for a further examination of Cobham that took place on 22 November.[2] At what was to be Cobham's last interrogation, Cecil succeeded in extracting what he had no doubt been looking for: a fresh and devastating allegation that Ralegh had returned from the court at Greenwich one night after a blazing row with Cecil, and had suggested to Cobham that he should approach Aremberg 'that he should do best to advertise and advise the King of Spain to send an army against England to Milford Haven'.[3] If true, this outburst may have followed Ralegh's dismissal from the captaincy of the guard in late April when, according to de Beaumont, he erupted in fury against Cecil whom he accused of being responsible for his dismissal.[4] Whatever the background to Cobham's story, the First Secretary now had colourful material with which to blacken Ralegh's name.

Cobham was tried on 25 November before his peers, consisting of eleven earls and twenty-nine barons, with the Lord Chancellor Ellesmere presiding as High Steward. Sir Dudley Carleton (later Lord Dorchester) reported that Cobham 'heard his indictment with much fear and trembling' and conducted himself so abjectly that 'he discredited the place to which he was called'.[5] Cobham elaborated on his latest allegation against Ralegh who, he claimed 'had once propounded to him a means for the Spaniard to invade England which was to bring down an army to the Groyne, under pretence to send them into the Low Countries, and land them at Milford Haven'.[6] This would have been just what Cecil wanted, as was Cobham's insistence that Aremberg was innocent of any ill intent and desired only to further the peace. To excuse Aremberg and placate

Spanish sensitivities further, the Attorney General stated in open court that the earlier evidence touching Aremberg was designed only to show the intentions of the accused and in no way questioned the ambassador's personal integrity.[7]

As far as his own defence was concerned, Cobham stuck to the argument that his plan to raise money from Spain was an inward conceit only and involved no overt treasonable act on his part. According to the foreign observer, La Renzi, the lords responded to this line of reasoning by asking the judges whether, in the absence of an open deed, the accused's conduct could be viewed as treasonable. The judges replied that the question was beside the point since Cobham's plan to travel back from Spain and consult with Ralegh in Jersey about the distribution of money constituted an overt act, thereby bringing him within the 1352 statute.[8] The judges' ruling had swept aside the legal defence which Cobham had so hopefully prepared, leaving little doubt about the outcome of the trial. When the peers delivered their verdict of guilty and after sentence of death had been pronounced, Cobham, according to Dudley Carleton, 'begged a great while for life and favour, alleging his confession as a meritorious act'.[9]

What is particularly interesting is Cecil's brief account of the trial included in his despatch to Ambassador Parry dated 1 December. According to Cecil, Cobham denied 'that Ralegh was privy to his purpose to go into Spain', and insisted that his plan to raise money for discontented persons was never communicated to anyone. However, he reaffirmed that Ralegh had sought a pension and had proposed to solicit Aremberg to persuade the King of Spain to send an army to Milford Haven.[10] According to Cecil, Cobham had denied vehemently the notorious remark attributed to him – 'that it would never be well in England till the King and his cubs were taken away'. In this letter too, Cecil was at pains to explain that Aremberg understood that the money he agreed to provide 'should be bestowed only for the gaining of friends to stand for the treaty, without any further reference'.[11]

Cecil had therefore achieved his twin objectives: Ralegh had been vilified and Aremberg's good name had been restored. But there are also indications of a third purpose evolving in Cecil's mind. He seems to have wanted to save Cobham's life and to prepare for this by minimising his misdeeds.

After Grey had been tried and convicted on the day following Cobham's arraignment, Carleton made a prescient observation:

> We cannot yet judge what will become of him [Grey] or the rest, for all are not likely to go one way. Cobham is of the surest side, for he is thought least dangerous, and the Lord Cecil undertakes to be his friend. They say the priests shall lead the dance tomorrow, and Brooke next after, for he proves to be the knot that tied together the … conspiracies, the rest being indifferent betwixt mercy and justice, wherein the King hath now subject to practice himself.[12]

As anticipated, the two priests, Watson and Clarke, were the first to be executed on 29 November. According to Carleton they both died bravely and unbowed, despite the fact that their despatch was 'very bloodily handled'.[13] La Renzi states that Watson was hanged until he was dead and then quartered while Clarke 'hanged longer but was cut down lively, speaking while the executioner did his office'.[14] The grisly detail of Clarke's ordeal is provided by the same account which says that although they hung on to Clarke's feet in order to strangle him, the rope broke and he fell fully conscious to the ground: 'When the executioner came to cut out his heart, he could still cry "Jesus help me"'.[15] Once the grim business was over, the priests' quarters were displayed on Winchester's gates and their heads on one of the castle towers.

Brooke was the next to go. He had insisted on several occasions that Cecil had offered him his life in return for accusing his brother, but the secretary was disinclined to help him. Brooke was the common link between the plotters; he had betrayed almost everyone, he had no friends left at court and because he was indiscreet he was liable to embarrass anyone who tried to intervene on his behalf. His strident letter to the lords claiming that both they and the king had promised him 'more than life' no doubt alienated them further.

However, it seems that Cecil may have wanted one more thing out of Brooke before he died. Even remote hopes of royal mercy could be used to sway a man on the eve of his execution and it seems that something may have passed between Brooke and Cecil after Cobham's trial. For on 4 December Anthony Watson, the Bishop of Chichester who was attending Brooke, reported to the lords that his charge now denied absolutely that Cobham had ever uttered the infamous words about the 'fox [or king] and his cubs'.[16] This retraction would suit Cecil very well if his purpose were to save Cobham because it would help to lessen his offence in the eyes of his peers. That Brooke was seeking favours when making his denial is suggested by his further statement, reported by the bishop: 'if there remain any doubt wherein he may further satisfy the King, or your Lordships, he professeth his readiness fully to accomplish.'[17] But there was to be no last-minute reprieve for Brooke. Unlike the priests he was to be allowed the privilege of a scaffold, as befitted his social status, and Sir Benjamin Tichborne, High Sheriff of Hampshire, reported that the scaffold he had erected was 12ft square and railed about – not so much to keep the prisoner in but to keep the crowds out. Brooke was also to be favoured with the axe rather than the full horrors of a traitor's death, and his body was to be buried in some local church rather than put on public display.

Cecil was evidently concerned that Brooke's last words should be kept to a minimum in order to avoid further embarrassments. This was made clear in a letter he wrote to the sheriff on 4 December: 'There shall be no need of any new questions to be asked at his death. For all is known, and it will be pity to trouble him at that time but with the best preparations for his soul …'[18] Brooke was executed on the morning of Monday 5 December, on the high ground of

Castle Green (now Beaumond Green), within sight of the Hospital of St Cross whose mastership Brooke had coveted. Among the spectators there was scarcely anyone of rank and when the headsman, after completing his task, cried out in the customary manner 'God save the King', only the sheriff's voice was to be heard in response.

Brooke's final public words, reported by Carleton, were to the effect that 'somewhat lay yet hid, which would one day appear for his justification'.[19] But at the very last, before the axe fell, something else was said privately to the Bishop of Chichester whom Brooke had asked to accompany him on to the scaffold. Whatever it was, it was reported to Cecil who, in a letter to Lord Shrewsbury a few days later, referred to a 'base and viperous accusation' the details of which, however, he declined to divulge.[20] Brooke had, it seems, accused his brother-in-law of dastardly betrayal in terms which struck home.

Friday 10 December was the appointed day for the execution of Cobham as well as two of those involved in the Priests' Plot – Markham and Grey – while Ralegh was due to follow on the Monday. Cobham was again in a state of anguish, no doubt desperately hoping that by accusing Ralegh he had done enough to obtain clemency. In the few days after his trial he wrote three letters to Cecil and two to the king, pleading for his life in the most abject terms. But then there was a very sudden change of tone. On 6 December Cobham, acting quite out of character, wrote a very restrained and dignified letter to the lords. He appeared now to accept his fate but was gratified to hear that Brooke had retracted his earlier charge regarding words allegedly spoken against the king:

> And now I may say ... conscience moved my brother to free me of those unworthy speeches I should speak of the King and his royal issue, which the Lord knoweth how innocent I was; yet though I die yet the more with peace I shall go to my grave being freed of so false and hateful an implication.[21]

Cobham ended with an acknowledgement that he was about to die and a final plea, not for his life, but for prayers for his soul:

> the Bishop of Winchester hath been with me, by whom I understand that my days shall not be many; therefore, my Lords, myself I recommend unto you, praying you to pray unto God for me. Patiently and in fear of God I will end my life.[22]

This letter bears the hallmarks of Cecil's intervention. Cecil apparently wanted to save his brother-in-law, partly, no doubt, because of the family connection but also because he knew that Cobham, left to himself, was harmless (as Carleton had pointed out) and that his great misfortune was to have been manipulated by Ralegh. Most importantly, Cobham had co-operated fully by providing the last minute accusation against Ralegh that had tilted the balance in favour of the prosecution. Now he had supplied further ammunition against Ralegh that would cause outrage amongst all patriotic Englishmen.

It seems that something was intimated to Cobham in the first week of December to encourage him to believe that he would be given his life; and that the letter to the lords was intended to clear the way with his peers and to make it easier for the king to exercise clemency on his behalf. By demonstrating Cobham's expectation of death, this final message to the lords was also perhaps designed to allay any suspicions that might later arise about a deal to give him his life.

In the days before the execution of Cobham, Grey and Markham, scheduled for 10 December, there was intense speculation at court as to who should or would be reprieved through royal favour. Carleton described the intense lobbying among courtiers and the king's determination to keep his distance from it all:

> Whilst [the prisoners] were so occupied at Winchester, there was no small doings about them at court, for life or death; some pushing at the wheel one way, some another. The Lords of the Council joined in opinion and advice to the King, now in the beginning of his reign, to show as well examples of mercy as severity ... the King held himself upright betwixt the two waters; and first let the Lords know, that since the law had passed upon the prisoners, it became not them to be petitioners, but rather to press for execution of their own ordinances.[23]

Cecil, as the king's principal and most trusted minister with an unequalled understanding of court politics, and as the man who had masterminded the exposure of the plotters, would of course be in a unique position to advise the king on such a delicate matter at the beginning of his reign. And while Cecil was undoubtedly inclined towards saving Cobham and had indeed already prepared the way, there was still unfinished business between Cobham and Ralegh. Their testimony was in direct conflict, and Ralegh had emerged from his trial with renewed credibility despite his conviction. Under the circumstances it would be very helpful if Cobham were to confirm his accusation of Ralegh from the scaffold, since a statement made in the face of death would be taken to be the truth.

Scaffold confessions had a very special status in the Tudor and early Stuart periods. It was a long-standing tradition that convicted traitors were granted the privilege of a farewell speech before suffering the punishment ordained – beheading for the nobility and hanging, drawing and quartering for commoners. As one student of the subject has put it: '... Confessions were pieces of public theatre, which to be effective required the co-operation of all involved – the people as the audience, the traitor in the leading role, and the state as the director.'[24] The drama was acted out on a stage, the scaffold, and there was added anticipation because the proceedings were unscripted and unrehearsed – though the conclusion was not in doubt.

Public executions of traitors attracted huge crowds. Broadsheets were sold describing events in macabre detail and flyers with the dead man's last words were eagerly snapped up. It is estimated that 10,000 attended the Earl of Northumberland's beheading in 1553 and 100,000, or a quarter of London's population, watched the Earl of Strafford's execution in 1641. While the general population may have been motivated largely by morbid curiosity, the prisoner's peers might by their presence offer sympathy and support to the condemned man. There were also those who wished to hear the final confession in case they themselves should be the target of some accusation.

For the prisoner, the speech from the scaffold was an opportunity for a degree of reconciliation – with the king or queen to whom great offence had been given and with God whose commandments had been broken. It also offered the prisoner a much larger audience than he could hope to have at his trial and, above all, it enabled him to address posterity. Scaffold speeches followed a well-established pattern, typically beginning with an acknowledgement of the legality of the sentence, then an admission of guilt, a plea for forgiveness, an expression of readiness to die and finally a commendation of the sovereign and his or her heirs. Of course, some might use the platform to justify themselves but it was always understood that this was an occasion for humility and submission before God. Most important of all, a man's last words, uttered in the hope of personal salvation in the world to come, were taken to be the truth.

From the state's point of view, the theatrical performance which it directed had important benefits. Of course in a troublesome case, if it was thought that the prisoner might cause embarrassment to the Crown, he could be prevented from making a public speech by having a private execution within the confines of the Tower of London. But in general the choreography of public execution was designed to strengthen the machinery of state. The public penance of the prisoner testified to the virtue of the Crown, the punishment to its authority and the prayers of the chaplain to its care for the offender's soul. The whole performance demonstrated that to conspire against the sovereign was a heinous crime against the monarchy and the state, but also against God and the natural order he had ordained.

The fate of the prisoners at Winchester presented James with a dilemma. On the one hand he wished to show at the outset of his reign that he was merciful. On the other hand, the final confessions of those convicted and the accompanying displays of penitence would underwrite the legitimacy of his succession and the authority of the new king. And there was a special reason for allowing Cobham to unburden his conscience on the scaffold: his final words regarding Ralegh would carry particular weight and might perhaps remove those remaining doubts in the public mind about the guilt of the late queen's favourite. Cecil, in a letter to Sir Ralph Winwood, who was later to become Secretary of State, emphasised the importance attached to Cobham's last words: the king, he said, 'pretended to forbear Sir Walter Ralegh for the present, till the Lord Cobham's death had given some light how far he would make good his accusation.'[25]

The elaborate charade that now ensued was designed to humble the king's enemies, to extract final confessions and to exhibit the new sovereign's inclination to mercy. On Monday 5 December the king signed three warrants for the execution of Cobham, Grey and Markham, to be carried out on the following Friday beginning at 10.00 a.m. However, on the Wednesday, James withdrew to the privacy of his study at Wilton and drafted a further warrant in his own hand, countermanding all his previous instructions. He then entrusted the warrant to a newly arrived page from Scotland, one John Gibb, whose presence among the crowds around the scaffold would not attract attention. Gibb rode to Winchester on Thursday, stayed the night there, and early the next morning made his way to Castle Green, where people were gathering, and found himself a convenient position close to the scaffold.[26]

Markham was the first to be led to his execution, to be followed by Grey and then Cobham. Three coffins had been laid out within view of the prisoners in case they should need reminding of what lay ahead. When Markham had delivered his last words and was kneeling down to pray, Gibb delivered his warrant discreetly to the sheriff, Tichborne, with verbal instructions on how to proceed. Tichborne then informed Markham that he had two hours' respite to further prepare himself for death and led him into the Great Hall where he was detained.[27] When Grey's turn came, he was accompanied to Castle Green by a large number of his supporters whose cheerfulness suggested a triumphal procession rather than the final rites of a condemned man. Grey was observed to stir the un-bloodied straw with his foot, so he may have had some inkling that all was not going to plan. After his speech he kept the onlookers in the rain for over half an hour while he prayed aloud for the king's prosperity. Then, as Grey was preparing himself for the block, Tichborne announced that the king's command had just been received, requiring that the order of execution be changed. Cobham was now to precede Grey, who was accordingly taken to the Great Hall to join Markham.

When Cobham appeared on the scaffold his manner was so out of character, so bold and so self-assured, that suspicions were later to be raised among onlookers that he might be aware of the charade that was being played out. Cobham prayed a good deal and removed a ring which he said had belonged to his father and was his dearest jewel so that it might be given to his wife. He then avowed before God that what he had said of Sir Walter Ralegh was true 'as I have hope of my soul's resurrection'.[28] It was possibly for this solemn affirmation that the whole performance had been contrived.

Tichborne required Cobham to remain on the scaffold while Grey and Markham were recalled. The three prisoners, standing together on the platform, were then asked a series of questions by the Sheriff concerning the gravity of their offence, the justice of their convictions and their preparedness to die – to which the answers were uniformly in the affirmative. The Sheriff then announced triumphantly: 'Then see the mercy of your prince who of himself hath sent hither a countermand and hath given you your lives!'[29] The crowd erupted with prolonged cheering although some, perhaps, were disappointed at being deprived of the spectacle they had come to see. The executioner, who was observed to be wearing the clothing of Clarke the priest, and the cap of Brooke, was reported to have wept because he had lost his fee.[30]

While this black comedy was being enacted at Winchester, a parallel drama was unfolding 27 miles away at the court in Wilton. Here members of the Privy Council and leading courtiers were called to the king's chamber, where His Majesty explained how he had been grappling with the problem of how to deal fairly with the convicted traitors. He gave his judgement on their conduct and character in pairs: he contrasted the resolute spirit of Grey with the craven and pitiful nature of Cobham, but then drew a different comparison between Grey's insolence and Cobham's humility in begging for his life. Having in this manner weighed up the merits and faults of the prisoners the king concluded by announcing his decision to save the lives of them all. The applause that followed spread all around the court.

Throughout these extraordinary scenes three principles had been observed. First the whole performance was carefully attributed to the king and the king alone, for it would be unseemly for Cecil or any other advisor to be seen to be meddling in men's lives. Second, the king's decision was expressly made on the grounds of justice: on the face of it no real-politick or state interest had entered into the royal deliberations, only the deservedness of the individuals concerned. Finally, it was crucial that the prisoners themselves should be seen to be preparing for their own imminent deaths in order that their confessions and conduct on the scaffold should be convincing to the beholders.

The reality, of course, was very different. Markham and Grey may well have been in the dark but there can be little doubt that Cobham was alerted in advance to his reprieve. La Renzi reported that 'it was vehemently suspected that Lord Cobham had some guess at the matter because he made no sign of sorrow but showed more courage at his death than ever he had in his life'.[31] De Beaumont also reported the suspicion of onlookers that some private warning had been given to Cobham.[32]

There are other suspicious circumstances pointing in the same direction. On 4 December the Bishop of Winchester wrote to Cecil to reassure him that Cobham, at his death, intended to maintain his accusation against Ralegh – including Ralegh's alleged proposal to land foreign armies at Milford Haven.[33] Two days later he reported that due to ill health he was withdrawing from his attendance on Cobham and that a new minister was replacing him. This was Dr

John Harmer, warden of Winchester College, who had taken holy orders and had already acted as spiritual advisor to Brooke.[34] Coincidentally it was also on 6 December that Cobham, in his final letter to the lords, revealed a transformation in his state of mind and a stated readiness to die. Then we have the extraordinary composure shown by Cobham when preparing himself for the block, and an intriguing comment by La Renzi on the role of Dr Harmer. According to La Renzi, Cobham, when on the scaffold, 'spake in profession of religion just as his minister did dictate unto him who, I since understand, did certainly foretell him of the good success that was to ensue'.[35] It seems possible, therefore, that Dr Harmer was the intermediary used to brief Cobham on what to expect and to remind him also of what was expected of him.

Once the decision had been taken to save Cobham, the rest followed, for if the other prisoners were to die it would give further credence to rumours already circulating that Cobham had been favoured in return for accusing Ralegh. Among those harbouring such suspicions was Ralegh himself, who was not slow to express his opinion that a deal had been struck with his accuser. At his trial he said he had seen the letter Lady Kildare had written to Cobham suggesting 'that there was no way to save his life but to accuse me'.[36] And in a postscript to a letter written to Cecil after his conviction, Ralegh said: 'Your Lordship will find that I have been strangely practised against, and that others have their lives promised to accuse me.'[37]

From his window in Winchester Castle Ralegh had a direct view of the scaffold on Castle Green, and he had witnessed the events that took place there on the morning of 10 December. According to Carleton he must have 'had hammers working in his head, to beat out the meaning of this stratagem'.[38] When he learned of the prisoners' reprieve he immediately wrote a letter to the lords rejoicing that 'we have this day beheld a work of so great mercy, and for so great offences, as the like had been seldom if ever known', and he trusted that the same compassion would be extended to himself. He said he feared it would be said 'that I, being now poor, would live but a discontented life', but he insisted he would be thankful to live humbly. He also made a pointed reference to Cobham's scaffold confession and his last accusation of Ralegh: 'I will not in charity condemn his faith, because he was nearer death, though not nearer the expectation, than I was.'[39]

Ralegh was left in doubt about his own fate until news was brought from Wilton that he had been included in the general stay of execution. He, along with Cobham, would now be imprisoned indefinitely at His Majesty's pleasure within the Tower of London. But he need not have concerned himself about having to live simply on modest means, because although he had been given his life he was, by law, dead and he had lost his liberty forever.

The curtain had now come down on the extraordinary drama that was played out in the provincial town of Winchester. On 12 December the king and court removed from Wilton to Hampton Court and on the same day Cecil, accompanied by Henry Howard, came to Winchester Castle to pay his last visit to the prisoners before they were despatched to the Tower of London. The courtiers, dignitaries and officials – together with their horses, carriages and servants – now drifted away from the town, leaving its inhabitants to resume their normal lives and to contemplate the unprecedented happenings of the past month.

There was one final matter to be addressed. The sheriff, Sir Benjamin Tichborne, evidently felt that he deserved some mark of gratitude for the services he had performed. He wrote to Cecil asking what was to become of Winchester Castle after the prisoners were gone, because it was falling into ruin and needed £500 or £600 spent on repairs. If the repairs were done and it were pleasing to His Majesty he was prepared to offer himself as the new constable at a fee of £50 per annum.[40] History records that his request was duly granted.

13

THE TOWER

For as no fortune stands, so no man's love
Stays by the wretched and disconsolate;
All old affections from new sorrows move.
Moss to unburied bones, ivy to walls,
Whom life and people have abandoned
Till th'one be rotten, stays, till th'other falls ...

Ralegh, poem from the Tower

The cavalcade of soldiers that had escorted the prisoners to Winchester in mid-November returned to the Tower with their charges on 16 December. Ralegh and Cobham now faced an indeterminate confinement in London's ancient fortress. This was, however, no ordinary prison. In the words of John Stow, writing in 1598:

> [The] Tower is a citadel to defend or command the city; a royal palace for assemblies or treaties; a prison of State for the most dangerous offenders; the only place of coinage for all England ... the armoury for warlike provision; the treasury of the ornaments and jewels of the Crown; and general conserver of the most records of the King's courts of justice at Westminster.[1]

He might have added that the Tower was also a menagerie where exotic wild animals, including lions and tigers, were caged – at first for the amusement of the king and his friends and then, in Elizabeth's reign, as a public attraction.

The conditions in which state prisoners were held in the Tower depended on their status, but generally they enjoyed far more privileges than their more humble fellow captives in, say, the Fleet. In Elizabeth's reign, for instance, the Earl of Northumberland had lived in some style in five large chambers opening onto 'two fair gardens within the Tower wall'.[2] Special arrangements were now made for Cobham to enable him to house his library of over 1,000 books. Ralegh was allotted two rooms on the second and third floor of the Bloody Tower, enabling him to accommodate not only his family – Bess and Wat – but also two live-in servants.

Ralegh had hopes that he might soon be pardoned, but for this to happen he would have to enlist the support of Cecil, the man he blamed for his present tribulations. In his farewell letter to Bess written some months before his arraignment, Ralegh had already pointed the finger at the secretary: 'and for my Lord Cecil, I thought he would never forsake me in extremity. I would not have done it to him, God knows. But do not thou know it, for he must be master of thy child and may have compassion of him.'[3] Here Ralegh was advising Bess to show a friendly face to the author of their sorrows in order to protect Wat, whose future lay in the hands of the Master of the Court of Wards. Now Ralegh himself wrote humble and ingratiating letters to Cecil appealing for an early release from his prison. He accepted that his freedom would have to be restricted and said he did not ask to be 'about London – which God cast my soul into hell if I desire'.[4] He would be content to be confined within the Hundred (district) of Sherborne, and if this were not permitted he was ready to live in Holland where he thought he could obtain employment connected with the Indies.

It was to be some time before reality sank in. Cecil had absolutely no intention of allowing Ralegh his liberty. He would be too dangerous to the State, but more particularly to Cecil himself. The diminutive First Secretary had the former royal favourite exactly where he wanted him: behind high walls and under constant surveillance.

Meanwhile, those who had brought about Ralegh's fall enjoyed spectacular favour under the new king. Cecil himself became Viscount Cranborne in 1604 and a Knight of the Garter before his elevation to the Earldom of Salisbury in 1605. The procession which celebrated his elevation apparently surpassed the coronation procession in its magnificence. In 1608, on the death of the Earl of Dorset, Cecil also succeeded to the post of Lord Treasurer while retaining both the role of Secretary of State and Master of the Wards – an unprecedented accumulation of executive power that exceeded even that of his illustrious father. Cecil also continued to acquire wealth, and among the great estates he added to his portfolio was that previously owned by Lord Cobham. He appears to have paid a very low price for all the Brooke property in Kent and elsewhere, prompting the suggestion by one modern historian that he might have deliberately 'first destroyed the main branch of the family and then, using subtle baits like interest-free loans, lured the heir to the family estates into a position from which there was no escape other than to turn them all over to him'.[5]

Cecil also had his eye on Durham House as part of his development plans for the area west of Salisbury House. Within two years of Ralegh's ejection from his

London residence, Cecil had secured a slice down the east side of the property on which to enlarge his own mansion. He then proceeded to acquire control of part of the Strand frontage of Durham House, including the stables and gatehouse, which he incorporated into the New Exchange, the great shopping mall designed to rival the city's Royal Exchange.

Henry Howard, whom Ralegh described as 'my heavy enemy', also received a multitude of favours from James. At the time of Ralegh's trial he had already been made a privy councillor. In January 1604 he was appointed to Cobham's former office of Warden of the Cinque Ports; two months later he became Earl of Northampton and Baron Marnhull of Marnhull in the County of Dorset. In the following year he was given the Garter and appointed Lord Privy Seal. Later on he was to become High Steward of the University of Oxford and Chancellor of the University of Cambridge. His finances prospered too: he built Northampton (later Northumberland) House at Charing Cross and he, like Cecil, enjoyed a pension from Spain in recognition of his contribution to the negotiation of the peace treaty in 1604. Finally, it was another member of the Howard clan, the Lord Admiral Earl of Nottingham, who acquired Ralegh's wine licence. This had been called in to determine whether it was a monopoly that should be prohibited, but the Council came to the conclusion that it was not, thereby enabling the king to re-grant it to his nominee.

The victors in the battle for James' favour had been able to gorge themselves, and the bones of their victims had been almost picked clean – but not quite. Cecil was content that Ralegh had been removed forever from court politics and he had no further wish to see his family ruined. When the Sherborne estate was under threat in 1604 Cecil therefore intervened to confirm Bess and Wat's right to the property subject to the control of trustees.

But that was not the end of the matter. The deed by which Ralegh had transferred the Sherborne estate to Wat at the end of Elizabeth's reign was found to be flawed. This meant that the legal ownership had remained with Ralegh and was then automatically forfeit to the Crown after his conviction for treason. In 1607 James wanted the estate for his new favourite, the young Scot, Robert Carr, and intimated his intention to have it forcibly confiscated as was his legal right. Thanks to a vigorous lobbying campaign by Bess, compensation was extracted from the king: a capital sum of £8,000 plus an annuity of £400 for the lifetime of herself and her son. Bess was secure but Sherborne had gone, and Ralegh's hopes of establishing a landed dynasty had been extinguished.

Ralegh was now caged and had to make an entirely new life for himself. For him the prospect of confinement must have been particularly daunting: as a man of action his tracks covered France, Holland, Ireland and South America, as well as the waters of the Atlantic; and even when at home he was accustomed to the great spaces afforded by Sherborne and Durham House. He was now restrained within a cramped apartment whose walls in winter exuded the foul damp and odours of the Thames. Yet after his early moments of despair, Ralegh began to make the most of his new environment. He had the leisure to enjoy his family, and it was here that his second son, Carew, was conceived. The register of the Tower chapel of St Peter ad Vincula records that Carew Ralegh was baptised there on 15 February 1605. Ralegh could call on the services of a serving man, Peter Dean; he had a well-educated secretary, John Talbot; and he was able to receive visitors much as he wished. Those who came to see him included his faithful retainer, Lawrence Keymis; his old friend, Thomas Hariot; his physician, Doctor Peter Turner; his Sherborne steward, John Shelbury; and a clergyman named Hawthorn.

Early in his captivity, Ralegh was given the liberty of the Tower, which meant that he could move freely within the Tower walls and its little village community. He also became friendly with the prison lieutenant or governor, Sir George Harvey, whom he dined with on occasion; and he was given access to the governor's garden where he was allowed to cultivate his own plot with exotic herbs and shrubs. He liked to pace the terraces and for the London populace he was a sight to behold from the wharfs below: opulently attired as always, he must have created quite an impression with his velvet and lace cap, rich gown, trunk hose and jewellery.[6] He was also given the use of a little shed or henhouse where he installed copper tubing and retorts and carried out chemical experiments. It was here that he concocted his 'Great Cordial' from the plants he cultivated and whose medicinal qualities now brought him fame as a pharmacist. Grateful users of his elixirs included Queen Anne, the wife of the French ambassador in London and other society ladies; the reputation of the Cordial was to continue for several generations after his death.

In August 1605 Sir William Waad replaced Harvey as governor and the easy-going prison regime came to an end. Waad complained to Cecil that 'Sir Walter doth show himself upon the wall in his garden to the view of the people who gaze upon him';[7] he issued an order forbidding Lady Ralegh to drive into the Tower courtyard in her coach; and he decreed that at the ringing of the afternoon bell at 5.00 p.m. all the prisoners and their servants were to withdraw to their chambers and were not to go out again until morning. For some time in 1610 Bess was not permitted to reside in Ralegh's apartment and had to move to a rented property on Tower Hill, putting further strains on the family's finances.

In a desperate attempt to secure his release, Ralegh approached Cecil in the summer of 1607 with a proposal.[8] He claimed that some stone he had brought back from Guiana had been assayed and found to contain traces of gold. He was prepared to travel as a private individual in a ship with a master and officers appointed by Cecil to the place where the gold seam was to be found. They would take bellows and bricks for a furnace so that the metal could be melted down in situ and brought back in ingots. The cost of £5,000 (surely an underestimate) could possibly be split between Ralegh, Cecil and Queen Anne. If not,

Ralegh would find the means to finance the expedition himself and present Cecil and the queen with half the profits. Cecil, however, was not to be drawn – he still had no intention of letting Ralegh out and the project came to nothing.

Wishing to maintain his connection with the world outside and subject as he was to a nightly curfew, Ralegh now began to use his evenings to write. He produced a scholarly dissertation on naval warfare and ship design dedicated to James' son and heir, Henry. He wrote two tracts on the proposed controversial marriages between James' children and the House of Savoy and, following the convention of the period, he set down his advice to his son which, when printed in the 1630s, quickly went through seven editions. Among other things, he counselled his son to avoid poverty because 'poverty provokes a man to do infamous and detested deeds'.[9] Was this perhaps an oblique reference to his own experience and the fact that both he and Essex had been provoked to unwise actions when faced with the prospect of financial ruin? Finally, he began research on his magnum opus, *The History of the World*, which was over time to establish his reputation as one of the foremost scholars and writers of his age.

Ralegh produced very little poetry while in the Tower, presumably because there was little point: neither court nor sovereign would now appreciate his verse. Nevertheless he did write one poem which captures his view of life as a brief tragic-comedy staged under God's watchful eye:

What is our life? A play of passion;
Our mirth, the music of division;
Our mothers' wombs the tiring houses be
Where we are dressed for this short comedy.
Heaven the judicious sharp spectator is,
That sits and marks still who doth act amiss;
Our graves that hide us from the scorching sun
Are like drawn curtains when the play is done.
Thus march we playing to our latest rest –
Only we die in earnest, that's no jest.[10]

For one performer in Ralegh's little theatre of life the curtains were soon to be drawn. Cecil, who had dominated the political stage for some twenty years, died in May 1612 after a long and agonising illness – an event which was to have a huge impact on affairs of state and which removed one important obstacle to Ralegh's eventual release.

In August 1611 the king's French physician, Sir Theodore Mayerne, had examined Cecil and found two large tumours, the painful effects of which were compounded by symptoms of dropsy and scurvy. Numerous doctors were called in to advise and a host of remedies applied: benzoin from Sumatra, musk from Tibet and china root, camphor and rhubarb from China. All was to no avail, and in his increasing distress Cecil decided in April 1612 to take the waters in Bath. Accompanied by sixty horse, he was carried by coach but the discomfort and pain caused by the jolting carriage was such that he had, on occasion, to be born on his litter and at other times on a specially designed sedan chair. It took the sad little party a whole week to reach Bath where Cecil was lowered into the water up to his waist on a padded chair suspended from a pulley.

After a brief respite his excruciating pains returned, and the dying statesman and his escort retraced their steps. He was in a hurry to get back because he feared political manoeuvrings against him. According to John Chamberlain:

> He found so little good at the Bath that he made all the haste he could out of that suffocating, sulphurous air as he called it, though others think he hastened the faster homeward to countermine his underminers and, as he termed it, to cast dust in their eyes.[11]

At Marlborough the cavalcade came to a halt. Cecil was carried into the parsonage and here on Sunday, 24 May, he died between 1 and 2 in the afternoon. A contemporary observer recorded the end:

> though sinking rapidly, he insisted on standing erect with the aid of his crutches while prayers were being offered … then, lying with his head on two pillows and his body in a swing [he] called for Doctor Poe's hand which he gripped hard when his eyes began to settle and he sank down without a groan, sigh, or struggle.[12]

It was reported by Chamberlain that during his final illness, Cecil became an increasingly isolated figure as friends and colleagues began to desert him. The political game was moving on and ambitious courtiers had no time for a dying man, however great his office.

It seems that while at Bath and increasingly conscious of his impending death, Cecil was overtaken by spiritual fears. In his final interview with his son who visited him there, he gave a solemn warning: 'Take heed, by all means, of blood, whether in public or in private quarrel.'[13] Was this, at the very last, his expression of remorse for the beheading of his own brother-in-law, George Brooke, who, while on the scaffold and at the edge of death, had accused his kinsman of dastardly betrayal?

While news of Cecil's passing at the age of 48 no doubt raised Ralegh's hopes of freedom, the tragic death of Prince Henry just six months later dashed his expectations of royal forgiveness. In the previous four years he had established a close friendship with the heir to the throne. With the approval of Queen Anne he had taken on the role of informal mentor and tutor to the young prince, advising him on matters ranging from marriage to naval warfare. His *History of the World* was intended, above all, as a great work of instruction for the benefit of the monarch-to-be as well as his fellow countrymen.

But Henry became seriously ill after swimming in the foul waters of the Thames. 'Looseness' affected him fifteen times a day and Doctor Mayerne was summoned to apply his remedies, one of which was a syrup made up of snails, frogs and crawfish boiled up in water of coltsfoot. Not surprisingly, Henry, almost certainly a victim of typhoid, did not respond and as a last resort the queen sent for Ralegh's Cordial – to no avail. After a brief revival the prince died on 6 November 1612, aged 18. Henry's death occurred just as Ralegh was completing his great masterpiece, *The History of the World*, which was fulsomely dedicated to the young prince. This scholarly work of some one million words and nearly 700 references first appeared in printed form in March 1614. The narrative began with the creation of the world and ended in 146 BC, covering first biblical history and then the story of Greece and Rome. Ralegh had originally intended to continue his narrative up to more recent times but was wary of writing about the immediate past because, as he said 'Whosoever in writing a modern history, shall follow truth too near the heels, it may happly strike out his teeth'.[14]

The History of the World was destined to become a best-selling publication: it went through eleven editions in the seventeenth century – which was twice as many as the works of Shakespeare. However, King James took exception to Ralegh's monumental opus. In December 1614 agents of the Archbishop of Canterbury began seizing copies which had been circulating for some months, and further publication was prohibited for the next two years because, according to John Chamberlain, the king thought the book was 'too saucy in censoring the acts of Princes'.[15] It may be that James recognised himself in the portrait of Ninias, successor of a famous queen, a man 'esteemed no man of war at all, but altogether feminine and subjected to ease and delicacy'.[16] Or he may have objected to the preface which catalogued the misdeeds of English kings up to Henry VIII and the divine retribution which followed – in Henry's case the extinction of the Tudor dynasty through the failure of his children, Edward, Mary and Elizabeth, to produce any children.

But James's fundamental objection to *The History* was no doubt based on its underlying philosophy – which was that God intervenes in human affairs to punish monarchs who abuse their power. Kings who govern with the approval and love of their people flourish; tyrants who oppress those they rule are subject to the wrath of God. Even the mightiest are laid low when confronted with death which is the divine punishment for their sins. The mortality of kings was eulogised in Ralegh's final declamation:

Oh eloquent, just and mighty Death! Whom none could advise, thou hast persuaded; that none hath dared, thou hast done; and whom all the world hath flattered, thou only hast cast out of the world and despised: thou hast drawn together all the far stretched greatness, all the pride, cruelty and ambitions of man and covered it all over with these two narrow words: Hic Jacet [Here lies] …[17]

For James, who upheld the divine right of kings and insisted on the subordinate role of parliament and people, the tone of Ralegh's *History* was provocatively judgemental, subversive and insolent.

The History no doubt served to deepen James' profound dislike and distrust of its author and all he stood for. Yet within two years of its publication, Ralegh was to be released from the Tower and allowed to prepare for the great expedition to Guiana which he had been pressing for during all his years of imprisonment. How had this extraordinary transformation in fortune come about?

To begin with, Ralegh had become something of a national treasure. He was the last surviving romantic figure from a more heroic age. He had kept himself in the public eye through his writings, his known connections with the royal family and his renowned elixirs. Furthermore, his most determined enemies had died – Cecil in 1612 and Henry Howard, Earl of Northampton, two years later – while the king's new Principal Secretary, the Puritan Sir Ralph Winwood, was well disposed towards the Tower's most famous prisoner. There was also the question of money. Ralegh claimed to know where to find gold and James was desperately trying to raise funds to cover £700,000 of royal debts. The king dared not call a parliament which was almost certain to oppose him, and his attempts to sell off his son Charles as a husband to the Infanta of Spain had run into difficulties. The prospect of a financial deal with Ralegh, in which the great adventurer would bear the cost of an expedition to Guiana while the Crown received a large share of any gold brought back, became increasingly attractive.

Court politics also played a role. The king's favourite, Robert Carr, having become embroiled in a scandalous intrigue involving the notorious poisoning of Sir Thomas Overbury, was disgraced and committed to the Tower in 1615. Carr was a member of the pro-Spanish faction at court but his replacement as favourite, George Villiers, a young Buckinghamshire gentleman, came under the influence of an anti-Spanish group which included Sir Ralph Winwood and George Abbott, the Archbishop of Canterbury. James was now encouraged to follow a more robust approach to Spain, and Ralegh's proposed Guiana adventure fitted well with the new policy. To seal matters, Ralegh evidently bribed Villiers to the tune of £1,500 in order to ensure that the case for his release was presented forcefully to the king.

So a deal was struck. Ralegh was to be released from the Tower on licence but not pardoned. He would be able to prepare an expedition to Guiana at his own expense with no financial contribution from the Crown other than the tonnage money that was allowed by act of parliament for the encouragement of shipbuilding. He was to be given a royal commission to exploit lands in South America 'inhabited by heathen and savage people' but the authority to subdue such lands contained in his earlier Guiana commission was deliberately struck out by James: the king did not want fighting. Ralegh was also appointed sole commander of the expedition with full powers to discipline his men. Finally, and most crucially, one fifth of all gold, silver, pearls and precious stones brought back, together with customs dues on the remaining valuables, was to be paid to the Crown.

On 19 March 1616 a royal warrant was issued requiring the lieutenant of the Tower to 'permit Sir Walter Ralegh to go abroad to make preparations for his voyage'.[18] He was allowed to live in his own accommodation in the city but he was attended by a keeper and his movements were restricted, as a letter to him from the Privy Council made clear:

> His Majesty being pleased to release you out of your imprisonment in the Tower, to go abroad with a keeper, to make your provisions for your intended voyage we admonish you that you should not presume to resort either to his Majesty's Court, the Queen's or the Prince's, nor go into any public assemblies wheresoever without a special licence.[19]

Immediately on his release Ralegh took time off, as John Chamberlain relates, to do a sight-seeing trip around London and view all the new buildings erected since his imprisonment over twelve years ago. But, ever the showman, he also wanted to be seen by Londoners: according to one contemporary '[Ralegh] entreats that he may have some time to walk about the town to show himself, for the comfort of being free is not so much as that others should take notice of it'.[20] Immaculately dressed, limping slightly and with the support of a stick (the result of his Cadiz wound) the great Elizabethan would have seen Cecil's New Exchange now occupying the Strand frontage of Durham House, the rebuilt Banqueting Hall in Whitehall replacing the Tudor building where he used to dine with the queen, and the great mansion, Northumberland House, built by his old enemy Henry Howard at Charing Cross.

Ralegh now had to devote his energy to raising finance, fitting out his fleet and enlisting crews and officers. The estimated cost of the expedition was £30,000 and Ralegh and Bess between them appear to have raised around one third of this from their own resources: Bess sold a property in Mitcham for £2,500 and called in a £3,000 loan to the Countess of Bedford, while Ralegh sold everything he had and persuaded his wife to part with some of the capital sum she had received as compensation for Sherborne. The financing was completed by asking each gentleman volunteer on the expedition to contribute up to £50. Meanwhile, the Earls of Huntingdon, Pembroke and Arundel between them provided £15,000 as sureties to ensure Ralegh's good conduct and return.

The flagship of the fleet of a dozen vessels was the *Destiny*, a 440-ton warship with thirty-six guns which was commissioned from the royal shipbuilder, Phineas Pett, at Deptford. The fleet would carry a total of around 1,000 men of whom maybe 150 were gentleman volunteers and the rest sailors, servants, labourers and miners. Those accompanying Ralegh included his old friend and aide, Lawrence Keymis, and his own son, Wat – now in his early twenties and named as Captain of the Admiral's flagship. Ralegh was released from his keeper at the end of January 1617 when the king issued a warrant 'fully and wholly enlarging him'.[21] Four months later the expedition was ready to sail, having taken a year to fit out and provision. Seamen and gentlemen volunteers had flocked to the flag, testimony to the powerful draw of Ralegh's name and to the belief in his Guiana goldmines. There was great excitement among the general population, too, and when James, prompted by objections from Spain, was having second thoughts about the project, he was warned by the Privy Council that the whole country would 'cry out' if it were stopped.[22]

The Guiana venture was Ralegh's last throw of the dice. Yet the odds were heavily loaded against its success. An expedition to South America led by Sir Thomas Roe in 1610 had found no evidence of the alleged site of El Dorado, although Roe did report on his return that Spain had established a military base at San Thome on the Orinoco, in the very area where Ralegh believed that gold was to be found. In one sense this was encouraging news: it suggested that the Spaniards, too, were convinced that there was gold to be mined in the region. But it also raised the prospect of a military clash between the English expedition and the Spaniards already in situ – an outcome that would be disastrous for Ralegh personally, given his commitment not to attack Spanish interests.

Ralegh would have been aware of the existence of the Spanish garrison at San Thome. Yet he may not have been too troubled by the possibility of a clash of arms because he appears to have had a plan B. The story was told that when walking in the gardens of Grays Inn with Sir Francis Bacon, Ralegh boasted that he would capture the Spanish Plate Fleet if he failed to find gold on the Orinoco. 'But that would be piracy' said Bacon, 'Oh no,' was the reply, 'Whoever heard of men being pirates for millions?'[23] Whether or not this conversation took place, an opportunistic attack on Spanish treasure ships with his heavily armed fleet would be entirely in keeping with Ralegh's previous track record. Such a stratagem is also suggested by a meeting he had with Des Marets, the French ambassador in London, on board the *Destiny* shortly before the fleet's departure. The possibility of France offering Ralegh asylum was evidently discussed because a letter was subsequently sent to Plymouth from the Duc de Montmorency, Admiral of France, intimating that Ralegh could on his return journey bring his fleet and any goods he might have acquired by trade 'or conquest' into a French port.[24] Ralegh was clearly taking precautions against James' possible displeasure at any predatory activities in which he and his company of treasure hunters and freebooters might become involved.

Gondomar, the Spanish ambassador, was also convinced that Ralegh intended to attack his country's treasure fleet. Why otherwise should his ships be so heavily armed? When he protested, James sought to appease him by requiring Ralegh to give a written undertaking that he would not harm Spanish subjects or encroach on Spanish territory. Ralegh was also asked to submit details of his ships and their armament together with a precise schedule of his voyage: information that James then passed on to Gondomar.

Ralegh was now engaged in a multiple gamble: that there was gold to be mined in Guiana; that he would be able to extract this without having to confront the Spanish; that if he failed to find gold he would be able to capture Spanish treasure; and that if he did breach the conditions of his royal commission – and thereby expose himself as an unpardoned traitor to re-incarceration or worse – he could find a safe haven in France.

He was also gambling on his health. Now in his mid-sixties, Ralegh was an old man by the standards of his time and he had been seriously ill in the Tower where the damp and cold of thirteen successive winters had taken their toll. On one occasion his physician, Doctor Turner, had described medical symptoms – numbness on his left side and virtual loss of speech – that suggested a stroke. It was asking a great deal of a man of his years and physical condition to lead a voyage of exploration across the Atlantic to the pestilential swamps of the South American jungle. There were indeed some at court who suspected that Ralegh himself knew that he had taken on too much. Among these was the Venetian ambassador who wrote to his government:

> I know very well that Sir Walter Ralegh's only object in embarking in this enterprise was to free himself from imprisonment. He would gladly change this scheme for any other.
> Many people know the fact as well as I.[25]

And some of Ralegh's own supporters warned him that he was embarking on a hopeless mission. His old friend, Sylvanus Scory, urged him in verse to 'cast anchor in this port; here art thou safe till Death enfranchise thee'.[26]

But Ralegh was too pre-occupied with final preparations to entertain doubts and gloomy thoughts. The fleet assembled in Plymouth and when Ralegh arrived he received a hero's welcome. The city's mayor, Robert Trelawny, was allowed £9 for 'entertaining Sir Walter Ralegh and his followers at his house' and a drummer was hired to beat the tattoo as Ralegh boarded his flagship.[27] The expedition sailed on 19 June under the command of the old Elizabethan adventurer who was setting out one last time 'to seek new worlds, for gold, for praise, for glory'.

14

THE FINAL GAMBLE

Hold thee firm here; cast anchor in this port;
Here art thou safe till death enfranchise thee.
Here neither harm, nor fears of harm, resort;
Here though enchained – thou livs't in liberty.
> Advice from Ralegh's friend, Sylvanus Scory, not to depart for Guiana

The Guiana expedition suffered a series of setbacks after sailing from Plymouth. The fleet was driven back to port by south westerly storms and then, on setting out again, it was driven back to Falmouth. The weather remained turbulent and when the ships were passing west of the Scilly Islands a severe gale scattered them: one was lost, two headed for Bristol and the rest ended up taking shelter at Cork in Ireland. The fleet remained holed up in port for the next few weeks and did not finally sail again, under a north easterly wind, until 19 August – a full two months after the original departure date. The delay was a serious blow: scarce provisions were depleted, the discipline of captains and of the men under their command was tested to breaking point and the most favourable time of year for crossing the Atlantic was missed.

Ralegh appears to have enjoyed his first taste of real freedom in Ireland. He went hawking and was generously entertained by Richard Boyle, later Earl of Cork, to whom he had sold his Irish lands in 1602. Boyle lent Ralegh £350 and helped with new provisions, in return for which Ralegh agreed to abandon certain outstanding claims on his old estate.

After sailing from Cork the fleet reached Lanzarote in the Canaries on 5 September, where three sailors were killed by unfriendly Spanish inhabitants. It was here, too, that Captain John Bailey deserted with his ship and headed for home, apparently because he was missing his wife. On the island of Gomera

Ralegh met with a more hospitable reception, and he was able to take on water and fresh fruit. But, ominously, sickness was already beginning to take hold among the sailors and by the time he left the Canaries, fifty men on the *Destiny* alone were laid low. Worse was to follow. After passing the Cape Verde Islands the fleet became becalmed and the rest of the Atlantic crossing, which should have taken two weeks, lasted forty days. At the outset of the voyage it had been south-westerly gales that had played havoc, but now it was the doldrums and stifling heat that took a terrible toll of the men. Ralegh's journal records the death of several of his closest associates, including John Talbot, his secretary; John Pigott, the fleet sergeant major; and John Fowler, a master refiner who was to have had a key role in prospecting for gold.

There were forty-two deaths on the *Destiny*, and the Reverend Samuel Jones, chaplain to the expedition, reported that throughout the fleet 'above 100 persons, gentlemen most of them, died between the [Cape Verde] islands and the continent of Guiana'.[1] At the end of October, Ralegh himself became seriously ill. He had fallen heavily in the night and inflamed his old leg wound, which appears to have become infected. He experienced a high fever and, by his own account, he received no solid food for three weeks and sweated so profusely 'as I changed my shirts thrice every day and thrice every night'.[2] When land was eventually sighted on 11 November he was too ill to leave his bunk.

Three days later the *Destiny* dropped anchor on the South American coast at the mouth of the River Cayenne, and Ralegh was able to leave his unsavoury ship 'pestered with many sick men which being unable to move poisoned us with a most filthy stench'.[3] However, he was still too weak to walk and had to be carried around in a chair.

Ralegh's health had not survived the trials of the voyage and he was in no physical condition to command the next and most crucial phase of the mission: the search for gold around San Thome. Death and sickness had removed several of the most likely candidates to lead the inland expedition and the choice eventually fell on Lawrence Keymis. Command of the land forces was given to George Ralegh, an experienced officer and Walter's nephew, while the impetuous Wat Ralegh was appointed one of the five company commanders. When the fleet had reassembled at the mouth of the Orinoco, Ralegh with the *Destiny* and several other of the larger ships stood watch off Trinidad to counter a feared Spanish naval attack. On 10 December five of the smaller ships, each having a draught shallow enough to navigate the Orinoco delta, began to make their way up river towards San Thome carrying 400 men. Their written instructions were to avoid direct confrontation with the Spanish garrison.

Precisely what happened thereafter is the subject of conflicting accounts, but the essential facts are not in dispute. It took three weeks for Keymis to negotiate the mud banks and shifting currents of the Orinoco delta, but on 3 January his ships anchored opposite the town of San Thome and a shore party set up camp. There was then some sort of confrontation outside the town walls in which musket shots were fired, whereupon the English force overran the Spanish settlement – but not before Wat Ralegh, leading from the front, had been fatally wounded by a musket ball. On the Spanish side, the governor of the garrison was killed along with four other officers while many houses were burned.

With San Thome secured, Keymis began the search for gold. Two launches were despatched up river but quickly returned when fired on by the retreating Spanish, aided by local indians with bows and arrows. Two Englishmen were killed and seven wounded. George Ralegh and Keymis then took a party of men on another river expedition which eventually travelled some 180 miles upstream – even though the gold mine was supposed to be only 3 miles from San Thome. By the time the search party had returned empty-handed after three weeks, it was painfully clear that Keymis had no idea where the supposed gold mine was to be found. Meanwhile, a combination of disease, sporadic Spanish attacks on the town and ambushes against foraging parties had taken a severe toll on the English occupying force. Keymis decided that there was no alternative but to abandon the project and, after setting fire to the remains of the town and carrying off as much loot – especially tobacco – as he and his men could lay their hands on, they prepared to rejoin the main fleet.

The mission had failed on all fronts. No gold mine or gold-bearing ore had been discovered; San Thome had been sacked and Spaniards killed in direct contradiction of the king's instructions; as many as half of the original 400 landing party had been lost; and there was mutiny in the air among the demoralised men, the officers and the ships' captains. For Ralegh personally there was also the devastating blow of the loss of his eldest son.

While these calamities had been unfolding at and around San Thome during December and January, Ralegh had been coasting off Trinidad in relative comfort. Then on 1 February he received a letter from Keymis giving him news of the storming of San Thome, the death of Wat and the futile search for gold. Keymis himself and the remnants of his party rejoined the admiral on 2 March at Trinidad and here there was a bitter confrontation between Ralegh and his humiliated commander on board the *Destiny*. When Ralegh blamed his long-standing and faithful friend for the disastrous failure of the mission, Keymis replied 'I know, then, Sir what course to take'. He retreated to his cabin and shot himself but since the wound was not fatal he took a knife and stabbed himself in the heart.

Ralegh had been physically broken by the transatlantic voyage. He was now mentally shattered by the death of his son and the collapse of all his hopes of rehabilitation, honour and riches. From this point on he lost his capacity for decisive action – a state of mind which no doubt communicated itself to his followers. Anchored off what is now St Kitts, Ralegh wrote a letter to his wife on 22 March which was to be carried home by a flyboat under the command of his cousin,

William Herbert. He could not bring himself to tell Bess of Wat's death in so many words:

> I was loathe to write because I know not how to comfort you. And God knows I never knew what sorrow meant till now. All that I can say to you is that you must obey the will and providence of God and remember that the Queen's majesty bore the loss of Prince Henry with a magnanimous heart ... Comfort your heart (dear Bess). I shall sorrow for us both and I shall sorrow the less because I have not long to sorrow, because not long to live.[4]

Faced with the prospect of humiliation and probable death on his return to England, Ralegh appears to have toyed with the idea of executing his plan B. According to Chaplain Jones, he told one of his senior commanders, Sir Warham St Leger, that he would sail for Newfoundland to victual and trim his remaining ships, make for the Azores where he would seize the treasure of homeward bound Spanish vessels and then head for France.[5] Another officer, Charles Parker, confirmed that Ralegh was thinking along these lines. In his letter to Bess, too, Ralegh hinted as much, when he expressed the hope that 'God will send us somewhat ere we return'.[6] However, now an ill and broken man, he eventually decided to head straight for home – perhaps influenced by the fact that large sums had been pledged by his friends as a guarantee of his good conduct.

But Ralegh had lost control of his fleet and was shortly to lose control of his ship. At Nevis on 12 March two more of his captains deserted, apparently to engage in some privateering on the way home, leaving him, after the despatch of his flyboat, with only four ships. There was then a mutiny on the *Destiny* and he was forced to make landfall at Kinsale in Ireland where he set men ashore. In the second week of June the undermanned *Destiny* eventually limped alone into Plymouth harbour carrying not newly mined gold but looted tobacco. The home-coming was without fanfare or celebration; a year had passed since the fleet had set out with such high hopes 'for gold, for praise, for glory'; but intervening events had destroyed the Guiana dream, discredited its chief promoter and provoked Spain into demanding that Ralegh be publicly hanged in the Plaza Majore in Madrid.

By the time Ralegh returned to Plymouth the king and Privy Council had already been informed of the events at San Thome. Ralegh himself had written to Sir Ralph Winwood giving his own account; Samuel Jones' report had also been received and Captain North, who had returned with Ralegh's letter, was able to brief the Privy Council personally in the final week of May. The Spanish ambassador, Gondomar, had meanwhile been given lurid accounts of the English depradations against the Spanish settlement via his masters in Madrid. He now demanded action from James who was relying on Spanish goodwill to secure a profitable marriage alliance for his son, Charles.

Accordingly James, on 9 June, issued a proclamation 'concerning Sir Walter Ralegh and those who had ventured with him'.[7] While the king had given them a licence for a voyage to Guiana 'to make discovery of certain gold mines for the lawful enriching of themselves and these our kingdoms', he had forbidden acts of hostility against the territories or subjects of friendly princes 'and more particularly those of our dear brother the King of Spain'. He referred to the reported killing, sacking and burning and expressed 'our own utter mislike and detestation of the same insolences and excesses' if such had been committed. He called for anyone with information to come forward with their testimony so that the guilty parties could be tried, convicted and punished.

Bess had travelled down from London with her surviving son, Carew, in order to join her husband at Plymouth. The reunited family appears to have stayed outside the city at Radford, the home of an old friend, Sir Christopher Harris. Here Ralegh was able to recuperate for two or three weeks despite the fact that on 12 June orders for his arrest had been given by the Lord Admiral to Sir Lewis Stukeley, Vice-Admiral of Devon. There was an unaccountable delay in executing this instruction which suggests that those in high places found the prospect of dealing with Ralegh, still a popular figure in the country, politically awkward. Giving him the opportunity to escape abroad was perhaps the most convenient option.

In fact Bess did arrange for one of Ralegh's old privateering captains, Samuel King, to provide a French boat to take them across the Channel, but her husband's nerve failed at the last moment. It seems that, old and ill as he was, he no longer had the stomach to make a new life for himself on the continent. Instead, he decided to await his arrest and to take on his detractors by providing a detailed written justification of his conduct. On 15 July Stukeley duly executed his warrant and he, the Raleghs, their servants, Samuel King and a doctor named Manourie, began their journey to London.

Ralegh passed by Sherborne for one last time and then the party moved on to Salisbury. Here Ralegh learned that James would shortly be arriving on his summer progress, and he saw an opportunity to present the king with the formal defence he was preparing. The problem was that he needed more time to complete his treatise which was to be entitled *Apologie for his voyage to Guiana*.[8] So he took Manourie into his confidence and persuaded him to collaborate in some outrageous play-acting. The doctor gave Ralegh an emetic, rubbed the inside of his chamber pot with a substance that turned his urine black, and gave him an ointment which produced blotches and pustules all over his face and upper body.[9] Exhibiting all the symptoms of extreme sickness Ralegh could not be moved and, writing frantically day and night, he was able to finish his *Apologie* in time for James' arrival at Salisbury on 1 August.

The essence of Ralegh's lengthy defence was that Guiana was English because of his 'conquest' of the region in 1595, and that the Spanish had in any case been the first to attack the English at San Thome. He concluded that:

if Guiana be not our sovereign's, the working of a mine there and the taking of the town there had been equally perilous to me, for by doing the one I had robbed the King of Spain and had been a thief and by the other a disturber and breaker of the peace.[10]

The implication was clear; if James had really wished to avoid a clash with Spain he should not have approved the expedition.

James evidently declined to read the *Apologie*. He was not interested in Ralegh's attempts at self-justification because he had had enough of this slippery and troublesome man and wanted to be rid of him. Stukeley was ordered to remove his charge immediately from Salisbury and to continue to London while Ralegh, now recovered from his feigned 'illness' but sensing that he stood in grave peril of his life, began to reconsider the possibility of escape. Somewhat recklessly he again took Manourie into his confidence and then sought Stukeley's co-operation by offering him a large bribe to help him cross to France. Finally, he enlisted the services of Samuel King and also his former servant Cottrell to arrange for river and sea transport.

With so many in the know it is hardly surprising that the planned escape was leaked to James' government – which decided to allow the plot to develop unchecked so as to catch Ralegh red-handed. On reaching London he was allowed the comparative liberty of his wife's lodgings in Broad Street for five days to order his affairs before entering the Tower. Here he was subject to round the clock surveillance. On the evening of 9 August, Ralegh, heavily disguised with a false beard, rode down to Tower Dock accompanied by Stukeley who was now playing a double agent's role as co-conspirator and government informer. Captain King was waiting for them at the waterside as was Cottrell who had two wherries moored at Tower Stairs to take the party down river to Gravesend. Here there would be a Thames ketch ready to carry the fugitive across the Channel. But government agents had been fully briefed and as the two wherries passed Woolwich a larger boat, which had been following them at a discreet distance, came alongside and ordered them back to Greenwich. Here Stukeley revealed his true colours as he arrested Ralegh in the name of the king.

On the morning of 10 August 1618, Ralegh was escorted back to the Tower of London. The Bloody Tower was occupied so he was given one of Cobham's rooms in the Beauchamp Tower, Cobham himself being seriously ill after suffering a stroke (later Ralegh was to be given more secure accommodation in the Brick Tower). The diamonds, gold and jewellery that Ralegh had been carrying in his cloak-bag to finance his intended new life in France were confiscated, while the ever-faithful Bess was placed under house arrest in Broad Street before herself being sent to the Tower. Ralegh must have realised that the game was now finally up, and in desperation he wrote forlorn letters to the king, the queen and the king's favourite, Villiers (now Duke of Buckingham) pleading for his life.

James had already decided that Ralegh must be executed – not least because he had given his word to Spain that if their old adversary could not be brought to Madrid for punishment there, he would be made to suffer a traitor's death at home. There were, however, difficulties. It was well known that the Spanish ambassador, Gondomar, a hated figure among the London populace, was demanding Ralegh's head. It was therefore necessary to ensure that there was an appearance of due process in determining Ralegh's fate so that it could not be said that the king had caved in to Spanish wishes.

But this political consideration in turn raised a legal difficulty. On what grounds could Ralegh be found guilty of capital offences? He could not be made personally responsible for the sacking of San Thome when he had not even been there; he may have talked recklessly about taking the Spanish Plate Fleet but he had not attempted this and in any case claimed that his only purpose in discussing the possibility was to keep his fleet together and prevent his captains going off on privateering expeditions. It was known that Ralegh had had some murky dealings with France before his departure from Plymouth, but there was insufficient evidence to point to a conspiracy.

The king appointed a commission of six privy councillors, including two skilful lawyers, Sir Francis Bacon and Sir Edward Coke, to build a case against Ralegh. The commission members worked through August and September and finally presented their recommendations on 18 October. It was their opinion that Ralegh, having been convicted of high treason in 1603, could not be judged for any offence committed since, but that the old death sentence, dating back fifteen years, was still valid and could be revived.[11] This could be done in one of two ways. The old warrant for his execution could be implemented and a printed narrative of his 'late crimes and offences' published in order to justify the decision to the general public. Alternatively, Ralegh could be made to answer for himself before the lords of the Council, senior judges and a handpicked group of nobles and gentry. He would be denounced, given his opportunity to reply, and then executed.

The king wanted some sort of judicial procedure but was anxious to avoid a public hearing before the Council: 'We think it not fit, because it would make him too popular, as was found by experiment at the arraignment at Winchester, where by his wit he turned the hatred of men into compassion for him'.[12] Accordingly James proposed a middle course, involving a further and final private hearing in front of the commissioners who had already examined the prisoner, followed immediately by execution and then publication of a declaration to justify the deed.

On 22 October Ralegh was taken from the Tower to confront his accusers. The Attorney General, Sir Henry Yelverton, charged him under three headings, distinguishing those offences committed before his last voyage, during the voyage and those committed since. He was accused of never intending to discover a gold mine, planning to start a war between the Kings of England and Spain, abandoning his men and behaving unfaithfully to his king. Since his return to England he had tried to escape both before and after his arrest, deceived the king and State and made insolent speeches against His Majesty. Ralegh answered the accusations, using many of the arguments he had presented in his *Apologie*, but matters had already been decided. He was escorted back to the Tower and two days later, on 24 October, he was told that he must be punished by execution and so should prepare himself for death.

On the morning of 28 October he was again removed from the Tower and taken by coach past St Paul's, down Ludgate Hill and along the Strand to Westminster Hall, where he was brought before the justices of the King's Bench. The Attorney General began the proceedings by referring back to the prisoner's original conviction for high treason at Winchester. He went on:

> Sir Walter Ralegh hath been a statesman and a man who in regard to his parts and quality is to be pitied. He hath been a star at which the world has gazed; but stars may fall, nay they must fall when they trouble the sphere wherein they abide. It is, therefore, his Majesty's pleasure to call for execution of the former judgement, and I now require order for the same.[13]

The prisoner was asked why execution should not be awarded against him, but there was now little more to be said. The Lord Chief Justice, Sir Henry Montague, then pronounced judgement, but in terms very different from the words used by Lord Justice Popham at Winchester fifteen years before:

> I pray you attend what I shall say unto you. I am here called to grant execution upon the judgement given you fifteen years since; all which time you have been as a dead man in the law, and might at any minute have been cut off, but the King in mercy spared you. You might think it heavy if this were done in cold blood, to call you to execution; but it is not so; for new offences have stirred up His Majesty's justice, to remember to revive what the law hath formerly cast upon you. I know you have been valiant and wise, and I doubt not but you retain both these virtues, for now you shall have occasion to use them. Your Faith hath heretofore been questioned, but I am resolved you are a good Christian, for your book which is an admirable work, doth testify as much. I would give you counsel, but I know you can apply unto yourself far better than I am able to give you … Fear not death too much, nor fear death too little; not too much, lest you fail in your hopes; not too little, lest you die presumptuously. And here I must conclude with my prayers to God for it, and that he would have mercy on your soul.[14]

Ralegh's application for a few days delay so that he might put his affairs in order was denied, but he was given two concessions: he was to be beheaded rather than hung, drawn and quartered; and at his particular request he was to be allowed to make a speech from the scaffold. He was to be taken straight away to the Gatehouse Prison near the west end of Westminster Abbey and executed the very next morning. As he was escorted across Old Palace Yard where his scaffold was about to be erected, he encountered an old friend, Sir Hugh Beeston, and asked him whether he would be present at the spectacle next day. Beeston said he would be there if he could find a place in the crowd. Ralegh replied: 'I do not know what you may do for a place. You must make what shift you can. But for my part, I am sure of one.'[15]

That night Bess was allowed to visit her husband at the Gatehouse and the couple said their last farewells. When she left just after midnight he sat down to write a few lines of poetry and then, being the great stage actor he was, he prepared himself for the final curtain fall.

15

The Last Act: Old Palace Yard, 29 October 1618

He hath purchased here, in the opinion of men, such honour and reputation, as, it is thought, his greatest enemies are they that are most sorrowful for his death, which they see is like to turn so much to his advantage.

Rev. Thomas Lorkin on Ralegh's execution

The prisoner was taken from the old Gatehouse close to Westminster Abbey at around 8.00 a.m. by an armed guard of pikemen. He was dressed in a black embroidered velvet nightgown, a hare-coloured satin doublet and a black embroidered waistcoat. He wore a ruff-band, a pair of black taffeta breaches and ash-coloured stockings. The whole ensemble combined the wearer's taste for magnificence with a proper regard for the solemnity of the occasion.

The crowds were such that the escort had to push its way through as it made its way towards Old Palace Yard where a scaffold had been hastily erected the night before. Onlookers noted that the condemned man had a curiously jaunty air, a fact which earlier visitors to the Gatehouse prison had also observed. The Dean of Westminster, Dr Tounson, when sent to take the final confession the previous evening had found the inmate unrepentant and inclined to make light of his fate. The dean had rebuked him gently for his insouciance in the face of death, but on receiving communion the next morning the prisoner was again cheerful and said that he hoped to persuade the world that he died an innocent man, though he confessed 'Justice had been done and by course of law he must die'.[1] After eating a hearty breakfast and smoking his beloved pipe he had been offered a glass of sack, and on being asked how he liked it replied: 'I will answer you as did the fellow who drank of St Giles' bowl as he went to Tyburn: "It is a good drink, if a man might tarry by it".'[2]

The prisoner had asked that his execution be in public so that he might make a short address. The prosecutors had reluctantly agreed to this but because they feared his way with words and wanted to limit the crowds, they insisted that the execution take place as early as possible on the next morning after his sentencing. The appointed day also happened to coincide with the Lord Mayor's pageant which would attract people towards the city and away from Westminster. Nevertheless, once the word was out that one of England's most illustrious figures was to be put to death, the crowds gathered around the scaffold in Old Palace Yard to watch the grim drama that was about to unfold. Some noblemen sat on horses to get a better view while others stood at windows or on balconies overlooking the place of execution.

The prisoner was accompanied onto the scaffold by the two sheriffs of London and the Dean of Westminster and after a proclamation for silence he began to speak:

> I was yesterday taken out of my bed in a strong fit of fever, which hath much weakened me, and whose untimeliness, forbearing no occasion nor place, I likewise expect today. And I do, therefore, first desire the Almighty God to keep sickness from me, that I may have time to deliver my mind; and my next desire unto you all is that if disability in voice or dismayedness in countenance, shall appear, you will ascribe it to sickness rather than to myself.[3]

Then, sensing that some of the nobles standing on a balcony opposite were having difficulty hearing him, the prisoner invited them down onto the scaffold where they all shook hands. He began his speech again by thanking God:

> that he hath brought me into the light to die before the eyes of so many honourable and worthy personages; and that he hath not suffered me to die in obscurity in the dark prison of the Tower where, for the space of fourteen years together, I have been oppressed with many miseries, and have suffered much affliction and sickness.[4]

The prisoner then spoke for some twenty-five minutes, rebutting in some detail several accusations made against him and professing his loyalty to his king and country. At this point the sheriff asked whether he would like to come down from the scaffold for a few moments to warm himself by the fire that had been lit for the occasion, before saying his final prayers. The response was resolute: 'No good Mr Sheriff let us dispatch, for within this quarter of an hour mine ague will come upon me, and if I be not dead before then, mine enemies will say that I quake for fear.'[5] He concluded by asking all those present to join with him in prayer:

> I now entreat that you will all join me in prayer to the great God of Heaven, whom I have grievously offended, being a man full of vanity, who has lived a sinful life in such callings as have been most inducing to it; for I have been a seafaring man, a soldier and a courtier and in the temptations of the least of these there is enough to overthrow a good mind and a good man.[6]

After a proclamation was made that all should leave the scaffold, the prisoner gently dismissed the assembled nobility: 'I have a long journey to go, therefore I must take my leave of you.'

When the scaffold had been cleared the prisoner again spent some time in prayer before taking off his night gown and doublet in preparation for the final act. He asked to see the axe which was concealed under the executioner's cloak and when, with reluctance, this was shown to him he felt the edge of it with his thumb, commenting to the sheriff, 'This is a sharp medicine, but it is a sure cure for all diseases.'[7] The executioner then kneeled before the prisoner and received forgiveness in the customary manner. A blindfold was offered but refused with a mild rebuke, 'Think you I fear the shadow of the axe, when I fear not the axe itself?'[8]

He stretched himself across the block with some difficulty, and when his head was in place the executioner ripped his shirt and waistcoat with a knife in order to expose the neck. The prisoner signalled with his hands that he was ready but when the executioner appeared to hesitate he called out 'What doest thou fear? Strike man, strike!'[9] Two blows were struck and as the head was severed the lips still moved. The executioner displayed the head on each side of the scaffold, before putting it into a red leather bag and wrapping both the bag and the body in the dead man's velvet night-gown. The gown and its contents were carried away in a black mourning coach, drawn by two white horses. The theatrical performance now over, the crowds dispersed, leaving an empty but bloodied stage.

In the fly leaf of the dead man's bible left at the Gatehouse they found his last written words – the final verse from a love poem he had penned many years before and to which he had added two lines:

Even such is time, that takes in trust
Our youth, our joys, our all we have,
And pays us but with earth and dust;
Who, in the dark and silent grave,
When we have wandered all our ways,
Shuts up the story of our days;
But from this earth, this grave, this dust
My God shall raise me up, I trust.[10]

So ended the life of Sir Walter Ralegh – one of the greatest figures of the Elizabethan age. He made his mark as a soldier, sailor, explorer, colonist, man of business, alchemist, poet, and historian, but above all as a courtier who had dazzled his queen and his contemporaries with his wit, his style and his flamboyance. Theatrical to the last, he had stage-managed his own death, impressing all those who witnessed it with his courage, dignity and eloquence. The battle for his reputation, however, had only just begun.

EPILOGUE

During his lifetime Ralegh never courted popularity and disdained those who did. He was a man who liked to be admired, even feared, rather than loved by his fellow men; it was the plaudits more than the affection of the crowd that he sought. At his death, too, as at his trial, he craved not sympathy but the respect of his peers, the favourable verdict of posterity and, above all, honour. So it was that in his speech from the scaffold he aimed to win over his audience by rebutting the three main charges that public opinion had levelled against him: that he had been disloyal to the king and state; that, in a Christian world, he was an unbeliever; and that he had been instrumental in the death of his great rival, Essex.

Ralegh professed his loyalty to James, rehearsing the arguments he had used in his *Apologie*. He also spoke much of the great and incomprehensible God, though one acute observer noted that he spoke not one word of Christ, concluding that 'he was an a-Christ, not an atheist'.[1] It was when defending his conduct at Essex's execution that he made reference to Sir Robert Cecil, the man he held responsible for the original judgement against him and for which he was now about to suffer the ultimate penalty: 'It was said that I was a persecutor of my Lord of Essex, and that I stood in a window over against him when he suffered and puffed out tobacco in disdain of him'. But Ralegh insisted that he had withdrawn to the armoury 'where I saw him, but he saw not me'. He went on to say: 'I confess I was of a contrary faction. But I knew that my Lord Essex was a noble gentleman and that it would be worse with me when he was gone. For those that set me up against him did afterwards set themselves against me.'[2] Here is a glimpse of the true face of Elizabethan court politics. Cecil had used Ralegh to neutralise an over-mighty favourite of the queen and then, when the mission had been accomplished, saw to it that his remaining court rival, the very instrument of his earlier policy, was in turn eliminated. What Ralegh omitted to say was that he was a more than willing partner in the scheme to bring down Essex and had himself begun to build a faction against Cecil once the royal favourite was removed.

The persuasive power of Ralegh's last speech was, perhaps, due less to its content than its manner of delivery and the speaker's general demeanour. One spectator observed that the victim 'seemed as free from all manner of apprehension as if he had come thither to be a spectator than a sufferer'.[3] He was a man acting out the final moments of a play while visualising his own performance from the gallery. The young Sir John Eliot, later to die in the Tower as an unrepentant defender of parliamentary privileges, was similarly affected:

> All preparations that were terrible were presented to his eye. Guards and officers were about him, the scaffold and the executioner, the axe and the more cruel expectations of his enemies. And what did all this work on the resolution of our Ralegh? … His mind became the clearer, as if it had already been freed from the cloud and oppression of the body.[4]

The Spanish agent in London, when reporting the scaffold scene to King Philip in Madrid, said 'Ralegh's spirit never faltered, nor did his countenance change'. In code he added that 'the death of this man has produced a great commotion and fear here, and it is looked upon as a matter of the highest importance, owing to his being a person of great parts and experience, subtle, crafty, ingenious, and brave enough for anything'.[5]

Ralegh, as at his trial, had through his composure and eloquence turned the tables on his enemies. It was perhaps because of the way he had swayed the crowd that the decision to allow his wife to bury his body at her family home at Beddington was reversed. In a letter to her brother, Sir Nicholas Carew, written on the day of the execution, Bess had said:

> Let me bury the worthy body of my noble husband in your church at Beddington, where I desire to be buried. The Lords have given me his dead body, though they denied me his life. This night he shall be brought to you with two or three of my men.[6]

But it seems that this dispensation was at the last moment withheld – the body being taken straight from the scaffold to the nearest possible burial site at St Margaret's Church close by. The authorities evidently did not want mourners jostling the funeral cortege of a newly created martyr.

James, stung by the groundswell of opinion in favour of Ralegh and against himself as well as the Spanish marriage, commissioned a lengthy treatise, largely written by Sir Francis Bacon, which sought to elaborate on the case against the victim and to justify the king's own conduct. The document was laboriously entitled: *Declaration of the Demeanour and Carriage of Sir Walter Ralegh, as well in his voyage as in and since his return, and the true motives and inducements which occasioned his Majesty to proceed in doing justice upon him, as hath been done.*[7] In his preface James explained that 'although Kings be not bound to give account of their actions to any but God alone,' in this particular case he was content to 'manifest unto the world how things appeared unto himself, and upon what proofs' since it not only concerned his own people, 'but also a foreign prince and state abroad'. He went on to say that it was Sir Ralph Winwood, the late Secretary of State, who had persuaded him to approve Ralegh's search for gold in Guiana even though 'his Majesty, in his own princely judgement, gave no belief unto it'. And because 'Sir Walter Ralegh had so enchanted the world with his confident asseveration of that which every man was willing to believe' he, James, did not wish to deny his people 'the adventure and hope of so great riches'.

Having excused the king's own role in the Guiana debacle the declaration provided a familiar litany of complaints against Ralegh, supported by statements from some of his captains on the voyage. The final assertion that James' 'just and honourable proceedings' had been intended to satisfy his 'dearest brother the King of Spain' was not calculated to dampen anti-Spanish feelings now running high among the populace.

James's propaganda machine failed to dent Ralegh's newly enhanced reputation, however. Indeed, he had become something of a national hero and his death was to remain a cause célèbre for many generations, a symbol of defiance in the face of royal oppression and an inspiration to those who championed the rights of Parliament and the individual against the tyranny of kings.

It was James who had initiated the new proceedings against Ralegh and who, in his eagerness, had signed the death warrant even before the judges had made their final determination. He had done so partly because of pressure from Spain and his desire to save his son's proposed marriage to the Infanta, together with the half million pound dowry that was expected to come with it. Just as concerns over money had induced Ralegh to engage in dangerous practices in 1603, so it was money that motivated James's conduct: both in allowing Ralegh his freedom to explore for gold and in bending to Spanish demands for his execution after the gold mission had failed. On the other hand it was thanks to his conviction at Winchester in 1603 that Ralegh was already legally dead in 1618, thereby enabling James to avoid a proper trial and to go straight to execution with only the barest semblance of judicial process. The true origins of the grim proceedings at Old Palace Yard can therefore be traced back to the court rivalry at the end of Elizabeth's reign which had prompted Cecil to 'heap coals' on his adversary's head and to bring him to the edge of the scaffold.

The struggle for power, favour and fortune between the two unlikely protagonists – the diminutive, deformed secretary and the flamboyant courtier/adventurer – appeared at the time to have ended in outright victory for Cecil. It was he, after all, who went on to embellish his political career under James while his opponent languished in the Tower. The graves of the two men bear witness to their divergent fortunes. Cecil is buried in a magnificent sculpted tomb in St Ethelred's Chapel, Hatfield, on which lies his white marbled gisant. Ralegh's decapitated remains are interred in a makeshift grave, which for many years remained unmarked, beneath the chancel of St Margaret's, Westminster. Cecil left extensive estates, three great houses and wealth on a scale that enabled him to establish a landed dynasty which flourishes to this day. Ralegh had Sherborne taken from him and left nothing, his family reliant on the modest pension that James allowed them by way of compensation. Cecil's glittering political career was marked by several important achievements, notably his deft handling of the succession in 1603 and the Spanish peace treaty of the following year. Ralegh's career was a catalogue of failures: he never attained high political office, his loss-making colonising ventures in Ireland and North America did not take root, while his voyages of exploration to Guiana were financially ruinous and ended in disaster.

Yet it is Ralegh's name and not Cecil's that has come down to us today. Posterity venerates him not because he represented any great cause, but because he was a man of dazzling brilliance and indomitable spirit who was eventually shipwrecked by his own visionary dreams of new worlds and undiscovered riches. And at the very end the world was reminded of his consummate skill as a dramatic artist: he wrote the script, set the stage, assured himself of an audience, and gave a performance which has stamped itself on the public imagination ever since.

As for the rest of the cast, James died unlamented just six years later at Theobalds during a violent attack of dysentery. His son, Charles I, did not marry the Infanta and was beheaded in Whitehall in 1649, only a short distance from Ralegh's place of execution. Cobham lingered on in the Tower, a sick, disconsolate and pitiful figure until his death in January 1619. Stukeley, having received over £900 from the Crown for taking charge of Ralegh and playing the role of double agent, was later convicted of clipping the coinage. He died, insane, on Lundy Island in the summer of 1620. The redoubtable Bess lived on, battling to salvage something from the financial wreckage of her husband's last voyage. She obtained some £3,000 from her share of the *Destiny*, recovered a £750 loan to the Earl of Huntingdon and, with her annuity, lived in some comfort in a large house in Broad Street. She died in 1647 at the age of 82, having by then acquired some considerable wealth, suggesting that she and her wily husband may have hidden some of their assets from James's investigators.[8]

Carew Ralegh married a wealthy young widow and, as a parliamentarian, prospered during the Commonwealth. He was killed in mysterious circumstances in 1666 at the age of 61 and buried alongside his father in St Margaret's, Westminster. In 1680 his body was disinterred and reburied in West Horsley, close to the manor he had inherited from the Throckmorton side of the family. Tradition has it that Ralegh's head, which Bess had bequeathed to her son, is buried there with Carew under the floor in the chapel of St Mary's Church.

APPENDICES

A

THE PRISONER'S DILEMMA

The 'Prisoners Dilemma' is a fundamental problem in game theory that demonstrates why two people might not co-operate, even if it is in both their interests to do so. A classical example of the dilemma is as follows:

Two suspects are arrested by the police. The police have insufficient evidence for a conviction, and, having separated both prisoners, visit each of them to offer the same deal. If one testifies for the prosecution against the other (betrays them) and the other remains silent (co-operates with the other) the betrayer goes free and the silent accomplice receives the full ten year sentence. If both remain silent, each prisoner is sentenced to only six months in jail for a minor charge. If each betrays the other, both receive a five year sentence. Each prisoner must choose to betray the other or to remain silent. Each one is assured that the other would not know about the betrayal before the end of the investigation. How should the prisoner act?

In this situation each prisoner has an incentive to betray the other, the essential point being that no matter what the other prisoner does they themselves would be better off if they choose the betrayal option rather than the co-operation option. The rational prisoner will therefore always betray his or her accomplice, with the result, in this case, that each prisoner will receive a five year sentence – longer than the six months sentence that would be imposed had they both co-operated and remained silent. The dilemma can be summarised in a simple matrix:

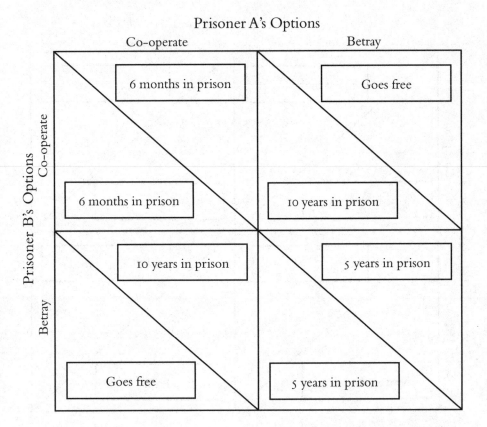

Prisoner A's Options

In the above set of choices and outcomes each prisoner, acting rationally, will betray the other but the resulting outcome for both is worse than the outcome that they would have obtained if each had remained silent. This paradox has attracted considerable interest because it shows that actions determined by self-interest are not necessarily in the group's interest and that better outcomes for all can be achieved through co-operative behaviour.

The situation facing Ralegh and Cobham was rather more complicated than in the example, but can be described roughly as follows. Each man faced execution if convicted of treason. Cobham was, however, offered his life if he betrayed Ralegh whereas Ralegh was not to be given his life if he betrayed Cobham. Nevertheless, there was a chance that if Ralegh did try to put the blame wholly on Cobham *and* Cobham did not betray him, he would escape conviction for treason and get away with a limited prison sentence.

Cecil and Coke did hot have enough evidence to charge either prisoner with treason without a confession or betrayal – or so the suspects may have believed. But it is reasonable to assume that if neither prisoner betrayed the other some lesser offence could be charged for which, say, one year in the Tower would be the punishment. The matrix of choices and outcomes for the two men were therefore as follows:

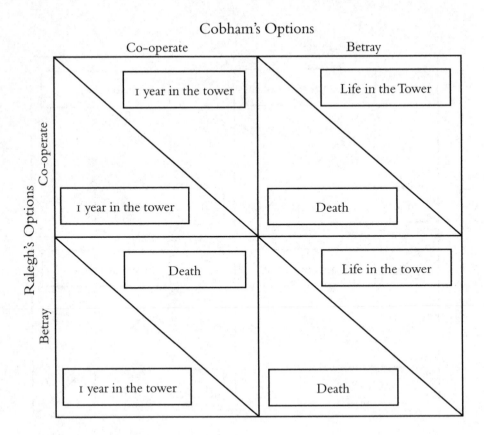

Cobham's Options

Both Cobham and Ralegh had an incentive to betray each other and initially this is what happened. In his correspondence with Cecil after his detention, Ralegh pointed the finger at Cobham. But when this correspondence was shown to Cobham the latter immediately denounced Ralegh. Crucially, by revealing to each prisoner the confessions of the other, Cecil was removing a key assumption underlying the prisoners' dilemma – that one prisoner's betrayal is not made known to the other – and thereby creating an incentive for both Cobham and Ralegh to co-operate with each other. This is because they would both now know that if they opted for betrayal this would be revealed to their accomplice who would certainly retaliate by betraying them, the outcome being life imprisonment for Cobham and death for Ralegh.

We can pinpoint the very moment at which Cobham and Ralegh realised that their best interests were served by mutual co-operation rather than betrayal. When Cobham saw the son of the lieutenant of the Tower talking to Ralegh he later remarked to him: 'I saw you with Sir Walter Ralegh – God forgive him! He has accused me but I cannot accuse him'. The Warder replied 'He doth say the like of you: that you have accused him, but he cannot accuse you.'

Thereafter, Cobham and Ralegh presented a common front of denial (insisting that the Spanish money was 'for the peace') and it was only when Cobham realised that his own earlier confessions had already fatally jeopardised his own position that he again accused his accomplice in order to save his life. Significantly, because of the a-symmetrical treatment of the two men (only Cobham being offered his life for betrayal), it was Ralegh who had the greater incentive to seek a co-operative solution, as his behaviour in desperately trying to hold Cobham to a common defensive line demonstrates.

B

EXTRACT OF LETTER FROM ROBERT CECIL TO SIR THOMAS PARRY, 4 AUGUST 1603

And now, because I doubt not but you may have heard also of other matters, and therein peradventure much hath been multiplied, you shall understand, that although the Lord Cobham was no particular actor nor contriver of this conspiracy [the Bye Plot], yet he had another iron in the fire, which, in general terms, he let fall to his brother and some others, though he used them not particularly in this project, no more than they had done him in theirs; always this being common to them all, that if one sped not, another might, so far had God blinded their eyes, when the king had no way wronged any of these by taking from them any matter of profit or credit, which ever they enjoyed. But it was not enough not to take away, because he did not suddenly give what they desired. To be short, therefore, the Lord Cobham meant to go over to the Spa, thereby to have had access to the archduke, to whom he meant to have intimated his discontentment, and withal to have represented the general disposition of others in this country on whom he would have pretended that good sums of money would have taken great hold. From thence he should have gone into Spain, and there have seen what the king would have embraced; and, at his return, he would have passed to Jersey, where Sir Walter Raleigh would have met him, and so have conferred together what course to take for advancement of those intentions which his overtures should have begot; leaving it not altogether hopeless but that some of these surprises, or some other accident in the mean time, might have happened to have saved his labour; always, if no such thing had followed in the interim, such sums of money as he could have procured the King of Spain to disburse, should have been employed *selon l'occasion*.

If now you will ask whether the Count of Aremberg had any hand in this matter, I must answer you truly, that the Lord Cobham privily resorted to him; first, to confirm former intelligence concerning the peace; and, as an argument to prepare him to believe him, if he offered any greater services, he stuck not to advertise him daily how things passed at court, with as many particulars as he could come by: what success the States had at the king's hands, or were like to have. And not three days before his commitment, he wrote to the count, in general terms, that, if he would do his master service, he should not be inveigled with conceit of peace; for, though the king had a good disposition to it, yet most of the principal counsellors were obstinate for the war; concluding that if the count would procure 4 or 500,000 crowns to be disposed as he would, he could show him a better way to prosper than by peace. To which letter, before the count could make any direct answer, the Lord Cobham was apprehended. And therefore, when you shall speak with the king, you may assure him that, whatsoever is advertised, more or less of those things is false; only the first conspirators had likewise resolved to carry the king to the Tower, to have forced him to a proclamation to justify their actions, with divers such pretences usual in such cases.

Concerning Sir Walter Ralegh's commitment, this hath been the ground. First, he hath been discontented *in conspectus omnium*, ever since the king came; and yet, for those offices which are taken from him, the king gave him £300 a year during his life, and forgave him a good arrearage of debt. Secondly, his inwardness, or rather his governing the Lord Cobham's spirit, made great suspicion that in these treasons he had his part. Whereupon, being sent for before four or five of the council, and asked of some particulars, before he was sent to prison, he w rote a letter secretly to the Lord Cobham, advising him, if he were examined of anything, to stand peremptory, and not to be afraid; for one witness could not condemn him. After which, the Lord Cobham being called in question, he did first confess his own treasons as above said; and then did absolutely, before eleven councillors, accuse Raleigh to be privy to his Spanish course, with further addition and exclamation, that he had never dealt herein but by his own incessant provocation. Whereupon he [Raleigh] was committed to the Tower, where, though he was used with all humanity, lodged and attended as well as in his own house; yet one afternoon, whilst divers of us were in the Tower examining some of these prisoners, he attempted to have murdered himself. Whereof, when we were advertised, we came to him, and found him in some agony, seeming to be unable to endure his misfortunes, and protesting innocency with carelessness of life; and, in that humour, he had wounded himself under the right pap, but no way mortally, being, in truth, rather a cut than a stab, and now very well cured, both in body and mind. What to judge of this case yet, we know not; for how voluntarily and authentically soever the Lord Cobham did, before us all, accuse him in all our hearing and most constantly; yet being newly examined, he seemeth now to clear Sir Walter in most things, and to take all the burthen to himself; so as the matter concerning the blood of a gentleman, how apparent soever it is *in foro conscientiae*, yet you may be assured, that no severity shall be used towards him, for which there shall not be sufficient proof; which is very likely there will be, notwithstanding this retraction, because it is confessed that since their being in the Tower, intelligence hath passed from one to another, wherein Raleigh expostulated his unkind using him.

C

EXTRACT OF LETTER FROM ROBERT CECIL TO SIR THOMAS PARRY, 1 DECEMBER 1603

Concerning Sir Walter Raleigh, he was brought to his trial the 17th day, at the place aforesaid. He was indicted for joining with the Lord Cobham in entertaining of another practice, to dispossess His Majesty and his royal issue of this crown, and to have set up the Lady Arabella Stuart. For better accomplishing whereof, it was said they intended to have craved the assistance of the King of Spain, and the Archduke Albert for borrowing of five or 600,000 crowns, to be bestowed here upon discontented persons, and such as should otherwise seem fit to be entertained for this purpose. And the Lord Cobham took upon him the rather to induce the King of Spain to the loan of this money (under colour of a licence, which he had obtained of the king, to travel beyond the seas), to have gone personally to the archduke, and into Spain to the king, and to have procured letters from the Lady Arabella unto them both, and to the Duke of Savoy; by which she should have promised, first, to publish a perfect peace and confederacy with them; next, to grant a toleration of Popish religion; and, thirdly, to promise not to marry herself but with the consent and good liking of them three.

Furthermore, Sir Walter was accused to have dealt with the Lord Cobham for an invasion to be made in England from Spain: all which accusations Sir Walter Raleigh diffidently denied, and did as much as wit of man could advise to clear himself. Yet the accusation of the Lord Cobham being of that nature, as it implied the accusing of his own self withal, (than which kind of proof the law regardeth none greater) he was found guilty of treason upon that accusation, with other circumstances precedent and subsequent. For, although the Lord Cobham did retract his former accusation, yet that was upon intelligence in the Tower betwixt him and Sir Walter Raleigh, who got a letter for testimony of his own innocency under the Lord Cobham's hand, which would have swayed the jury much, if the Lord Cobham had not, the night before Sir Walter's arraignment, laid open how Sir Walter practised for that letter by one Harvey, a son of the now lieutenant, accusing him freshly of being an instigator of him to deal with the Count Aremberg for a pension of

£1500 a year only to be a spy for Spain, if the peace went not forward. Which, when Sir Walter heard, notwithstanding many of his former denials, that he never knew the Lord Cobham Spanishly affected in any thing, he had no other evasion, but confessed at the bar, that the Lord Cobham indeed moved that to him, but not he to the Lord Cobham.

You shall also understand that, at the first beginning, before ever the Lord Cobham was suspected, Sir Walter, having been examined only about himself, immediately wrote a letter to the Lord Cobham, that he had been examined upon him; and that he had cleared him to the Lords, wishing him to be wary; if he were examined to remember that one witness could not overthrow him: which being done before ever Lord Cobham was called in question, and being added to the accusation of the Lord Cobham, was argument that Raleigh's denials of other things were also false. Besides, it may be remembered, upon Raleigh's first commitment to the Tower, how suspiciously he carried himself in offering to stab himself with a knife, as heretofore you have heard.

The Friday after the Lord Cobham was arraigned before thirty-one of the peers, the lord chancellor sitting as high steward. He denied then, that Raleigh was privy to his purpose to go into Spain; and, for the matter of money to be gotten for discontented persons, he confessed it was a conceit of his own thoughts, never communicated to any, but died in him almost as soon as it was harboured in his mind, though he did reveal it to the lords of the council, when they examined him about other matters. Concerning the setting up of the Lady Arabella, he fastened it upon his brother, George Brooke. And for Sir Walter Raleigh, though he confessed that in many things he had done him wrong, yet he maintained still the pension sought for by him: and withal that Sir Walter moved to solicit Aremberg to persuade the King of Spain to send an army into Milford Haven. For, being privy to the undutiful speeches of the king, where-with he was also charged, as namely, that it would never be well in England, till the king and his cubs, meaning his royal issue, were taken away; he took damnation upon him if ever he thought such a matter.

D

Extract from Sir Edward Coke's Prosecution Document[1]

The course of proof to be observed in the evidence against Sir Walter Ralegh

Wherein it is to be agreed that the matter to be objected against him is matter of treason, which requireth not that direct and precise proof as is requisite in other actions of honest and lawful nature, for four general reasons:

First, for that the matter now to be discovered is in his nature treason, whereunto honest witnesses are never called to testimony as in other lawful actions they are, and therefore condemnation will seldom or never be if it may not be without honest and direct testimony

Secondly, for that it is a work (as all other criminal offences are) of darkness and practised in obscurity, and therefore requireth not that clearness of proof as honest works of light do

Thirdly, for that it is of that vile and horrible nature in the sight of men and so capitally dangerous to the practisers that they ever bend the spirit of their wits to secrete and conceal it, and therefore both law and reason alloweth violent concurring presumptions for concluding proof

Fourthly, for that the nature of this unlawful offence (excluding all lawful testimony) the law alloweth the approvement or accusation of a co-offender to be as strong as an indictment by the oath of twelve jurors

There is also a particular reason in this particular case to be observed and drawn from the person of the offender:

Who is Sir Walter Ralegh? A man by nature of an extraordinary wit, and thereby the better furnished to shadow his misdoing

Secondly, a man of too much more than ordinary policy, and thereby the better provided to prevent the discovery of his secret unlawful purposes

13 August, Cobham's confession: Thirdly, out of his own false doctrine (being in this his deceiving devil) preached to his unhappy disciple the Lord Cobham, which was that one witness could never hurt him

The course of the proof against him consisteth in three parts, the first direct proof, the second inferences, the third violent concurring circumstances

First, the proof:

The discovery whereof grew, first out of Cobham's confession moved by a letter of Ralegh's written to the lords in these words: 'If your honours apprehend the merchant of St Hellens the stranger will know that all is discovered of him, which perchance you desire to conceal for some time; all the danger will be lest the merchant fly away, if any man know any more of the Lord Cobham, I think he trusted George Wiet of Kent.'

Which letter being showed Cobham by the Lords, he at his second reading of it, suspecting that Ralegh had discovered the matter, said: 'Oh wretch, oh traitor', iterating the same three or four times, and then said: 'I will tell you all truly', and thereupon accused both himself and Ralegh as followeth:

20 July: The Lord Chief Justice's certificate that upon Cobham's second view of Ralegh's letter, Cobham break out into these passions: 'Oh Wretch, oh Traitor', iterating the same three or four times, and then said: 'I will tell you all truly', confessing his purpose was to go into Flanders and into Spain, and spake of getting five or six hundred thousand crowns, and that he and Ralegh agreed to meet in Jersey upon his coming out of Spain, and then they would take the advantage of the discontentments of the people, and thereupon resolve what was to be done

20 July: The Lords' certificate that at Cobham's first beginning of his speech he breathed out many exclamations and oaths against Ralegh, calling him traitor and affirming that he was privy to this purpose, and that he had never entered into this course but by his instigation, and that he would never let him alone, which accusation if it stand true, then consequently it followeth Ralegh is guilty

Which direct accusation is strongly approved by these reasons following:

First, what colour of cause should move Cobham jointly to accuse himself and Ralegh of high treason, ruinating thereby his own honour, life and estate, except they thereof were guilty, against whom before that his confession nothing was proved?

Secondly, Ralegh was as dear to Cobham as his hand and his heart and therefore it was not the accusation of an enemy but of a avowed and dearly beloved friend

Thirdly, Cobham by accusing Ralegh seeketh not to excuse himself, but by the same his accusation condemneth himself guilty of the self same treason

If it be objected that this accusation of Cobham's grew out of sudden passion upon his perusal of Ralegh's letter, conceiving thereby that Ralegh had accused him, it is fully answered thus:

First, what colour of occasion was there that Cobham should doubt that Ralegh had accused him, except he knew cause whereof Ralegh could accuse him?

Secondly, is it to be imagined that Cobham's sudden mislike of Ralegh should occasion [him to accuse] himself and Ralegh falsely of treason, and thereby to overthrow himself to be revenged of Ralegh?

Thirdly, the several circumstances of Cobham's accusation stand confirmed by the proofs following, which violently argueth the same to proceed out of truth, though discovered in passion

George Brooke 23 August; Watson 22 and 23 August: Fourthly, to take away all shadow of doubt that the matter whereof Cobham accused Ralegh was not then out of sudden passion devised, it standeth plainly proved that Cobham two months before had discovered the same unto George Brooke, and Brooke to Markham and Watson, as they all three confessed

Which direct accusation is also secondly approved by these circumstances following:

First out of the nature of the offence and quality of the person

The nature of the treason is violent and bloody, and not to be executed but by the sword and arms, Cobham of himself is neither of the sword nor ever professed arms, and therefore it [is] probable (as he affirmeth) that Ralegh being a man of both was the inciter of him thereunto as he confesseth

Secondly, these treasons could not be either plotted or performed but out of an extraordinary wit and policy, but Cobham of himself is far from them, but Ralegh owner of them all, and therefore more probable that these treasons as Cobham affirmeth are arrows drawn out of Ralegh's quiver rather than of his own, he wanting both the motive and the means thereof

Thirdly, the long known and approved inward affections and passages between Cobham and Ralegh strongly presumeth that Cobham neither could not would attempt things of this high nature without the privity and advice of Ralegh, whom he held his second self, of whose love, fidelity, wit and policy he had so great an opinion and belief

Fourthly, George Brooke affirmeth and so it seemeth true that he was not in this treasons until they were determined and agreed on, and then is it not probable that all these several treasons could or should both proceed, be plotted and performed by Cobham only, which if Ralegh be not therein, then it so followeth for anything yet appearing no other person being touched therewith?

The third course to approve Cobham's accusation to be true is to be drawn out of the concurrence in circumstances between Cobham and Ralegh himself:

20 July Lords' certificate: First, Cobham confesseth he was to travel to the archduke, from thence to Spain for the money, for that archduke was but poor and from thence to return to Jersey to Sir Walter Ralegh, until which time that he so there met with Ralegh nothing should be done, but thereupon the rest of the proceedings should have followed for the distribution of the money according to the occasions and opportunity which the discontentments in England should have afforded in that time

2 August Ralegh in his declaration: Ralegh in his examination confesseth that it was agreed that Cobham from Spain should return to Jersey to him

Secondly, Cobham in his later declaration under his hand confesseth and sayeth that the money was to be employed as the discontentments of England which he expected, should occasion, and so the said money to be employed as time and occasion was offered

Ralegh confesseth he was to have ten thousand crowns of the money

Whereby it followeth he was to have it for the purpose declared by Cobham both in his first and last declaration

Although he sayeth he was to have it for procuring of peace, whereof as there is no probability, so it appeareth as aforesaid manifestly untrue, except the peace he meaneth that George Brooke 19 July confesseth was meant to be promised to the King of Spain by the Lady Arabella's letters, which Cobham practiced from her to procure, which if so then his words stand true, and yet he guilty of the treason

23 August: Thirdly, Cobham affirmeth Ralegh delivered him a book written against his Majesty's title and his line to the crown, after Ralegh returned from the king, which George Brooke explaineth to be fortnight before his apprehension

24 August: Ralegh confesseth his having the book, but what became of it he knoweth not

So that although Ralegh denieth the main yet he confesseth and agreeth with Cobham's accusation in the material circumstances

The fourth course of proof is drawn out of these inferences and circumstances following:

19 July: First Renzi confesseth that he carried four several letters from Cobham to Aremberg, and like letters from Aremberg to Cobham, that Ralegh one night supped with Cobham, and Cobham late in that evening brought Ralegh from the Blackfriars to Durham House being only accompanied with Renzi, and from thence Cobham returned with Renzi (only) secretly to St Mary Overies to Aremberg's lodging, and was brought up a back way in the night time

That at another time when he delivered letters to Cobham from Aremberg, whereby Aremberg promised the money aforesaid, Ralegh was present, and Cobham and he went with the letter up into a chamber privately, and left him below and alone

Whereby it is strongly to be conceived that Cobham did not conceal from Ralegh the cause of his so secret going to Aremberg and the contents of the letter promising the money

23 August: Secondly, George Brooke confesseth that Cobham told him that the Lord Grey and Brooke were but upon the Bye, but he and Sir Walter were upon the Main, whereby was meant the taking away the King and his issue by Cobham and Ralegh

Which words he at several times related to Watson the priest as Watson also confesseth 22 and 23 August

20 July, the Lords' report: Thirdly Cobham confesseth in these words, he was of long time doubtful of Ralegh lest he should betray him, and for proof thereof he told a friend of his not long ago that he thought sometimes that when Ralegh had him in Jersey he would send him to the King

13 August: And in his later confession being examined who that friend was, he answered it was himself, and for Ralegh's betraying him to the King he thinketh he said so to George Brooke

Whereby it necessarily followeth that Ralegh did know and was acquainted with Cobham's treasons, or else there was no colour of cause why Cobham should fear Ralegh's betraying of him, for except he knew he could not betray

13 August: Fourthly, Cobham confesseth that Keymis brought him a letter from Ralegh, but had torn the words of the Lords of the Council out thereof wherein was contained that he had been before the Lords and was asked divers questions of his lordship, but he had cleared him in all, whereas in truth the lords will affirm he was never asked one question of Cobham, but it seemeth he wrote the same to assure Cobham he neither had nor would accuse him

13 August: And also confesseth that with the same letter he received a message by Keymis from Ralegh, which was that one witness could not hurt him, and therefore Keymis wished him not to be dismayed

Whereby it appeareth probable that Ralegh endeavoured to settle in him a resolution that he had excused him and then although that Brooke the third actor in this traitorous tragedy (for more than they three it appeareth not) should accuse him, yet his testimony being but one could not hurt him, otherwise there was no cause moving that message

13 August: Fifthly there appeareth there passed secret intelligence and advertisements between Cobham and Ralegh, for as soon as Copley was apprehended, Ralegh thereof advertised Cobham, and as soon

13 August: as himself was stayed he forthwith informed Cobham, with directions as aforesaid, but the letter was resent by Cobham and by Ralegh burned, whereby it appeareth it was not convenient for them to have it seen

19 July: and as soon as Cobham was stayed, he instantly and secretly informed Ralegh

Lastly, Ralegh's purpose and attempt to murder himself, strongly presumeth the guiltiness of his own conscience, for so the civil law construeth the same.

These observations are also to be noted:

20 July, the Lords report: That Cobham at the time he accused Ralegh seeing Sir Arthur Gorges used these words as an argument that he would as well clear the innocent as accuse the offender, he cleared Sir Arthur Gorges for that they never durst trust him (which they was himself and Ralegh)

20 July, the Lords report: Cobham confessed he was to present to the Archduke overtures, and to advertise how he did accept of them, to whom should he so advertise but unto Ralegh?

NOTES

Introduction Brought to Bay

1   Edward Edwards, *The Life of Sir Walter Ralegh*, (MacMillan, London, 1868), Vol. I,
    p. 386
2   4 July, Institute of Historical Research, Hatfield State Papers,
3   D. Jardine, *Criminal Trials* (1832–5), Vol. I, p. 401

1 Sir Walter Ralegh

1   Ralegh has attracted numerous biographers but among the most important works
    are Edward Edwards, *The Life of Sir Walter Ralegh*, 2 volumes (MacMillan, London,
    1868); William Stebbing, *Sir Walter Ralegh* (Oxford, 1891); Robert Lacey, *Sir Walter
    Ralegh* (Phoenix Press, London, 1973); and Raleigh Trevelyan, *Sir Walter Raleigh*
    (London, 2002)
2   Lacey, *Sir Walter Ralegh*, p. 37
3   Ibid., p. 39
4   Trevelyan, *Sir Walter Raleigh*, p. 46
5   Id.
6   Letter of 5 June 1573, in Harris Nicolas, *Memoirs of the Life and Times of Sir
    Christopher Hatton* (London, 1847), p. 26
7   Trevelyan, *Sir Walter Raleigh*, p. 52
8   Stebbing, *Sir Walter Ralegh*, p. 36
9   Edwards, *The Life of Sir Walter Ralegh*, Vol. I, p. 84
10 Oliver Lawson Dick (ed), John Aubrey, *Brief Lives* (London, 1972), p. 416
11 Mark Nicholls and Penry Williams, 'Sir Walter Ralegh', in *Oxford Dictionary of
    National Biography*, p. 4
12 Aubrey, *Brief Lives*, p. 417
13 Ibid., p. 420
14 Trevelyan, *Sir Walter Raleigh*, p. 354
15 Ruth McIntyre, 'William Sanderson: Elizabethan Financier of Discovery', *William
    and Mary Quarterly* (1944), Vol. 13.2, p. 194

16 For a biographical portrait of the feisty Lady Ralegh see Anna Beer, *Bess: the Life of Lady Ralegh, wife to Sir Walter* (Constable, London, 2004)

17 Gerald Hammond (ed), *Sir Walter Ralegh, Selected Writings* (1984), p. 34

18 Edwards, *The Life of Sir Walter Ralegh,* Vol. II, p. 46

19 Hammond, *Selected Writings,* p. 38

20. For Ralegh's own financial calculations regarding the Madre de Dios see Edwards, *The Life of Sir Walter Ralegh,* Vol. II, pp. 67–69; 75–78

21 Hammond, *Selected Writings,* p. 38

22 Nicholls and Williams, 'Sir Walter Ralegh', p. 11

23 John Shirley, 'Sir Walter Ralegh's Guiana Finances', *Huntington Library Quarterly* (1937), Vol. 13, pp. 59–61

24 Ibid., p. 57

25 Lacey, *Sir Walter Ralegh,* p. 232

26 Stebbing, *Sir Walter Ralegh,* p. 165

27 Shirley, 'Guiana Finances', pp. 59–69

28 Lacey, *Sir Walter Ralegh,* p. 112

2 Sir Robert Cecil

1 P.M. Handover, *The Second Cecil: The Rise to Power 1563–1604 of Sir Robert Cecil, later First Earl of Salisbury* (London, 1959), p. 5

2 Ibid., pp. 42–3

3 Stowe MSS 143.14, British Library

4 Handover, *The Second Cecil,* p. 69

5 Ibid., p. 57

6 Francis Bacon (Viscount St Alban), *The Essays or Counsels Civil and Moral of Francis Lord Verulam* (London, 1625; reprinted Macmillan, 1883), pp. 178–9

7 Thomas Birch, *The Court and Times of James the First* (London, 1848), Vol. I, p. 214

8 Handover, *The Second Cecil,* p. 34

9 Ibid., p. 79

10 Ibid., p. 126

11 Catherine Bowen, *The Lion and the Throne: the Life and Times of Sir Edward Coke 1552–1634* (London, 1957), p. 69

12 Handover, *The Second Cecil,* pp. 80–1

13 Ibid., p. 152

14 Bowen, *The Lion and the Throne,* p. 105

15 Handover, *The Second Cecil,* p. 191

16 Thomas Birch, *Memoirs of the Reign of Queen Elizabeth, from the Year 1581 till her death* (London, 1754; reprinted General Books, 2009), Section 9, pp. 68–9

17 Id.

18 Alan Haynes, *Robert Cecil, First Earl of Salisbury* (London, 1989), p. 39

19 Handover, *The Second Cecil,* p. 278

20 Birch, *Memoirs,* Section 15, p. 149

21 T.B. Howell et al (eds), *A Complete Collection of State Trials* (1816–28) Vol. II, p. 205

22 Bowen, *The Lion and the Throne,* p. 135

23 Ibid., p. 284

24 Handover, *The Second Cecil,* p. 227

25 Lawrence Stone, *Family and Fortune: Studies in Aristocratic Finance in the Sixteenth and Seventeenth Centuries* (Clarendon Press, 1973), p. 12

26 Ibid., p. 22

27   Ibid., p. 14
28   Ibid., p. 15
29   Haynes, *Robert Cecil*, p. 79
30   Ibid., pp. 177–180
31   Stone, *Family and Fortune*, p. 27
32   Haynes, *Robert Cecil*, p. 73
33   Stone, *Family and Fortune*, p. 32
34   Bacon, *Essays*, pp. 207–8

3 Shifting Alliances

1   Handover, *The Second Cecil*, p. 73
2   Letter to Lord Treasurer Burghley, 12 May 1583, in Edwards, *The Life of Sir Walter Ralegh*, Vol. II, pp. 21–2
3   Letter to Sir Robert Cecil, 10 March 1592, in ibid., p. 46
4   Edwards, *The Life of Sir Walter Ralegh*, Vol. I, p. 138
5   Letter to Cecil, July 1592, in ibid Vol. II, p. 51
6   Ibid., Vol. I, p. 151
7   Ibid., p. 154
8   Id.
9   Id.
10   Letter to Cecil, 10 May 1593, in Edwards, *The Life of Sir Walter Ralegh*, Vol. II, p. 80
11   Letter to Cecil, 20 Sept 1594, in ibid., p. 100
12   Lacey, *Sir Walter Ralegh*, p. 226
13   Letter to Cecil, in Edwards, *The Life of Sir Walter Ralegh*, Vol. II, pp. 161–2
14   Beer, *Bess*, p. 109
15   Ibid., p. 128
16   Id.
17   Beer, *Bess*, p. 107
18   Edwards, *The Life of Sir Walter Ralegh*, Vol. I, p. 226
19   Letter to Cecil, 6 July 1597, in ibid., Vol II, pp. 169–70
20   Lacey, *Sir Walter Ralegh*, p. 244
21   Handover, *The Second Cecil*, p. 156
22   Id.
23   Ibid., p. 166
24   Ibid., p. 182
25   Ibid., p. 193
26   Letter to Cecil, undated *c.* 1600, in Edwards, *The Life of Sir Walter Ralegh*, Vol. II, pp. 222–3
27   Stebbing, *Sir Walter Ralegh*, p. 148
28   Letter to Cecil, August 1601, in Edwards, *The Life of Sir Walter Ralegh*, Vol. II, pp. 226–7
29   Handover, *The Second Cecil*, p. 219
30   Letter to Sir George Carew, June 1601, in *Camden Society* (1864), p. 85
31   Memorandum from Howard to Cecil, Spring 1602, in Edwards, *The Life of Sir Walter Ralegh*, Vol. II, p. 439
32   Handover, *The Second Cecil*, p. 247
33   Letter to Sir George Carew, 30 June 1602, in *Camden Society* (1864), p. 116

4 Preparing for the Great Day of Mart

1   Handover, *The Second Cecil*, p. 232
2   Ibid., p. 235
3   Ibid., p. 236
4   Ibid., p. 238
5   Birch, *Memoirs*, p. 569
6   Handover, *The Second Cecil*, p. 239
7   Ibid., pp. 239–40
8   Memorandum from Howard to Cecil, 1602, in Edwards, *The Life of Sir Walter Ralegh*, Vol. II, pp. 436–44
9   Ibid., p. 440
10   Id.
11   Ibid., p. 443
12   Ibid., p. 444
13   Id.
14   Howard to Mar, 4 June 1602, in *The secret correspondence of Sir Robert Cecil with James VI, King of Scotland* (Edinburgh, 1766), p. 127
15   James to Howard, May 1602, in ibid., p. 116
16   Howard to Bruce, 4 Dec 1601, in ibid., p. 50
17   Howard to James, 24 August 1602, in ibid., p. 168; 195
18   Howard to Bruce, 4 Dec 1601, in ibid., p. 29
19   Howard to Bruce, April 1602, in ibid., p. 68
20   Id.
21   Howard to Bruce, April 1602, in ibid., p. 88
22   Howard to Bruce, 1 May 1602, in ibid., pp. 107–8
23   Howard to Mar, 4 June 1602, in ibid., p. 125
24   Handover, *The Second Cecil*, pp. 277–8
25   Edwards, *The Life of Sir Walter Ralegh*, Vol. I, pp. 313–4
26   Handover, *The Second Cecil*, p. 249
27   Howard to Bruce, 4 Dec 1601, in *The secret correspondence of Sir Robert Cecil with James VI, King of Scotland* (Edinburgh, 1766), p. 47
28   Id.
29   Id.
30   Ibid., pp. 49–50
31   Ibid., p. 45
32   Ibid., p. 52
33   Handover, *The Second Cecil*, p. 285
34   A.L. Rowse, *Ralegh and the Throckmortons* (Macmillan, London, 1962), p. 232
35   Edwards, *The Life of Sir Walter Ralegh*, Vol. II, pp. 252–3
36   Ibid., Vol. I, p. 336
37   Ibid., p. 335

5 The Death of a Queen

1   J.B. Black, *The Reign of Elizabeth* (Oxford, 1936), p. 194
2   Birch, *Memoirs*, pp. 556–7
3   Ibid., p. 557
4   Ibid., p. 558
5   Bowen, *The Lion and the Throne*, p. 151

6   Handover, *The Second Cecil*, p. 295
7   Ibid., p. 296
8   Samuel Gardiner, *History of England from the Accession of James I to the Outbreak of the Civil War, 1603–1642* (Longmore, London, 1905), p. 84
9   Bowen, *The Lion and the Throne*, p. 152
10 Handover, *The Second Cecil*, p. 299
11 Beer, *Bess*, p. 141
12 Bowen, *The Lion and the Throne*, pp. 153–4
13 John Stow, *Annales* (1631), p. 815
14 Stebbing, *Sir Walter Ralegh*, p. 181
15 Edwards, *The Life of Sir Walter Ralegh*, Vol. I, p. 363
16 Id.
17 John Chamberlain to Dudley Carleton, 30 March 1603, in Birch, *The Court and Times*, p. 5
18 John Chamberlain to Dudley Carleton, 12 April 1603, in ibid., p. 7
19 Edwards, *The Life of Sir Walter Ralegh*, Vol. I, p. 357
20 Ibid., p. 358
21 Memorandum to Cecil, in *The Life of Sir Walter Ralegh*, Vol. II, p. 441
22 Ibid., Vol. I, p. 358

6 The Lion Provoked

1   Birch, *The Court and Times*, p. 8
2   Edwards, *The Life of Sir Walter Ralegh*, Vol. I, p. 363
3   Gardiner, *History of England*, p. 95
4   Stebbing, *Sir Walter Ralegh*, p. 182
5   Gardiner, *History of England*, p. 102
6   Handover, *The Second Cecil*, p. 300
7   Letter to Cecil, 7 April 1603, Hatfield Papers
8   Edwards, *The Life of Sir Walter Ralegh*, Vol. II, p. 263
9   Letter to Egerton, 8 June 1603, in ibid, p. 265
10 Ibid., pp. 269–70
11 Egerton Papers, in *Camden Society* (1840), p. 380.
12 Undated letter to the lords of the council from The Tower, in Edwards, *The Life of Sir Walter Ralegh*, Vol. II, pp. 298–300

7 Treason: The Raptor strikes

1   Letter from John Chamberlain to Dudley Carleton, 30 March 1603, in Birch, *The Court and Times*, p. 1–2
2   For the Priests' plot, also known as the 'Bye plot', see Mark Nicholls, 'Treason's Reward: the punishment of conspirators in the Bye plot of 1603', *The Historical Journal* (38:4, 1995), pp. 821–42; Mark Nicholls, 'Two Winchester Trials: The Prosecution of Henry Lord Cobham and Thomas Lord Grey of Wilton, 1603', *Institute of Historical Research* (Feb., 1995), pp. 26–48; Francis Edwards, *The Succession, Bye and Main Plots of 1601–1603* (Four Courts Press, 2006), pp. 157–96
3   Nicholls, 'Two Winchester Trials', p. 39
4   Id.
5   Nicholls, 'Treason's Reward', p. 831

6   Jardine, *Criminal Trials*, Vol. I, p. 434

7   Patrick Tytler, *Life of Sir Walter Raleigh* (Edinburgh, 1833), p. 449

8   Edwards, *The Succession, Bye and Main Plots*, p. 184

9   Ibid., p. 236

10   Public Record Office: PRO SP 14/2/64

11   Public Record Office: PRO SP 14/2/55

12   Public Record Office: PRO SP 13/2/56

13   Cobham's attempt to communicate covertly with Aremberg got off to a false start. Just after the count's arrival in London Cobham asked his servant, Matthew Questor, to inform Aremberg that he wished to see him but Questor returned saying that the count would only see him by official appointment notified to Cecil. Cobham then dismissed Questor angrily and went off with Ralegh who was waiting 'in the outer chamber'. Presumably Aremberg was only prepared to communicate secretly through his own trusted agent, La Renzi. 'July' 1603, in Hatfield State Papers

14   Public Record Office: PRO SP 14/2/65

15   Edwards describes this last act of courtiership in *Life of Sir Walter Ralegh*, Vol. I, p. 367

16   *The Arraignment and Conviction of Sir Walter Ralegh*, copied by Sir Thomas Overbury (1648), p. 14

17   Howell, *State Trials*, Vol. II, p. 216

18   Birch, *The Court and Times*, p. 13

19   Mark Nicholls, 'Sir Walter Ralegh's Treason: A Prosecution Document', *English Historical Review* (Vol. 100, 1995) p. 922

20   Birch, *The Court and Times*, p. 12

21   Edwards, *The Succession, Bye and Main Plots*, p. 210

22   Ibid., p.209

23   Nicholls, 'Sir Walter Ralegh's Treason', p. 915

24   Edwards, *The Succession, Bye and Main Plots*, p. 233

25   Jardine, *Criminal Trials*, p. 397

26   Cobham said he burned his letters from Aremberg which, if true, meant that any surviving correspondence had been intercepted. In ibid., p. 467

27   Jardine, *Criminal Trials*, p. 433

28   This letter to Cecil, a key piece of evidence referred to by the prosecution at Ralegh's trial, was never produced, suggesting that it may have referred to Cecil's private questioning of Ralegh about Cobham, Aremberg and La Renzi whose disclosure would be embarrassing to the secretary. In ibid., p.412

29   Ibid., p. 919

30   Letter of 9 November 1605, in Edwards, *The Life of Sir Walter Ralegh*, Vol. II, p. 388

31   Jardine, *Criminal Trials*, p. 412

32   Ibid., p. 425

33   We may be sure that this examination took place at Richmond because in his subsequent confession of 29 July, Cobham begins by saying 'Mindful of that faithful promise I made unto your Lordships at my last being at Richmond' he will now tell all he knows. In Public Record Office: PRO SP/14/294. The implication is that the statement in Levinus Munck's diary, that Cobham was sent to the Tower on 18 July, may be in error – unless Cobham was taken downriver from the Tower to Richmond on the following two days. In Levinus Munck, 'The Journal of Levinus Munck', *English Historical Review* (Vol. XVIII, 1953), p. 244

34   Nicholls, 'Sir Walter Ralegh's Treason', pp. 914–15

35   Edwards, *The Life of Sir Walter Ralegh*, Vol. II, pp. 449–50

36 According to the diary of Cecil's secretary, Levinus Munck, the prisoners in the Tower were examined on 27 July. See Munck, 'The Journal of', p. 245
37 Public Record Office: PRO SP 14/2/94
38 Jardine, *Criminal Trials*, p. 422
39 Birch, *The Court and Times*, p. 12
40 Id., this could be interpreted as an oblique reference to Aremberg's response being intercepted
41 Ibid., p.13
42 Id.
43 Edwards, *The Life of Sir Walter Ralegh*, Vol. I, pp. 376–7

8 Holding the Line

1   Jardine, *Criminal Trials*, p. 412
2   Edwards, *The Life of Sir Walter Ralegh*, Vol. I, p. 373
3   Ibid., p. 381
4   According to Cecil, Cobham said that he and Ralegh were in daily communication. In ibid., p. 243
5   Public Record Office: PRO SP 14/3/24
6   Jardine, *Criminal Trials*, p. 425
7   Howell, *State Trials*, Vol. II, p. 218
8   It is clear from Cobham's outburst on 20 July that he did not altogether trust Ralegh. He said he was afraid that if he returned by Jersey 'Ralegh would then have had him in his power, and have delivered him and the money to the King'. In Jardine, *Criminal Trials*, p. 415
9   Edwards, *The Life of Sir Walter Ralegh*, Vol. II, p. 485
10 Jardine, *Criminal Trials*, p. 447
11 Ibid., p. 448
12 This correspondence is set out in full in ibid., pp. 437–441
13 Ibid., p. 440
14 Edwards, *The Succession, Bye and Main Plots*, p.238
15 October 1603, Hatfield State Papers
16 Edwards, *The Succession, Bye and Main Plots*, p. 238
17 Ibid., p. 232
18 Stebbing, *Sir Walter Ralegh*, pp. 194–5
19 Birch, *The Court and Times*, p. 13
20 Edwards, *The Life of Sir Walter Ralegh*, Vol. II, pp. 381–7
21 23 July 1603, Hatfield State Papers
22 Birch, *The Court and Times*, p. 13
23 Agnes Latham, (ed), *The Letters of Sir Walter Ralegh* (University of Exeter Press, 1999), pp. 257–8

9 Preparing for the Trial

1   John Bellamy, *The Tudor Law of Treason* (Routledge, London, 1979), p. 9
2   Gardiner, *History of England*, p. 126
3   Bellamy, *The Tudor Law of Treason*, p. 156
4   Ibid., p. 66
5   Ibid., p. 161

6   Annabel Patterson, (ed), *The Trial of Nicholas Throckmorton* (Toronto, 1998), p. 21;
     from Raphael Hollinshead, *The Chronicles of England, Scotland and Ireland* (London,
     1587)

7   This estimate is based on treason trials during a sample period of 1532–40, when
     there were thirty-two acquittals out of 600 arraignments. In Bellamy, *The Tudor
     Law of Treason*, p. 171

8   Edwards, *The Life of Sir Walter Ralegh*, Vol. I, p. 377

9   4 May 1603, Hatfield State Papers

10   Jardine, *Criminal Trials*, p. 415. According to Howell, *State Trials*, p. 217, Cobham, in
     his 'second examination': '... being required to subscribe to an examination, there
     was showed a note under Sir Walter's hand ...'

11   A note to Cobham's 17 July examination states that the examiners warned him
     that 'the Lord Chief Justice before his Majesty did absolutely deliver his opinion,
     that it is a high contempt in his lordship or any other man [not] to subscribe
     such answers ... to such interrogatories as by his Majesty's appointment shall be
     demanded of him or any party'. In Public Record Office: PRO SP 14/2/56

12   Nicholls, 'Two Winchester Trials', p. 40

13   Nicholls, 'Sir Walter Ralegh's Treason', pp. 902–25

14   Ibid., p. 918

15   Ibid., p. 919

16   Ibid., p. 918

17   Id.

18   Ibid., p. 920

19   Id.

20   Patterson, *The Trial of Nicholas Throckmorton*, p. 46

21   Ibid., p. 59

22   Ibid., p. 64

23   Ibid., p. 72

24   Jardine, *Criminal Trials*, p. 418

25   Hill favours the two witness rule, in L.M. Hill, 'The Two-Witness Rule in
     English Treason Trials: Some Comments on the Emergence of Procedural Law',
     American Journal of Legal History (Vol. XII, 1968), pp. 110–111; whereas Bellamy
     supports Popham's view that this did not apply in Ralegh's case, in Bellamy, *The
     Tudor Law of Treason*, p. 157

26   The lawyers decided that for indictments brought under any post-1352 treason
     act two witnesses were required, but that if the offence were within the act of
     1352 such witnesses were not necessary. In the event, this was the interpretation
     of the law followed by the Lord Chief Justice at Ralegh's trial. In Bellamy, *The
     Tudor Law of Treason*, p. 77

27   Jardine, *Criminal Trials*, p. 413

28   Ibid., p. 414

29   Id.

30   Edwards, *The Succession, Bye and Main Plots*, p. 235

31   Jardine, *Criminal Trials*, p. 438

32   Edwards, *The Succession, Bye and Main Plots*, p. 235

33   Ibid., p. 260

34   Ibid., p. 236

35   Ibid., p. 269

36   Public Record Office: PRO SP 14/4/38. I

37   Jardine, *Criminal Trials*, p. 438

38   Edwards, *The Succession, Bye and Main Plots*, p. 233

39 Ibid., p. 234
40 Ibid., p. 265
41 Ibid., p. 254

10 The Trial

1 Howell, *State Trials*, p. 213
2 Jardine, *Criminal Trials*, p. 404
3 Sir Edward Coke, *Institutes of the Laws of England* (M. Flesher, London, 1644), pp. 25–6
4 Jardine, *Criminal Trials*, p. 406
5 Ibid., p. 410
6 Howell, *State Trials*, p. 216
7 See, for instance, Edwards, *The Life of Sir Walter Ralegh*, Vol. I, p. 272
8 Nicholls, 'Sir Walter Ralegh's Treason', pp. 914–16; 919; 921
9 Jardine, *Criminal Trials*, p. 415
10 Contrast Jardine, *Criminal Trials*, p. 416, and Howell, *State Trials*, p. 217
11 Howell, *State Trials*, p. 217
12 Jardine, *Criminal Trials*, p. 463
13 Id.
14 Ibid., p. 418
15 Id.
16 Ibid., p. 419
17 Ibid., p. 420
18 Id.
19 Ibid., p. 421
20 Ibid., pp. 421–2
21 Ibid., p. 429
22 Howell, *State Trials*, p. 221
23 Jardine, *Criminal Trials*, pp. 434–5
24 Ibid., p. 435
25 Id.
26 Howell, *State Trials*, p. 427
27 Jardine, *Criminal Trials*, p. 427
28 Howell, *State Trials*, p. 225
29 Jardine, *Criminal Trials*, p. 436
30 Edwards, *The Succession, Bye and Main Plots*, p. 257
31 James Fitzjames Stephen, *History of the Criminal Law of England* (Macmillan, London, 1883), p. 333
32 Edwards, *The Succession, Bye and Main Plots*, p. 257
33 Jardine, *Criminal Trials*, p. 466
34 Id.
35 Id.
36 Munck, 'The Journal of', p. 247
37 Jardine, *Criminal Trials*, p. 443
38 Ibid., p. 445
39 Ibid., p. 446
40 Id.
41 Ibid., p. 449
42 Ibid., pp. 450–1
43 Howell, *State Trials*, p. 225

44   Ibid., pp. 225–6
45   Munck, 'The Journal of', p. 247
46   Jardine, *Criminal Trials*, p. 452
47   Ibid., pp. 453–5

11 Was he Guilty?

1   Birch, *The Court and Times*, p. 19
2   Ibid., p. 16
3   Ibid., p. 13
4   Ibid., p. 17
5   Jardine, *Criminal Trials*, p. 416
6   Birch, *The Court and Times*, pp. 16–17
7   In this letter Ralegh said that in the light of Cobham's new accusation the lords now knew that the original accusations – for which he was committed, indicted and arraigned – were false. See Edwards, *The Life of Sir Walter Ralegh*, Vol. II, pp. 274–7
8   Jardine, *Criminal Trials*, p. 463
9   Stebbing, *Sir Walter Ralegh*, p. 206
10   Jardine, *Criminal Trials*, p. 517
11   Gardiner, *History of England*, p. 89
12   Jardine, *Criminal Trials*, p. 450
13   Ibid., p. 425
14   Edwards, *The Life of Sir Walter Ralegh*, Vol. I, p. 359; Vol. II, p. 450
15   Birch, *The Court and Times*, p. 17
16   Cobham 'was of long time doubtful of Ralegh lest he should betray him … and he thought some times that when Ralegh had him in Jersey he would send him to the King'. In Nicholls, 'Sir Walter Ralegh's Treason'
17   Handover, *The Second Cecil*, p. 143
18   Edwards, *The Succession, Bye and Main Plots*, p. 209
19   Stone, *Family and Fortune*, p. 17.
20   Id.
21   Ibid., p. 18

12 The Aftermath

1   F.E. Halliday, *A Shakespeare Companion 1564–1964* (Penguin, Baltimore, 1964), p. 531
2   Munck, 'The Journal of', pp. 247–8
3   Nicholls, 'Sir Walter Ralegh's Treason', p. 908
4   Gardiner, *History of England*, p. 94; n. 2
5   Jardine, *Criminal Trials*, p. 466
6   Ibid., p. 467
7   Edwards, *The Succession, Bye and Main Plots*, p. 270
8   Letter from La Renzi to Giovanni Antonio Frederico, 31 January 1604, in Public Record Office: PRO SP 14/6/37
9   Jardine, *Criminal Trials*, p. 468
10   Birch, *The Court and Times*, p. 18
11   Ibid., p. 19
12   Jardine, *Criminal Trials*, p. 469

13 Ibid., p. 470
14 Letter of La Renzi, in Public Record Office: PRO SP 14/6/37
15 Edwards, *The Succession, Bye and Main Plots*, p. 284
16 Edwards, *The Life of Sir Walter Ralegh*, Vol. II, p. 466–7
17 Ibid., p. 467
18 Ibid., p. 466
19 Carleton, Letter of 11 Dec, in Jardine, *Criminal Trials*, p. 471
20 Edwards, *The Life of Sir Walter Ralegh*, Vol. I, p. 442
21 Letter of 6 December, Hatfield State Papers
22 Id.
23 Jardine, *Criminal Trials*, p. 472
24 Charles Carleton, 'The Rhetoric of Death: Scaffold Confessions in Early Modern England', *The Southern Speech Communication Journal*, (Vol. 49, Fall, 1983), p. 69. This section draws on Carleton's study of scaffold speeches
25 Stebbing, *Sir Walter Ralegh*, p. 237
26 Edwards, *The Succession, Bye and Main Plots*, p. 287
27 Id.
28 Edwards, *The Life of Sir Walter Ralegh*, Vol. I, p. 453
29 Id.
30 Letter of La Renzi, in Public Record Office: PRO SP 14/6/37
31 Id.
32 Edwards, *The Life of Sir Walter Ralegh*, Vol. I, pp. 452–3
33 4 Dec 1603, Hatfield State Papers
34 6 Dec 1603, Hatfield State Papers. Dr John Harmer was also designated as 'Harmar' in some contemporary records
35 Letter of La Renzi, in Public Record Office: PRO SP 14/6/37
36 Jardine, *Criminal Trials*, p. 449
37 Edwards, *The Life of Sir Walter Ralegh*, Vol. II, p. 280
38 Jardine, *Criminal Trials*, p. 475
39 Edwards, *The Life of Sir Walter Ralegh*, Vol. II, p. 283
40 10 Dec 1603, Hatfield State Papers

13 The Tower

1   John Stow, *A Survey of London* (1598), p. 23
2   Bellamy, *The Tudor Law of Treason*, p. 95
3   Edwards, *The Life of Sir Walter Ralegh*, Vol. II, p. 385
4   Stebbing, *Sir Walter Ralegh*, p. 245
5   Cecil paid £36,700 for the Brooke estates; when they were sold after Cecil's death they yielded over £70,000. In Stone, *Family and Fortune*, pp. 47–8
6   Aubrey, *Brief Lives*, p. 421
7   Stebbing, *Sir Walter Ralegh*, p. 250
8   Trevelyan, *Sir Walter Raleigh*, p. 419
9   Stebbing, *Sir Walter Ralegh*, p. 241
10 Hammond, *Selected Writings*, p. 55
11 Birch, *The Court and Times*, p. 169
12 Haynes, *Robert Cecil*, p. 212
13 Stone, *Family and Fortune*, p. 54
14 Trevelyan, *Sir Walter Raleigh*, p. 428
15 Edwards, *The Life of Sir Walter Ralegh*, Vol. I, pp. 517–8

16   Lacey, *Sir Walter Ralegh*, p. 330

17   Hammond, *Selected Writings*, p. 272

18   Stebbing, *Sir Walter Ralegh*, p. 295

19   Ibid., p. 298

20   Trevelyan, *Sir Walter Raleigh*, p. 456

21   Stebbing, *Sir Walter Ralegh*, p. 298

22   Trevelyan, *Sir Walter Raleigh*, p. 469

23   Stebbing, *Sir Walter Ralegh*, p. 303

24   Ibid., p. 308

25   Edwards, *The Life of Sir Walter Ralegh*, Vol. I, p. 599

26   Ibid., p. 598

27   Trevelyan, *Sir Walter Raleigh*, p. 475

14 The Final Gamble

1   Paul Hyland, *Ralegh's Last Journey* (London, 2004), p. 30

2   Trevelyan, *Sir Walter Raleigh*, p. 484

3   Ibid., p. 485

4   Edwards, *The Life of Sir Walter Ralegh*, Vol. II, p. 359

5   Hyland, *Ralegh's Last Journey*, p. 33

6   Edwards, *The Life of Sir Walter Ralegh*, Vol. II, p. 359

7   Hyland, *Ralegh's Last Journey*, p. 34

8   Sir Walter Ralegh, *Apologie for his voyage to Guiana*, London (1650)

9   Trevelyan, *Sir Walter Raleigh*, p. 524

10   Ibid., p. 525

11   Hyland, *Ralegh's Last Journey*, pp. 189–90

12   Ibid., p. 190

13   Trevelyan, *Sir Walter Raleigh*, pp. 541–2

14   Ibid., pp. 542–3

15   Ibid., p. 544

15 The Last Act: Old Palace Yard, 29 October 1618

1   Edwards, *The Life of Sir Walter Ralegh*, Vol. II, p. 491

2   Edwards, *The Life of Sir Walter Ralegh*, Vol. I, pp. 697–8

3   Jardine, *Criminal Trials*, p. 502

4   Ibid., p. 503

5   Ibid., p. 508

6   Stebbing, *Sir Walter Ralegh*, p. 378

7   Id.

8   Ibid., p. 379

9   Id.

10   Lacey, *Sir Walter Ralegh*, p. 378

Epilogue

1   Aubrey, *Brief Lives*, p. 422

2   Edwards, *The Life of Sir Walter Ralegh*, Vol. I, pp. 703–4

3   Lacey, *Sir Walter Ralegh*, p. 382

4   Hyland, *Ralegh's Last Journey*, p. 216

5   Ibid., p. 215

6   Edwards, *The Life of Sir Walter Ralegh*, Vol. I, p. 697

7   Stebbing, *Sir Walter Ralegh*, pp. 391–2

8   Beer, *Bess*, p. 257

Appendices

1   I am grateful to Dr Mark Nicholls and to the publishers of the *English Historical Review* for permission to reproduce this extract from Mark Nicholls, 'Sir Walter Ralegh's Treason: A Prosecution Document', *English Historical Review* (1995), pp. 918–924. Some spelling has been modernised but the punctuation of the original manuscript has been preserved.

SELECT BIBLIOGRAPHY

Primary Sources

Institute of Historical Research, Hatfield State Papers
Public Record Office (PRO)

Oliver Lawson Dick (ed), John Aubrey, *Brief Lives* (London, 1972)
Francis Bacon, *The Essays or Counsels Civil and Moral of Francis Lord Verulam* (London, 1625; reprinted Macmillan, 1883)
Thomas Birch, *Memoirs of the Reign of Queen Elizabeth, from the Year 1581 till her death* (London, 1754; reprinted General Books, 2009)
————, *The Court and Times of James the First*, 2 volumes (London, 1848)
Sir Edward Coke, *Institutes of the Laws of England* (M. Flesher, London, 1644)
Egerton Papers, *Camden Society* (1840)
Gerald Hammond, (ed), *Sir Walter Ralegh, Selected Writings* (1984)
T.B. Howell et al, (eds), *A Complete Collection of State Trials*, 34 volumes (1816–28)
D. Jardine, *Criminal Trials*, 2 volumes (1832–5)
Agnes Latham, (ed), *The Letters of Sir Walter Ralegh* (University of Exeter Press, 1999)
Letters from Sir Robert Cecil to Sir George Carew and John McLean, *Camden Society* (1864)
Levinus Munck, 'The Journal of' Levinus Munc', *English Historical Review* (Vol. XVIII, 1953)
Mark Nicholls, 'Sir Walter Ralegh's Treason: A Prosecution Document', *English Historical Review* (Sept., 1995)
Annabel Patterson, (ed), *The Trial of Nicholas Throckmorton* (Toronto, 1998); from Raphael Hollinshead, *The Chronicles of England, Scotland and Ireland* (London, 1587)
Sir Walter Ralegh, *Apologie for his voyage to Guiana* (London, 1650)
John Stow, *Annales* (1631)
————, *A Survey of London* (1598)
The Arraignment and Conviction of Sir Walter Ralegh, copied by Sir Thomas Overbury (1648)
The Secret Correspondence of Sir Robert Cecil with James VI, King of Scotland (Edinburgh, 1766)

Secondary Sources

Books

Anna Beer, *Bess: the Life of Lady Ralegh, wife to Sir Walter* (Constable, London, 2004)

John Bellamy, *The Tudor Law of Treason* (Routledge, London, 1979)

J.B. Black, *The Reign of Elizabeth* (Oxford, 1936)

Catherine Bowen, *The Lion and the Throne: the Life and Times of Sir Edward Coke 1552–1634* (London, 1957)

Edward Edwards, *The Life of Sir Walter Ralegh*, 2 volumes (MacMillan, London, 1868)

Francis Edwards, *The Succession, Bye and Main Plots of 1601–1603* (Four Courts Press, 2006)

Samuel Gardiner, *History of England from the Accession of James I to the Outbreak of the Civil War, 1603–1642* (Longmore, London, 1905)

F.E. Halliday, *A Shakespeare Companion 1564–1964* (Penguin, Baltimore, 1964)

P.M. Handover, *The Second Cecil: The Rise to Power 1563–1604 of Sir Robert Cecil, later First Earl of Salisbury* (London, 1959)

Alan Haynes, *Robert Cecil, First Earl of Salisbury* (London, 1989)

Paul Hyland, *Ralegh's Last Journey* (London, 2004)

Robert Lacey, *Sir Walter Ralegh* (Phoenix Press, London, 1973)

Mark Nicholls and Penry Williams, 'Sir Walter Ralegh', *Oxford Dictionary of National Biography*

William Stebbing, *Sir Walter Ralegh* (Clarendon Press, Oxford, 1891)

James Fitzjames Stephen, *History of the Criminal Law of England* (Macmillan, London, 1883)

Lawrence Stone, *Family and Fortune: Studies in Aristocratic Finance in the Sixteenth and Seventeenth Centuries* (Clarendon Press, 1973)

Raleigh Trevelyan, *Sir Walter Raleigh* (London, 2002)

Patrick Tytler, *Life of Sir Walter Raleigh* (Edinburgh, 1833)

Articles

Anna Beer, 'Textual Politics: The Execution of Sir Walter Ralegh', *Modern Philology* (Vol. 94, 1996)

Alan D. Boyer, 'The Trial of Sir Walter Ralegh: The Law of Treason, the Trial of Treason and the Origins of the Confrontation Clause', *Mississippi Law Journal* (Vol. 74, 2005)

Charles Carleton, 'The Rhetoric of Death: Scaffold Confessions in Early Modern England', *The Southern Speech Communication Journal* (Vol. 49, Fall, 1983)

Pauline Croft, 'Robert Cecil and the Stuart Monarchy', *Royal Stuart Society* (Paper LXVIII, 2005)

———, *Robert Cecil and the Early Jacobean Court*, in Linda Peck, (ed), *Mental World of the Jacobean Court* (Cambridge, 1991)

———, 'The Reputation of Robert Cecil: libels, political opinion and popular awareness in the early seventeenth century', *Transactions of the Royal Historical Society* (6th series, 1991)

Rosalind Davies, 'The Great Day of Mart: Returning to the Texts at the Trial of Sir Walter Ralegh in 1603', *Renaissance Forum* (Vol. 4, No. 1, 1999)

L.M. Hill, 'The Two-Witness Rule in English Treason Trials: Some Comments on the Emergence of Procedural Law', *American Journal of Legal History* (Vol. XII, 1968)

Pierre LeFranc, 'Ralegh in 1596 and 1603: Three Unprinted Letters in the Huntingdon Library', *Huntingdon Library Quarterly* (Vol. 29, 1937)

Ruth McIntyre, 'William Sanderson: Elizabethan Financier of Discovery', *William and Mary Quarterly* (Vol. 13.2, 1944)

Mark Nicholls, 'Treason's Reward: the punishment of conspirators in the Bye Plot of 1603', *The Historical Journal* (38:4, 1995)

———, 'Two Winchester Trials: The Prosecution of Henry Lord Cobham and Thomas Lord Grey of Wilton, 1603', *Institute of Historical Research* (Feb., 1995)

———, 'Sir Walter Ralegh's Treason: A Prosecution Document', *English Historical Review* (Vol. 100, 1995)

John Shirley, 'Sir Walter Ralegh's Guiana Finances', *Huntington Library Quarterly* (Vol. 13, 1937)

INDEX

Other titles published by The History Press

Napoleon is Dead: Lord Cochrane and the Great Stock Exchange Scandal
Richard Dale £18.00

Early on 21 February 1814, an army officer revealed that the French had been defeated and Napoleon killed. When the London Stock Exchange opened at 10.00 a.m., the City was full of rumours of an allied victory. Napoleon is Dead tells the tale of one of the earliest stock market scams; a story of greed, deceit and the public humiliation of Lord Cochrane.

978-0-7509-4381-9

Tropics Bound: Elizabeth's Seadogs on the Spanish Main
James Seay Dean £17.09

'For the first time, and long awaited, we have the view from the gun deck of the wide world that opened to the Elizabethans on the Spanish Main and among the islands of the Caribbean. The tang of salt air stings the story … *Tropics Bound*, rich in documentary research, reveals in triumph and failure the lives of privateers who deserve to be remembered.' – Barry Gough

978-0-7524-5096-4

The Elizabethan Secret Services
Alan Haynes £8.99

The England of Elizabeth was a nation under threat, spies and spy networks became of cardinal importance. By stealthy efforts at home and abroad, the Elizabethan spy clusters became forces to be feared. Kidnapping, surveillance, conspiracy, counter-espionage, theft and lying were just a few of the methods employed to defeat the ever-present threat of regicide. This book challenges many stale notions about espionage in Renaissance England.

978-0-7524-5046-9

The House of Tudor
Alison Plowden £8.99

The Tudors ruled England for little more than a century, but no other dynasty has so impressed itself on the English consciousness. In a personal rather than political history, Alison Plowden tells the story of the five Tudor monarchs, as well as lesser known members of the family; four turbulent, passionate, tragic and prodigious generations.

978-0-7509-3240-0

Visit our websites and discover thousands of other History Press books.

www.thehistorypress.co.uk